Diamond Fiddler

New Traditions for a
New Millennium

Why Fiddler on the Roof *Always Wins*

Who is this book for? This book is for all the directors and dramaturges, all the cast members on stage, and all the crew members behind the scenes, who will pool their talents to present new productions of *Fiddler on the Roof* from 2018 to 2039 (the year *Fiddler on the Roof* will celebrate its 75th anniversary).

As you gather in high schools, colleges, and community theaters, as you travel to cities and towns on road tours, whatever country you live in and whatever language you speak, I hope this book will be a reliable companion. I hope you will find answers in these pages to the many questions I know you will have. I hope my words will help you beckon to the Fiddler, so that you can bring him with you on your journey. And most important, I hope that through you, new audiences will come to see the many facets of this brilliant Jerome Robbins diamond.

And to the rest of you, to budding feminists and learned academics and lovers of Broadway, be you Papas, Mamas, Sons, or Daughters, if you are rabbis or butchers or any profession in between, whether you are a rich man or only the wife of a poor tailor, you are entitled to some happiness… so I hope you like this book too.

*This book is dedicated to my husband Richard Bayard Miller
and to our grandmothers:*

Sophie Slotnick Hecht
Audrey Berryman Miller
Fanny Silverkeit Hatoff
Isabel Hayes Richards

*Contemporaries of Tevye's daughters,
they all traveled far from the homes they loved,
and—collectively—they gave us life.*

TABLE OF CONTENTS

This lecture—delivered in 2014—celebrates the 50th anniversary of the first Broadway performance of *Fiddler on the Roof* in 1964. "From Gold to Diamond" explores the original historical context and explains why *Fiddler on the Roof* is so pertinent now. It attacks Conventional Wisdom, and predicts that *Fiddler on the Roof* will continue to retain its relevance far beyond its 75th Diamond Anniversary in 2039.

This lecture—delivered in 2009—locates the source of inspiration for the fiddler character, a klezmer musician named Stempenyu, who is the subject of Marc Chagall's iconic painting *Green Violinist*. Though we know very little about Stempenyu, we do know he was definitely a real person, and that Sholem Aleichem's novella—*Stempenyu*—was the catalyst for Marc Chagall's painting. Together, these two sources—Sholem Aleichem's novella and Marc Chagall's painting—provided the title for *Fiddler on the Roof*.

This lecture—delivered in 2010—analyzes the character called "Yente-the-Matchmaker." The Ashkenazi name "Yente" gave rise to the Yinglish noun "yenta" that is commonly used today. If you know your Sholem Aleichem, you know there is no Yente-the-Matchmaker in any of his eight Tevye stories, making Yente the only major character specifically created for *Fiddler on the Roof*.

In this lecture—delivered in 2011—Jan presents a seemingly outrageous claim: the main character in *Fiddler on the Roof* is Tevye's second daughter Hodel. Based on her extensive research into the personal life of Solomon Rabinowitz (aka Sholem Aleichem), Jan draws parallels between Sholem Aleichem's life, his stories, and Joseph Stein's *Fiddler on the Roof* libretto.

In this lecture—delivered in 2012—Jan argues that **five** is the winning number of daughters for *Fiddler on the Roof*, even though Sholem Aleichem originally gave Tevye **seven** daughters in *Tevye the Dairyman*. To reach this conclusion, Jan provides links between between the novel *Pride and Prejudice*, the musical *First Impressions*, and the TV series *Downton Abbey*, showing how they all tie back to the five Daughters of Zelophehad in the Bible's Book of Numbers.

In this lecture—delivered in 2013—Jan discovers crucial differences between the 1964 Robbins version onstage and the 1971 Jewison version onscreen. Jerome Robbins was already working on a radical conception of how to present *Fiddler on the Roof* onscreen, but producer Walter Mirisch chose Norman Jewison as his director. Although the two versions obviously share common elements, *Fiddler on the Roof* onstage and *Fiddler on the Roof* onscreen differ in critically important ways.

In this lecture—delivered in 2014—Jan explores her personal obsession with *Fiddler in the Roof*. How did this material come to dominate the life of a Jewish Femnist for almost two decades? In the end, Jan concludes that not only does *Fiddler on the Roof* have "legs," it is a classic that sustains us in the throes of today's fight against bigotry and prejudice.

a full understanding of *Fiddler on the Roof* requires more than just a female-centered analysis.

7. Was Kitty Genovese Jewish? 267

This section explores the echoes of the Kitty Genovese case in Joseph Stein's libretto. Of course, the answer to this question as stated is an emphatic "No!" Kitty Genovese was not Jewish. Nevertheless, Jan asserts that the coverage of her murder in March 1964—especially by the *New York Times*—had more to do with what happened in Auschwitz in the mid-1940s than what happened in Queens in the mid-1960s.

SECTION 10 Epilogue: 275
The "Me Found" through the Research

In this final section, Jan writes to the future. The Golden Anniversary events of 2014 are now history. The title *Diamond Fiddler*—chosen sometime in 2013—reflects the belief that the Diamond Anniversary in 2039 (honoring the 75th anniversary of the first Broadway performance) and then the Centennial in 2064 (honoring the 100th anniversary) will prove the power of *Fiddler on the Roof* to transcend time. *Fiddler on the Roof* will always defy barriers of gender, race, class, and ethnicity.

PHOTOS & ILLUSTRATIONS

The Jerome Robbins Centennial Edition

What is a Book?

When I started my research on *Fiddler on the Roof* way back in 2002, I would never have thought to ask such a question. I thought everyone already agreed that "a book" was a physical object with many pages of text that were bound together and encased by some kind of cover.

Sometimes there were pictures and other graphic elements and sometimes there weren't, but there were always words—thousands and thousands of words—words that became sentences, sentences that became paragraphs, and paragraphs that were typically divided into sequential chapters.

Seventeen years later, as we approach the middle of the 21st century, the question no longer has such an easy answer. Except for academic books—and sometimes novels—most books are no longer linear. In the non-fiction case, "books" are often collections (collections of articles, interviews, web posts, whatever). In the fiction case, "books" are also often collections (typically short stories and novellas but sometimes including poems and "fragments" as well). And though they may still appear on paper—either hard cover or soft cover—many "books" today are actually read on screens (on e-readers like Kindle and Nook, on computer workstations, and even on mobile devices like laptops and "smart" phones). Sometimes we even say we are "reading" a book when someone else is reading to us in an "audio book."

My book does not have sequential chapters. It is a collection of lectures followed by thoughts on those lectures based on numerous question/answer sessions. And it is not linear. Each lecture always begins with an introduction that assumes I am speaking to a new audience, but then it quickly branches off in its own direction. Then the Questions Asked/Questions Answered section circles back on a topic in one (or more) of the lectures and adds to what I have learned about the topic since I wrote the original lecture.

For older readers who are used to reading books with sequential chapters, this book will no doubt be somewhat frustrating. But for "digital natives" who grew up reading most "books" on a screen rather than on a page, circling around and around a topic probably won't be so disorienting. But just to make sure, I have included an index so readers can skip from topic to topic based on what is of most interest to them, and hopefully, they will find more that might be interesting and keep reading.

Note that according to anthropologist Mary Catherine Bateson (the daughter of Margaret Mead and Gregory Bateson), most women in almost every culture "compose a life" that is cyclical rather than linear. This is not just because their essential physicality means that adult women plan their lives according to monthly cycles when they are menstruating and nine-month cycles when they are not. Cultural expectations help define an even deeper layer.

Even though I was already post-menopausal when I began my research on *Fiddler on the Roof*, and even though I have never given birth to a child myself, it seems those same patterns are deeply embedded in my own nature. I originally planned this as a linear book with sequential chapters that began with "introduction" and ended with "conclusion." I wrote proposals with that exact structure for several agents to no avail.

Only now do I see that I was destined to write a book that keeps spiraling around an axis of analysis not only because I am a woman, but because this is a book about women. No wonder the male critics who wrote the first reviews of *Fiddler on the Roof* were frustrated. They thought they were watching a musical about a man named Tevye, but *Fiddler on the Roof* is, in fact, the story of a father who is narrating the stories of his daughters.

The characters who drive the plot of *Fiddler on the Roof* are Tevye's three eldest daughters: Tzeitel, Hodel, and Chava. Tevye, on the other hand, is a character who is forced to react—again and again and again—once he learns of the decisions his daughters have already made. They do not ask for his permission; they ask for his blessing. (Even Tzeitel—Tevye's eldest daughter—gave Motel-the-Tailor her pledge well before Tevye started singing about tradition.)

What is My Genre?

I did not know what to call this book when, after a decade of drafts, I started pitching it to agents. But in the interim, a new genre has evolved to accommodate books like mine. This book is a "bibliomemoir." And although my book, like most memoirs, contains references to my husband, our parents, and many of my teachers, this book is proof that one of the deepest relationships in life can be with a text. (In this case, however, the word text must be in quotes because the "text" of *Fiddler on the Roof* is not just a series of words, but images and music as well.)

One aspect I understand now—something I didn't really understand before—is that this lifelong engagement with a text is a very Jewish thing. We are the "People of the Book," and we read our book—a Torah—over and over again, starting anew each year. And the more devoted among us also develop a lifelong engagement with something called the Talmud (which is not quite a new book but a compendium of layers upon layers of commentary on the Torah).

For Jews, it always starts with the Torah (the first five "books" of the Hebrew Bible). Perhaps the glue that has kept us together as a people over so many millennia is the fact that our core text is actually very compact and portable. As Simon Schama famously says: "Judaism is a suitcase-ready religion."

What's Next?

After circling around the text of *Fiddler on the Roof* for almost two decades now, I am ready to answer four of my most basic questions:

- Why is Marc Chagall's work so important to *Fiddler on the Roof*?
- What are we to make of the invocation of "tradition" in *Fiddler on the Roof*?
- Is the film version of *Fiddler on the Roof* faithful to the stage version?
- Do fathers really know best?

Why is Marc Chagall's work so important to *Fiddler on the Roof*?

No matter which sections of this bibliomemoir you end up reading, at some point you will find yourself in the south of France in the middle of the first year of our new millennium. The significance of one specific day in my life—May 20, 2000—cannot be overstated. At approximately 7 AM, I had a sudden revelation and after this transformational moment, the trajectory of my life was never the same.

I had spent the afternoon of May 19th at the Marc Chagall Biblical Message Museum in Nice. I had gone in expecting to see kitschy paintings filled with flowers and birds. Colorful. Pretty. As easy on the mind as they would be on the eyes. But what I actually found inside were deeply-engrossing depictions of scenes from the Torah (known to Jews worldwide as "The Five Books of Moses").

On my way out of the museum, I grabbed a book about Marc Chagall, and the next morning, while I was reading it, I suddenly realized that Marc Chagall's *Green Violinist* was "the fiddler on the roof." But, so what? Why did it matter to me? Looking back now—almost twenty years later—I think what unsettled me most was the realization that my connection to Judaism had all but disappeared. Was I the only Jew who had failed to appreciate such a fundamental cultural connection?

Of course, the answer is no. The more research I did, the more I realized that the connection between *Green Violinist*—Marc Chagall's painting from the 1920s—and *Fiddler on the Roof*—a musical first performed in the 1960s—had become deeply buried by century's end. Some writers denied the connection outright; some writers obscured the connection by pointing out how many different fiddlers Marc Chagall painted; and some writers acknowledged that there was a connection, but then they mocked it (usually because they valued Chagall's work and thought it was *Fiddler on the Roof* that had turned it into kitsch).

All of these writers (almost all of whom are men) are wrong. Marc Chagall's *Green Violinist* was a major source of inspiration for the creators of *Fiddler on the Roof*, so there is definitely more than just "a connection." Although Marc Chagall did indeed paint many different fiddlers over the course of his long life, only *Green Violinist* is intimately related to the iconography of *Fiddler on the Roof.* American art critics started calling Marc Chagall's work "kitsch" in the 1950s (during the heyday of Abstract Expressionism), so the surprising success of *Fiddler on the Roof* in 1964 probably did more to elevate Marc Chagall's standing than diminish it (certainly in popular consciousness).

This story arc begins with a man named Stempenyu who was a mid-19th century klezmer musician from Berdichev (now in Ukraine). The story then moves to Sholem Aleichem, who wrote a novella about this very famous fiddler. The name of the novella was *Stempenyu* and it was very popular. It was, in fact, the first story Sholem Aleichem wrote that was translated and published in other languages.

And then Marc Chagall, inspired by *Stempenyu*, picked up the baton and made this very famous painting. Chagall actually painted this particular fiddler twice. He created a mural called *Music* when he was at the Moscow State Yiddish Theater (that was in the early 1920s), and then he did it again after he left what had just become the Soviet Union and moved to Berlin on his way back to Paris. So, there are actually two copies of the *Green Violinist.*

I discuss this background information at great length in the section called Questions Asked/Questions Answered: Which Fiddler is *the* Fiddler? The early version, which is simply called *Music* (the *Music* mural), is at the Tretyakov Gallery in Moscow. The second version—almost a copy but not quite—is at the Guggenheim Museum in Manhattan. That's where it has been for decades, and that's where it was when the *Fiddler on the Roof* team was working on *Fiddler on the Roof.* There is no doubt that *Green Violinist* is the painting that inspired the title *Fiddler on the Roof.*

The fourth and final part of this story connects us with Jerome Robbins and the fact that in the original casting, the part of the Fiddler was always played by a dancer. Now there's generally a musician—an actual violinist—on the stage dressed up to be the Fiddler. But originally, Jerome Robbins had conceived the character of the Fiddler as a dancer.

Why is this important? Because Jerome Robbins began his professional life as a dancer! Through some artistic alchemy, Robbins knew that the same Jewish essence that was captured in Stempenyu's music, in Sholem Aleichem's words, and in Marc Chagall's paintings (this "cry [that] is shrill and heartrending...

[from] the deepest depth of the soul") must also be present in the dancing Fiddler. With the passage of time, this symbolic fiddler on the roof character has been recognized as the most enduring of Jerome Robbins's creative accomplishments.

It is critical, therefore, that we understand that the title is not accidental, and the identification of which fiddler is *the* Fiddler is necessary if we are to understand the story behind the story of *Fiddler on the Roof*. And this is why Jerome Robbins (fiddling away while dressed in the clothing of Marc Chagall's *Green Violinist*) is on the cover of this second edition—the Jerome Robbins Centennial Edition—of *Diamond Fiddler: New Traditions for a New Millennium*.

What are we to make of the invocation of "Tradition" in *Fiddler on the Roof* ?

This second question has to do with tradition. What are we to make of the invocation of "Tradition!" in the Musical-Prologue? Short answer: This is, indeed, how *Fiddler on the Roof* begins. ("Because of our traditions, everyone knows who he is and what God expects him to do.") But three plus hours later—when the Jews of Anatevka are expelled and "the circle of [their] little village" becomes a fragmented stream of refugees—none of them know "what God expects [them] to do" next.

Now let's back up. Before the Musical-Prologue, the first thing we actually hear is the Fiddler playing the Daughters' Theme ("And who does Mama teach to mend and tend and fix…").

6

Most people think these notes constitute the Fiddler's Theme, but listen closely and you will immediately realize the Fiddler does not have his own theme. The Daughters' Theme and the Fiddler's Theme have the exact same structure.

So, the first thing we—in the audience—hear is the Daughters' Theme—as played by the Fiddler—and the very next thing we hear is the Fiddler playing the Papa's Theme ("Who day and night must scramble for a living").

In other words, from the very beginning of *Fiddler on the Roof*, this musical announces itself as a dialogue between fathers and daughters. As the story unfolds, we come to understand that fathers may try to constrain their daughters ("have the final say at home") but the daughters—who are initially reconciled to "marry whoever Papa picks"—will eventually decide that they want to make their own decisions and live their own lives. What is a father to do?

In the end, Tevye realizes that wherever he is going next, he must bring the Fiddler with him… but why? Because his daughters are the embodiment of tradition. There is no "future" for the Jewish People without daughters; there is no "future" for the human race without daughters. (Just look at what is happening in East Asia today. Decades of femicide—the selective abortion and starvation of infants just because they were born female—has created an enormous population imbalance with dire consequences.)

Somehow, by some magic alchemy, the *Fiddler on the Roof* team found this truth in both Sholem Aleichem's life and in his life's work. At the moment of his death in 1916, Solomon Rabinowitz (aka Sholem Aleichem) had four daughters, two granddaughters, and only one son. Somehow, in the fourth of his eight Tevye stories—a story called "Hodel" published in 1904—Sholem Aleichem anticipated this. The night before Hodel leaves home,

Tevye tries one last time to convince her to stay. He tells her a plaintive little story about a mother hen and her ducklings.

Hodel's reply?

> Of course, I feel sorry for the hen; but just because
> the hen squawks, is the duckling never to swim?

And how does Tevye respond to this? He is in awe.

> Now, is that an answer or isn't it?
> I tell you, Tevye's daughters don't mince words!

The next day, Tevye takes Hodel to the train station so she can join Perchik in Siberia. This is the story—the "Hodel" story—that ends with the famous line:

> Let's talk about something more cheerful.
> Have you heard any news of the cholera in Odessa?
>
> (Halkin, Pages 67–69)

When Tevye leaves Anatevka with Golde (his wife) and Bielke and Shprintze (their two youngest daughters) in the final minutes of *Fiddler on the Roof*, Golde is standing next to him and the two little girls are behind them. Then Tevye looks back and sees the Fiddler, and the expression on the Fiddler's face tells all: What about me? What am I supposed to do now? Tevye stops for a moment—as he so often does—to consider. What is the answer? Then Tevye beckons to the Fiddler: You are coming with us.

Cue Daughters' Theme/Fiddler's Theme in measure 35:

(Dictated)   cue: Tevye motions to fiddler.   [Curtain]

From beginning to end, this is the story of fathers and daughters.

Why? Because all fathers know that only their daughters can give birth to the next generation. It is the daughters who make "tradition" possible because without new generations, there will be no tradition. And, at least in principle, all Jews respect this as a fact of life; according to Jewish Law— Halakhah—the religion of the child is determined by the religion of the mother. The father can be anyone (literally anyone); even if the father is not a Jew, the child will be a Jew.

So, all fathers have a choice to make. Are they going to try to imprison their daughters in a version of "tradition" that is necessarily based on the past? Or are they going to raise their daughters as **people** in the hope that their own love of Judaism will bring "tradition" into the future?

This is Perchik's challenge in Act One, Scene 2:

Perchik: Do you have children?
Tevye: I have five daughters.
Perchik: Five?
Tevye: Daughters.
Perchik: Girls should learn too. Girls are **people**...
Tevye: Food for lessons? Good. Stay with us for the Sabbath.

(Stein, Page 30–31)

"Girls are people." By the end of *Fiddler on the Roof*, Tevye has accepted the fact that he is the one who has raised his daughters as people. They are the carriers of tradition, so if he wants tradition to endure, he must believe in them and all of the lessons they have learned from him and through him (for example, when he brings Perchik into the house).

This Tevye—the Tevye who understood that girls were "people" well before women had legal standing, voting rights, or the ability to participate as full citizens anywhere in the world—this Tevye comes directly from the pen of Sholem Aleichem: "Of course, I feel sorry for the hen," says Hodel. "But just because the hen squawks, is the duckling never to swim?"

And how does Hodel's father react to his daughter's words? He speaks with awe of this person he has created. "I tell you," says Tevye as he describes this incident to Sholem Aleichem, "Tevye's daughters don't mince words!"

Is the film version of *Fiddler on the Roof* faithful to the stage version?

Over and over again in the book that follows, I repeatedly ask some variant of the question "Is the film version of *Fiddler on the Roof* 'faithful' to the stage version?" My answer to this question is always no. No, Norman Jewison's version of *Fiddler on the Roof* on the screen is not "faithful" to Jerome Robbins's stage version.

Despite their many similarities, the differences between the two versions all point to patriarchal aspects of the film that were not present in Jerome Robbins's original production. For now, since you haven't read this book yet, I ask you to grant me the benefit of the doubt. Even so, so what?

First, we need to ask ourselves why this is even a question. Doesn't the creative team behind any adaptation have the right—one might even say the responsibility—to make the source material its own? Of course. But if you only learn one thing from reading this book, I hope you will learn that even though so many of the words and so much of the music is almost identical, in the end, Robbins's version and Jewison's version tell very different stories.

Fiddler on the Roof on the stage (as conceived by Jerome Robbins) is a drama about culture implosion. Even before the Fiddler plays his first notes, people like Fruma-Sarah's (unnamed) brother and Tevye's brother-in-law ("Uncle Avram") have already settled in America ("*Die Goldene Medina*"). Meanwhile, other Jews with different goals—both men and women—are leaving Russia to build a homeland in Palestine.

Hodel is the first cast member in *Fiddler on the Roof* to leave Anatevka. She makes a conscious choice to join Perchik in Siberia. No one is forcing her to go. Everyone in her family wants her to stay (most especially her father Tevye).

Sholem Aleichem—a man who came of age in an era of Jewish Enlightenment called the Haskalah—certainly didn't want to live his life in a shtetl like Anatevka. As soon as he had a bit of money in his pocket (more about that later), he moved his growing family first to Odessa and then to Kiev.

Sholem Aleichem left Kiev after the pogroms which followed the 1905 Revolution, and for the rest of his life—sometimes by design and sometimes by necessity—he traveled the world. He gave lectures throughout Europe and made two trips to the United States (where he eventually died in 1916).

On the other hand, *Fiddler on the Roof* onscreen (as directed by Norman Jewison) is a drama about expulsion. In Jewison's film, Jews would have stayed in Anatevka forever had they not been driven out. Everything would have been just fine if only the Russians had left the Jewish community in peace.

I certainly do not want to minimize the importance of expulsion. Jews were expelled from the Russian Pale of Settlement in huge numbers and millions of people in these same "Blood Lands" were murdered a few decades later during the Holocaust. These are facts and I would never deny them.

Nevertheless, Sholem Aleichem's Tevye stories are not about the Holocaust, and since *Fiddler on the Roof* is based on the Tevye stories, Robbins was discreet in his foreshadowing. His decision to emphasize the universality of the Tevye stories had enormous impact on *Fiddler on the Roof*'s initial success and astounding longevity.

In the Robbins version, Tevye narrates a story of cultural implosion in which his daughters are the key protagonists. Robbins knew that in the Tevye stories, there is no going backwards because there's no way back. If we truly believe in the future, then we must bring tradition with us ever forward.

But for Jewison, it's all Tevye all the time. Anatevka is his home and Anatevka will remain his home until he is forcibly expelled by men with guns. In the end, Tevye and his three remaining family members—Golde, Shprintze and Bielke—are herded onto a river raft. They float through the mist while trains whistle ominously in the background. The future is terrifying, so they console themselves by clinging to the past: "Anatevka, Anatevka, tumbledown, workaday Anatevka, dear little village, little town of mine" (Stein, Page 145).

Final Question: Do Fathers *Really* Know Best?

Did Sholem Aleichem believe that fathers always knew best? The way Sholem Aleichem presents the duckling anecdote in the text of his "Hodel" story, it should be clear to all readers that when Hodel challenges Tevye, Tevye knows that she is right and he is wrong. Painful as it is for him, Tevye does not try to stop Hodel from joining Perchik in Siberia. He goes home, waits for news, and treasures all the updates in her subsequent letters.

And the answer in *Fiddler on the Roof* is also no. No, fathers do not always know best.

Consider what would have happened if Tzeitel had married Lazar Wolf. This is what her father has agreed to when he turns to Lazar Wolf at Mordcha's Inn and says: "What do I think? It's a match!" But Tevye agrees to this match—against his own misgivings—because "with a butcher, my daughter will surely never know hunger." (Stein, Page 48)

While that was certainly a reasonable assumption in Act One, by the end of Act Two, Tevye would have known that Lazar Wolf had little ability to care for Tzeitel (not to mention any children who might have been conceived in their bed). When Lazar Wolf leaves Anatevka during the finale, he is an old man with one battered suitcase hoping that he can rely on the relatives of his long-dead wife—the irascible Fruma-Sarah—to take him in (should he even manage to find them in the big city of Chicago).

And what about Tzeitel? If she had left Anatevka as the wife of Lazar Wolf, would she have known hunger? The answer is almost certainly yes. But even more important, would she have been happy? The answer is almost certainly no. Tzeitel is in love with Motel-the-Tailor. When she leaves Anatevka as Motel's wife, at least she is leaving with the man of her choice—who, unlike Lazar Wolf, is a young man her own age—and they are both committed to working hard to build a life together.

Yes, I know: When Sholem Aleichem forces Tevye and his family to leave their home at the end of "Get Thee Out!" (the last of his eight Tevye stories), Motel is dead and Tzeitel is a widow. But in context, this happens years later, long after Tevye has buried both Golde and Shprintze (his fourth daughter). People die. At least for the time that Tzeitel is with Motel, she is in love, she is building a family, and she has given birth to two healthy children who are the embodiment of both Motel's legacy and her own future.

The two endings—the one written by Sholem Aleichem and the one written by Joseph Stein—therefore run parallel. In neither case does either author believe that Tzeitel would have been better off with Lazar Wolf. She would probably have had a miserable married life, and when forced to leave Anatevka, she would have been weighed down by a broken man. Even with Motel dead, Tzeitel has nonetheless eluded a sorrowful fate.

And this brings us to the most controversial topic anyone can address when discussing *Fiddler on the Roof*: Is Tevye right when he tries to separate Chava and Fyedka? After almost two decades of research on *Fiddler on the Roof*, I stand firm in my conviction that the answer is no. No, Tevye is not right to try to separate Chava and Fyedka. Once again, Tevye is wrong.

Specific details will be found in the section called "What about the guys?" But for now, let's start where we started with Tzeitel. What life is Chava planning to live when she and Fyedka leave Anatevka?

Wait. Back-up. Somewhere between Act Two, Scene 5 and Act Two, Scene 6, Chava (Tevye's third daughter) and Fyedka (the Russian youth who has been courting her) get married in some kind of offstage ceremony. We in the audience know nothing more than what Golde tells Tevye: "He [the priest] told me—they were married." (Stein, Page 134)

Where do Chava and Fyedka live after their marriage? When we're watching *Fiddler on the Roof*, the truth is that we really don't know. We do have one clue: Anatevka is a very small place. Therefore, it would have been very difficult for Tevye and his family to avoid them if they had stayed in Anatevka after their wedding. But all we really know for sure is that as soon as they hear that the Jews of Anatevka have been expelled, they come back to the place where Chava grew up so that they can say goodbye to her family—Tevye, Golde, Tzeitel, Shprintze, and Bielke—before they all leave.

Sholem Aleichem gives us another hint. At the end of his fourth story—the story called "Chava"—Tevye tells Sholem Aleichem that he went to the train station after the wedding to buy a ticket to Yehupetz (the name Sholem Aleichem used for Kiev), but the ticket seller told him that he had never heard of such a place.

> I know exactly where she and he are living and even what
> they are doing there… Once I put on my best clothes and
> went to the station in order to take a train there—I mean
> where he and she live.   (Halkin, Pages 81–82)

In Sholem Aleichem's final story "Get Thee Out!" Chava returns… but from where? And where is Fyedka? Is he even still alive? Tevye is so busy talking about himself that he never gives Sholem Aleichem any details. Chava was gone. Now she is back. In Tevye's telling, the only word she says when she returns is "Papa."

Are we to assume that Chava and Fyedka are living a Christian life (presumably a Russian Orthodox life) when they move to Kiev after their marriage? So many people insist on this: If Chava and Fyedka are married, then she must have converted.

But I see no evidence of this in any of Sholem Aleichem's stories, and there is certainly nothing to suggest an actual conversion in *Fiddler on the Roof*. Perhaps Chava had to say some "magic words" before the priest would agree to marry them? If so, everything I know about her character leads me to believe that if she did say these "magic words," she said them to achieve her goal (marrying Fyedka). There is never any suggestion that Chava has studied Russian Orthodoxy, or believes in Russian Orthodoxy, or has had any change whatsoever in her religious convictions.

On the other hand, Fyedka is always presented by both Sholem Aleichem and by Joseph Stein as a young man yearning for what many people would consider a Jewish life (at least intellectually). He is proudly self-educated and reads for self-improvement, and he's attracted to Chava precisely because he knows that she loves books too. Chava, for her part, tells Tevye that Fyedka is a "Second Gorky," invoking the name of a famous Russian novelist—Maxim Gorky—who was known as a philo-Semite.

When we—in the audience—first meet Fyedka in Motel's tailor shop in Act One, Scene 8, he tells Chava this ("I've often noticed you at the booksellers.") and then he hands her a book. "Go ahead, take the book. It's by Heinrich Heine. Happens to be Jewish, I believe." (Stein, Page 87)

We never see Fyedka attempting to pull Chava into his world. When he hands Chava the book by Heinrich Heine, he's implicitly saying he has read this Jewish book. It's a gift from him to her. This is Chava's tradition and Fyedka respects it.

Is marrying outside the faith a sin in Judaism? If yes, then why don't I find anything about intermarriage in the Ten Commandments?

In the Book of Genesis, we learn that Joseph's wife was an Egyptian woman named Asenith. Their sons—Ephraim and Manassah—gave their names to two of the Twelve Tribes of Israel.

In the Book of Exodus, we learn that Moses married Zipporah who was either a Cushite or a Midianite (the words in the Torah seem to contradict one another unless we are meant to understand that Moses married two different women). Regardless, neither of them—if there were two—was Jewish. But one way or the other, Moses also had two sons: Eliezer and Gershom.

In the Book of Ruth, Ruth—a Moabite—tells her mother-in-law Naomi: "Your people shall be my people, and your God my God." Then Ruth marries Naomi's kinsman Boaz and they become the great-grandparents of King David.

If intermarriage worked for all of these revered Biblical couples, then why should intermarriage be a fate worse than death for Chava and Fyedka?

Over the years, again and again, I have asked *Fiddler on the Roof* lovers why Chava and Fyedka tell Tevye that they are going to Krakow? Is there something special about this specific destination? But I never get an answer; instead of engaging with my question, people always react with rage. But clearly Chava and Fyedka have decided to move to a city. They are going to a place where they hope they can be together without all of their neighbors looking though their windows and making judgments about the lives lived within. And is it just a coincidence that they've decided to move near one of the most prestigious universities in Eastern Europe?

In 1964, very few people heading to a Broadway show—Jews included— would have been able to find Krakow on a map. But now, because of *Schindler's List*, Krakow has become a major philo-Semitic tourist destination, the host city for a world-renowned annual Klezmer festival. In *Schindler's List*, the Nazis want to destroy the Jewish community of Krakow precisely because it is the home of a prestigious university, therefore many educated Jews live in the area.

If Fyedka and Chava had indeed moved themselves to Krakow circa 1905, and if they had stayed there and had children, then all of their children and all of their grandchildren would have been considered Jewish when the Nazis arrived. That would have been the case even if Chava had converted and was actively living the life of a faithful Russian Orthodox wife.

So why should Jews in a *Fiddler on the Roof* audience refuse to accept Chava and Fyedka as Jews? Their children will be Halachically Jewish because their mother is Jewish. Their father will be a man who not only loves a Jewish woman, but a man who aspires to live a Jewish-style life of education and self-improvement.

And why would we expel people from our own community when we know that no matter what we say, the world is going to consider them Jewish anyway? Whatever we say, the world will force them to share our fate as Jews. What is the point?

Why Krakow? Chava and Fyedka are going to a place with an educated Jewish community. They are going to a place where they hope to live without outmoded traditions that would constrain them. They are going to a place where they can live as "people"—man and woman as well as husband and wife.

At the last possible moment, hearing this news, even Tevye relents. "God be with you!" (Stein, Page 151)

Me? I am just fine with the marriage of Chava and Fyedka, and I believe with my whole heart that Sholem Aleichem was too. Best to embrace our differences as Jews. Better to worship the spirit of our people than the letter of our law.

My conviction is not just practical, but based on personal experience. The man I married came from a Presbyterian family, but he converted to Judaism and he now attends a Talmud class every month. My sister married a man from a Catholic family. He converted too, and now my niece is raising a Jewish family in Denver (USA) while my nephew studies Mishnah in S'fat (Israel).

From my point of view, those who really care about the future of the Jewish people should embrace the Fyedkas rather than casting out the Chavas. The Daughters' Theme is the Fiddler's Theme; their music is the same. *Fiddler on the Roof* teaches us that the fathers who raise their daughters to be PEOPLE bring tradition from the past and point it towards the future.

I have now done all that I could do to elucidate the words and images of *Fiddler on the Roof*. But I have not done what I could not do, because I do not have the technical vocabulary to do comparable analyses of the music and dance which are so integral to the artistic triumph that is *Fiddler on the Roof*.

I have the ability to appreciate the music. I have the ability to appreciate the dance. But I do not have the ability to translate my appreciation into words that will convey the structural significance of the music and the dance in *Fiddler on the Roof*. Someone else will have to do that.

I end by leaving a "to-do list" for new generations. I am hoping that people will write about the music and the dance with a sophistication that is beyond my own capabilities. And I am also leaving important questions open about the text. For example: What did Joseph Stein know and when did he know it? I have relied on many sources that were not available to Stein (certainly not as texts in book form), so how did he pull all of this detail together so brilliantly?

Clearly much of his success was based on artistic alchemy, but I also believe that somewhere Stein left notes about conversations with both Frances Butwin and Marie Waife-Goldberg (and maybe others as well). And in that way, if in no other—that there's so much fruit left to harvest after almost two decades of research and writing—then *Fiddler on the Roof* is surely like *Hamlet*. It is a great work of art with unending riches and I have no regrets about having spent so much of my life and my energy trying to give you the answers that I hope you will find in this book.

Every end is a new beginning!

Jan Lisa Huttner
Brooklyn, New York
October 11, 2018

William James Hall

Scenes from Harvard University (Spring 1975)

Prologue:
The "Me" Search in the Research

When Solomon Rabinowitz died on May 13, 1916, his casket was accompanied by a funeral cortège that wound across four of New York City's five boroughs. People lined the streets from his home in the Bronx down through the caverns of Manhattan and across the hills of Brooklyn, all the way to his final resting place in Queens. The event is still on record as one of the largest public tributes in the history of America's largest city.

Today, 100 years later, a surprising number of people know this fact, even though they do not recognize this man's name. Solomon Rabinowitz? Who? Oh yes, right: When he died, the beloved Yiddish author—best known by his pen name Sholem Aleichem—had one of the largest funeral processions ever seen in the United States.

In this book, I will argue that we know all of this 100 years later—in 2016—because of the astounding and totally unexpected success of the Broadway musical *Fiddler on the Roof*. But first, I intend to tell you a bit about how I came to know so much about Solomon Rabinowitz and his family, and why *Fiddler on the Roof* has come to play such an important role in my own life story.

In later chapters, I will tell you quite emphatically that I have no memory of the first time I saw *Fiddler on the Roof* on the stage, nor do I have any memory of the first time I saw *Fiddler on the Roof* on the screen. In retrospect, this is quite astonishing because I have very vivid memories of comparable events from childhood, like seeing *Lawrence of Arabia* for the first time on screen with my father—in Chicago—in 1961, and seeing *Man of La Mancha* for the first time on stage with my mother—on Broadway—in 1966. Ironically, other people have memories that I do not have. For example, one of my college roommates is sure that I saw *Fiddler on the Roof* on the screen for the first time with her in 1972. I would never doubt Jessica's memory of this day, but I cannot confirm it either.

Memory plays a very large role in this book. I know I saw *Fiddler on the Roof* on Broadway at some point in the mid-'60s. Even though I may not remember anything about that performance now, nevertheless I am certain that I saw one. On the other hand, all these years later, many people have very fond memories of watching Zero Mostel play Tevye onstage in 1964 and 1965. They never believe me when I tell them their memories are significantly different from observations recorded by others at the time.

Human memory is fallible. I have known this theoretically for decades, but I know it now in a whole new and very personal way. One specific day—May 19, 2000—plays a huge role in **my** *Fiddler* story, and yet the way I talk about this day has changed over time. As I tidied up the lectures that comprise the bulk of this book, I was struck by the subtle differences in the way I tell the story of my trip to France. From one year to the next, the more I came to know about *Fiddler on the Roof*, the more I learned about the men who created it; the more I studied the sources and synergies they drew from as they put it all together, the more I came to understand why the trip to Nice had had such a profound impact on me.

It took more than a decade! I literally struggled with this question—*Why had the trip to Nice made such a profound impact on me?*—for more than a decade! Sounds crazy, no? But the pages of this book will prove just how much I struggled. I felt something at the Marc Chagall Biblical Message Museum that I could not explain, either to myself or to anyone else, for years. But as I struggled to understand the meaning of that day, I found unexpected answers not only about *Fiddler on the Roof*—and Sholem Aleichem and Marc Chagall and Jerome Robbins and all the rest—but also about myself and my world.

In May 2000, I knew myself to be Jewish-American even though I did not live a Jewish life. In May 2000, I knew myself to be a committed feminist even though I did not make much time in my life for activism. Now—in May 2016—my daily, weekly, and annual routines all revolve around my new understanding of myself as a Jewish Feminist.

What was latent all those years? What had been lying fallow for decades? How did the seeds planted at the Marc Chagall Biblical Message Museum in Nice blossom into the life I live today? And equally important, what is the source of the determination that leads me—again and again—to reject Conventional Wisdom and keep digging for deeper answers?

When: Spring 1975
Where: Harvard University

I had graduated from Livingston High School in Livingston, New Jersey, in June 1969, and then proceeded to break my mother's heart by attending St. John's College in Annapolis, Maryland (the "Great Books" school) rather than Barnard College in Manhattan (which had been her dream for me). Then I won a Thomas J. Watson Fellowship and left for Israel three weeks after receiving my BA in Liberal Arts from St. John's in May 1973. (The dean, Robert J. Goldwin, actually handed me the $6,000 Watson check at graduation, leading my proud father to tell all the relatives that I had graduated "Magna Cum Cash.")

My Watson project was called "The Concept of Cultural Deprivation." Sometime early in the fall of 1972, I had read an article in *Newsweek* magazine about "cultural deprivation." American college graduates would be sent to schools in inner cities and rural enclaves to work with students thought to be suffering from something called "cultural deprivation." Say what? I remember being very disturbed by this article. Didn't everyone have a culture? If yes, then how could someone be "culturally" deprived? So during my Watson Year, I spent a lot of time in Israeli and Iranian schools—in inner cities and rural enclaves—searching for Cultural Deprivation.

My Israeli mentor, Hertzel Fishman, urged me to continue my studies at Harvard (where he had received his own EdD), so I applied. Soon after, I flew off to Tehran to continue my Watson project. For the six weeks I was in Iran, I was basically incommunicado. But when I got to Istanbul and called my mother, I learned I had finally made good in her eyes. "You were accepted at Harvard," she said, "and I told them you were coming."

In the interim, I had learned a lot about economic hardship, cognitive deficit, and developmental disabilities. And although I was no wiser about "cultural deprivation," I came back more interested than ever in cognitive psychology… And that is what led me to study the work of Swiss psychologist Jean Piaget… And that is what led me to William James Hall.

During spring semester, I offered to assist Jane Platt—one of my professors—with her research. My job was to stand behind a screen while we showed movies to babies. The babies were 6 months old, 12 months old, and 18 months old. One at a time, they came into our research room and sat on their mothers' laps, facing three screens. The first movie played on the middle screen. A simple shape (we used squares, circles, and triangles) made a simple motion (up-and-down, side-to-side, and round-and-round). After 30 seconds, the middle movie switched off, and movies began running simultaneously on both the left and right screens. One screen showed the same shape in a different motion. The other screen showed the same motion but with a different shape. I think we sometimes varied the color combinations too.

I stood behind the screen—watching through a peephole—with two clickers that each had one button. When the baby looked at the left screen, I pressed the button on the clicker in my left hand. When the baby looked at the right screen, I pressed the button on the clicker in my right hand.

Now, in my mind's eye, I see myself doing a kind of rhythmic dance: click left, click right, freeze right, click left...

Afterwards, we fed the data from the two clickers into a machine that produced a long, curly piece of paper that looked something like an EKG strip. Then, we analyzed our data to see whether there was any discernable difference between left and right. Did babies appear to be more interested in shape, motion, or color? If yes, then what did they prefer—shape? motion? color?—and did their preferences change over time?

We were testing a theory called the discrepancy hypothesis, which is now known as the Goldilocks Effect. The overarching idea is that human beings have a cognitive "sweet spot." If something is "same old," then we quickly grow bored. If something is "too new," then we quickly recoil. But when something is new enough to hold our interest without boring us, then it is "just right."

Thinking about this experience now makes me laugh. Who would ever have guessed—way back in 1975—that one day I would become a film critic? And yet today, when people ask me why Hollywood is so heavily invested in making adaptations and sequels, my goal is always to answer the question succinctly without getting too pedantic.

Back to 1975: Much to my mother's dismay, I decided to leave Harvard in June. I decided to continue my studies with someone named Theodore Mischel at the State University of New York at Binghamton. ("Oh, Jan: Please think again! Do you really want to leave Harvard to go to SUNY Binghamton?!?") Professor Mischel was starting a new PhD program at SUNY Binghamton called "Hap-Sabs" for History and Philosophy of the Social and Behavioral Sciences (H.P.S.B.S.), and I was just the kind of iconoclast he was looking for to fill his first class.

I spent one year happily immersed in philosophy of science, philosophy of mind, and cognitive psychology, and then, at the beginning of my second year at SUNY Binghamton, Ted Mischel left campus on medical leave. Two months later, he was dead. Ted's brother Walter Mischel—internationally renowned now for his Marshmallow Test—has written eloquently about Ted's sudden death from stomach cancer in 1976. Me? I moved to Chicago to work on my dissertation with Professor Stephen Toulmin in a program called the Committee on the Conceptual Foundations of Science (C.F.S.) at the University of Chicago. That was August 1977.

In 1980, when Professor Toulmin learned that a journal called *International Studies in Philosophy* was planning a special issue on Piaget, he generously pulled some strings so that I could be one of the named contributors. My paper, which carries the very academic-sounding title "Egocentrism: A Defense of Pre-Reflexive Experience"—a title I barely understand myself now—allowed me to pay my deep intellectual debt to Professor Mischel through an articulation of the four principles that Mischel had derived from the work of Jean Piaget and passed on to me.

(1) What is observed depends on what is expected.

(2) What is anomalous depends on what is accepted.

(3) The continuity of thought depends on the "normal" tendency to assimilate anomalies to accepted paradigms through minor accommodations.

(4) The novelty of paradigms depends on a need to restructure the past in order to consolidate the present.

(1) What is observed depends on what is expected.

After more than a decade of work on the sources and synergies of *Fiddler on the Roof*, I now understand that when I walked into the Marc Chagall Biblical Message Museum on May 19, 2000, I was expecting kitsch. I was in Nice on vacation. All I really wanted to do was relax. Surely, Marc Chagall was not an artist to be taken seriously by a high-minded person like me.

(2) What is anomalous depends on what is accepted.

Once inside the museum, I was overwhelmed with emotion. It was immediately clear to me that the paintings on display at the Marc Chagall Biblical Message Museum were profoundly serious. I simply was not seeing the kitsch I had expected to see. Perhaps I was wrong about Marc Chagall? If yes, then maybe I needed to re-think my assumptions. But where had these assumptions come from anyway? I left the Marc Chagall Biblical Message Museum in a tizzy.

(3) The continuity of thought depends on the "normal" tendency to assimilate anomalies to accepted paradigms through minor accommodations.

In my lectures, you will see that I describe what happened to me at the Marc Chagall Biblical Message Museum on May 19, 2000, as the beginning of a "paradigm shift."

I was no longer able to see the work of Marc Chagall as kitsch. On my way out of the museum, I bought the book *Marc Chagall* by Andrew Kagan, which I began reading the next morning.

The next anomaly quickly presented itself on page 48:

> Hanging opposite *Introduction to the Jewish Theatre* in the auditorium [of Moscow's State Jewish Chamber Theatre] were four individual panels representing Jewish music, dance, theatre and literature. In the allegory of music, a theme Chagall repeated in the animated *The Green Violinist*, appears once again his fiddler on the roof, that stock character preserved from the world of the *shtetl* by Chagall and Sholem Aleichem. (Kagan, Page 48 [*sic*])

Say what? The character of the Fiddler in *Fiddler on the Roof* came from a painting by Marc Chagall? Well, if Chagall's work wasn't kitsch, then maybe *Fiddler on the Roof* wasn't kitsch either?

(4) The novelty of paradigms depends on a need to restructure the past in order to consolidate the present.

When I returned home from France, I started reading voraciously about Marc Chagall, Sholem Aleichem, and all things *Fiddler*. The more I read, the more doubts I had about my old paradigms, and the more obsessed I became with "restructuring the past in order to consolidate the present."

✡ ✡ ✡ ✡ ✡

"*Fiddler on the Roof* sets Village Theatre sales record," trumpeted a headline posted online on January 30, 2013, in the *Issaquah Press*. "Theatergoers embraced *Fiddler on the Roof* and propelled the classic musical to a Village Theatre sales record." The author, Warren Kagarise, continues:

> *Fiddler on the Roof* opened in Issaquah on November 8 to a
> standing ovation and enthusiastic reviews… [It] played at the
> downtown Issaquah theater through November and December,
> and then shifted to the Everett Performing Arts Center… In
> Issaquah, a record 32,726 audience members attended the show,
> including more than 14,000 single-ticket buyers—a significant
> number for a playhouse reliant on seasonal subscribers… In
> Everett, *Fiddler on the Roof* set more milestones. The show
> reached the revenue goals before opening night—a first for Village
> Theatre's Snohomish County stage—and broke the sales record
> for single-ticket revenue two weeks before *Fiddler on the Roof*
> closed January 27.

Issaquah? Everett? Snohomish? Kagarise is describing places somewhere east of Seattle, which is about as far from Manhattan as one can possibly go and still be in the continental United States. In November 2011, I even slipped across the border to attend a performance of *Fiddler on the Roof* at the Conexus Arts Centre in Regina, Saskatchewan. It was a Wednesday night, and this beautiful Canadian concert hall—which seats 2,031 people on three balconies—was packed full. Not bad for a musical that had made its Broadway debut almost 50 years ago! Not bad for a place with almost no Jews!

However unbelievable this fact sounds now, way back in 1964 *Fiddler's* backers expected a flop. Before investing, one worried prospect supposedly asked: "What will you do when you run out of Hadassah Ladies?" The critic from *Variety* who reviewed the very first public performance, held at the Fisher Theater in Detroit on June 27, 1964, wrote: "There are no memorable songs in this musical." He (known only as "TEW" and remaining forever anonymous) concluded his review with these damning words: "*Fiddler on the Roof* has a chance for moderate success on Broadway." When *Fiddler on the Roof* finally did open on Broadway, the reviews were mixed. The only element that really excited Howard Taubman, a critic from the *New York Times*, was Zero Mostel's performance as Tevye; and some of his colleagues went so far as to predict that the show would close once Mostel's contract expired.

Audiences embraced *Fiddler on the Roof* anyway. Just like the folks in faraway Snohomish County, Washington, people all around Metro New York purchased tickets (even though, in that pre Internet era, they had to wait in long lines that stretched around the corner). Then they raved about the show to all their friends when they got home. When *Fiddler on the Roof* finally closed in 1972—**after 3,242 performances**—it had become the longest-running show in the history of Broadway. It held that record for more than a decade until it was finally eclipsed by the success of *A Chorus Line* in 1984.

But that was just the beginning. More than 50 years later, *Fiddler on the Roof* is still a theatrical phenomenon that continues to play regularly on stages of every size, from high schools and colleges to community theaters and regional touring companies, all around the world. Norman Jewison's film adaptation, released in 1971, received eight Oscar nominations (including Best Picture) and won three. Gross domestic revenue in 1970s dollars was $10,404,330, and it is likely that millions of VHS tapes, CDs, and DVDs have been sold since. Meanwhile, a fifth revival opened on Broadway last year on December 20, 2015.

Searching Amazon today—April 15, 2016—I found innumerable CD and vinyl recordings, including cast albums in American English, British English, German, and Yiddish, as well as covers by artists as diverse as jazz musicians Cannonball Adderley and Eddie Gomez, and singers Jan Peerce and the Barry Sisters. There is a mellow option from the Boston Pops and an edgy option from the Knitting Factory. There are even multiple karaoke versions for all the aspiring Anatevkans who want to practice before an audition or just make their own fun at home.

Searching YouTube today—April 15, 2016—I found more than 455,000 results, most of which are snippets in American English that include hundreds of live performances of the much-loved Musical-Prologue "Tradition." There is also a Lego stop-motion version of it from 2010 set to music from 1964's Original Broadway Cast Recording. As of today, 56,412 people besides me have seen this Lego version. And 32,398 people have also watched the 1982 performance of "Tradition" in Japanese, which 95 people "like" (including me).

In 2010, when MacArthur Genius Lin-Manuel Miranda—creator of the Broadway hits *In The Heights* and *Hamilton*—married New York attorney Vanessa Nadal, the whole wedding party surprised her at the reception with a performance of "To Life" starring Miranda and his new father-in-law. The video, uploaded to YouTube on September 8, 2010, already has almost five million hits!

So how did the critics get it so wrong way back in 1964? What did audience members see onstage in 1964 that seems to have gone right over the critics' heads? There is a hint in this anecdote told by Joseph Stein—the man who wrote the *Fiddler on the Roof* libretto—in a 2003 lecture at Hofstra University.

> I must tell one story about that opening night [in Detroit] because we were very worried. This was a new show. It was a strange, strange subject. It was a very unusual musical. After the first act, I was standing in the lobby, eagerly listening to people's opinions. I was standing with [producer] Hal Prince, and **a lady ran over to an open phone booth**, and **she called**, evidently, **her husband**. We were both listening eagerly, and **she said**: "Harry, for one night you should have given up your gin game. It's a wonderful show. You won't believe it. In the middle of everything, they have a pogrom!" That was the first **review** I heard of *Fiddler on the Roof.*

But who were "the critics" in 1964? Here is a revealing fact: The Billy Rose Theatre Division at the New York Public Library's Library for the Performing Arts at Lincoln Center (NYPL)—a place in which I have spent countless wonderful research days—has a vast collection of *Fiddler on the Roof* materials. Over the years, I have scoured through boxes and boxes of reviews, beginning with the "TEW" review in *Variety* published way back in June 1964. As I read through boxes and boxes of materials from the 1960s, it quickly became clear to me that every single review in the NYPL file was signed by a man! The first review signed by a woman was Pauline Kael's review of Norman Jewison's film adaptation, a review she wrote for the *New Yorker* in 1972.

Are you skeptical? Then turn to page 207 of *Opening Night on Broadway: A Critical Quotebook of the Golden Era of Musical Theatre*, Oklahoma! (1943) *to* Fiddler on the Roof (1964) by Steven Suskin, and read the names there for yourself: John Chapman (*Daily News*), Walter Kerr (*Herald Tribune*), John McClain (*Journal-American*), Norman Nadel (*World-Telegram & Sun*), Howard Taubman (*New York Times*), and Richard Watts Jr. (*New York Post*). These are the **men** who determined "the critical consensus," and here is Suskin's summation:

BROADWAY SCORECARD / perfs: 3,242 / $: +				
Rave	Favorable	Mixed	Unfavorable	Pan
2	4	-	-	-

From Steven Suskin's *Opening Night on Broadway: A Critical Quotebook of the Golden Era of the Musical Theatre*, Oklahoma! (1943) *to* Fiddler on the Roof (1964)

The scholarly community has been equally male-dominated. In his highly influential article "Fiddling with Sholem Aleichem: A History of *Fiddler on the Roof*," Brandeis historian Stephen J. Whitfield cites his sources, which include the following: *A Century in the Life of Sholem Aleichem's Tevye* (Ken Frieden); *The Americanization of Tevye or Boarding the Jewish Mayflower* (Seth L. Wolitz); and Fiddler on the Roof: *The Making of a Musical* (Richard Altman with Mervyn Kaufman).

But when Whitfield makes the startling claim in this 2003 article that *Fiddler on the Roof* was "born in the era when fathers knew best," all the pieces begin to fall into place. CBS broadcast the last episode of the popular sitcom *Father Knows Best* on May 23, 1960. The premiere of *Fiddler on the Roof* was September 22, 1964. By that time, the "era when fathers knew best" was long over, and what we now call the Sixties was well underway. So perhaps Whitfield still longed for "the era when fathers knew best," but the creators of *Fiddler on the Roof* were already embracing President Kennedy's New Frontier. And then—after JFK's assassination—they were totally committed to the birth of President Johnson's Great Society.

No one will ever know the identity of that woman in Detroit, but her voice is alive in me. Today I am a life member of Hadassah—like my mother and her mother before me—and I take pride in the fact that "Hadassah Ladies" defied all those male critics, bought all those tickets, and refused to be intimidated by yet another uphill battle. I bet that woman in Detroit was a Hadassah Lady too, but even if she wasn't, there is no question that she was Jewish and spoke for women everywhere in an unmistakably Jewish voice.

It has taken me more than a dozen years to fully understand that what the male critics missed in 1964—and what so many male scholars still miss today—is that *Fiddler on the Roof* is not about the past; *Fiddler on the Roof* is about the future.

- Coming into my own as a Jewish Feminist has meant taking *Fiddler on the Roof* back from the men who think that *Fiddler on the Roof* is about Tevye, when it is really about Tevye's daughters.

- Coming into my own as a Jewish Feminist means helping others to appreciate that the *Fiddler on the Roof* created on stage by Jerome Robbins in 1964 is significantly different from—and significantly better than—the film adaptation released on screen by Norman Jewison in 1971.

- Coming into my own as a Jewish Feminist requires that I leave a roadmap for "Tevye's Daughters"—girls of every cultural, ethnic, national, and religious background—not just for the next generation but for all the generations to come.

"Girls should learn too. Girls are people." Perchik makes this declaration in Act One, Scene 2 of *Fiddler on the Roof*, and Tevye immediately agrees. "Food for lessons? Good. Stay with us for the Sabbath."

Far from being the man I was told about—a man described by other men as "desperately clinging to Tradition"—I have come to know Tevye as a father much like my own. I have come to appreciate that Tevye was a man who opened the door to the future by encouraging his daughters to read, educate themselves, and realize their potential as human beings. And wonder of wonders, miracle of miracles, I have even learned that Solomon Rabinowitz—the beloved Yiddish author best-known by his pen name Sholem Aleichem—was that kind of father to his many daughters too!

✡✡✡✡✡

My life did not turn out as expected. I never finished my PhD at the University of Chicago. I never became an academic. I never made any contributions to philosophy of science, philosophy of mind, or cognitive psychology. (Mommy: You were so right! Since I wanted to be a professor, I should have stayed at Harvard!) But I have lived a wonderful life, and this book is the culmination of the many subjects I have studied over the course of my life. It is propelled by intellectual curiosity and it breaks new ground.

Specifically, in this book, I will explain the astounding and totally unexpected success of the Broadway musical *Fiddler on the Roof* as a perfect example of the Goldilocks Effect. What its author, Joseph Stein, considered a "strange, strange subject… a very unusual musical" quickly became a new theatrical paradigm, so much so that by the time the film arrived on screen, no one even remembered that it had once been considered a risky endeavor.

And 50 years after its Broadway premiere on September 22, 1964, *Fiddler on the Roof* is more popular than ever. It has become one of the touchstones of world culture, just as relevant to the "sweet spot" of our current concerns as it was on the day of its debut. And even though I probably will not be alive to see it, I am totally confident that many will feel the same way about it on the 75th Diamond Anniversary and 100th Centenary Anniversary and beyond.

Helene and Eddie Huttner (1982)

So I invite you to join me on this journey, and maybe, by the end, you will learn to see some aspects anew too. I know my parents are "up there" somewhere with Solomon Rabinowitz, Marc Chagall, Jerome Robbins, their wives, and generations of Hadassah Ladies, and they are all cheering us on.

Jan Lisa Huttner
Brooklyn, New York
May 13, 2016

Perchik Tears down the Mechitzah

Act One, Scene 10

From Gold to Diamond: Moving Beyond Our Father's *Fiddler*

This lecture was originally presented to Brooklyn Hadassah at the Essen Deli in Brooklyn, New York, on June 24, 2014. It was subsequently presented to Congregation Tifereth Israel in Washington, D.C., on December 6, 2014.

One of the wonderful aspects about anniversary dates is that they focus the mind. Whether it is in our personal life, our professional life, or the life of our culture, an anniversary date prompts us to ask ourselves deep questions: Where am I now? Where did I come from? Where am I going?

A Golden Anniversary is a 50th anniversary. A Diamond Anniversary is a 75th anniversary. *Fiddler on the Roof* opened on Broadway on September 22, 1964, so September 22, 2014, will be the 50th anniversary of that Opening Night. And that fact also prompts us to ask ourselves deep questions: What is our current understanding of *Fiddler on the Roof* now, on its Golden Anniversary? What was our understanding of *Fiddler on the Roof* on that first Opening Night 50 years ago? What will our understanding of *Fiddler on the Roof* be on its Diamond Anniversary on September 22, 2039?

I believe we are at a critical point in world culture and we have it in our power to decide whether *Fiddler on the Roof* will go in one direction (let's call it a "progressive" direction) or in another (let us call it a "conservative" direction). I know these are provocative and polarizing labels right now, so please trust me when I say that I am not using them just for the sake of controversy. By using these words upfront at the beginning of my presentation, I am announcing the fact that I plan to say some things about *Fiddler on the Roof* today that might well surprise you.

Let us start with Conventional Wisdom. What does our Conventional Wisdom say about *Fiddler on the Roof* in 2014?

Here is a quote from Stephen J. Whitfield, a prominent professor of Jewish Studies, who published a very influential article called "Fiddling with Sholem Aleichem: A History of *Fiddler on the Roof*" in 2003:

> *Fiddler on the Roof*, born in the era when fathers knew best, had located a problem [tradition] at the heart of Sholem Aleichem's stories.

And here is a quote from the foreword to Philip Lambert's book, *To Broadway, To Life! The Musical Theater of Bock and Harnick*, published by Oxford University Press in 2011:

> And then came *Fiddler on the Roof* on September 22, 1964… When it closed eight years later, *Fiddler* had knocked *My Fair Lady* off her pedestal as Broadway's longest run… and it was followed by an elaborately faithful (and musically nearly complete) film in 1971.

These are two prevalent ideas, both of which encapsulate Conventional Wisdom about *Fiddler on the Roof* in 2014.

- *Fiddler* comes from the **era when fathers knew best**.
- The movie—made in 1971—is an **elaborately faithful** version of the stage production.

My goal today is to convince you that both of these two pieces of Conventional Wisdom about *Fiddler on the Roof* are totally wrong.

Who am I?

Who am I and how do I have the chutzpah to attack the Conventional Wisdom established by recognized experts such as Stephen J. Whitfield (a prominent professor of Jewish Studies) and Geoffrey Block (the editor of Oxford University Press's Broadway Legacies series)?

My story begins in Newark, New Jersey, in 1951. I was born at Beth Israel Hospital, and like most Jewish people in Newark, my parents—and many members of my extended family—lived in the Weequahic section. Our apartment was on Wainwright Street.

Has anyone here read Philip Roth's semi-autobiographical novel *The Plot Against America*? Good! In *The Plot Against America*, Philip Roth says he lived on Wainwright Street when he was a kid too! He describes our block—Wainwright Street between Chancellor Avenue and Lyons Avenue—perfectly. I went to Chancellor Avenue School, and we spent our summers at Kassack's Bungalow Colony in the Catskills. Has anyone here seen the film *A Walk on the Moon* with Diane Lane, Tovah Feldshuh, Liev Schreiber, and Viggo Mortensen? Good! That's exactly what Kassack's looked like when I was young.

In 1961, just before I turned ten, we moved to the booming suburb of Livingston, New Jersey. Some of you might remember that in *Goodbye, Columbus*, Neil lives in Newark, but Neil's cousin Doris lives in Livingston. That is how Neil gains admittance to the exclusive swim club where he meets Brenda. Doris invites Neil to join her one day at the club, and when Brenda asks him who he is, Neil tells Brenda that he is Doris's cousin. When Brenda says she doesn't know Doris, Neil says something like this: "Every year there is a fat girl at the pool reading *War and Peace*, and that girl is my cousin Doris."

The first time I read *Goodbye, Columbus* I flipped. I really was a fat girl who read *War and Peace* at the Livingston Community Pool every summer! But Roth's story was published in 1959, so Doris was that girl in the late '50s, whereas I did not become that girl until the mid-'60s. So how did Roth know? Even now, as I tell you about this, I am still asking myself if I am really **me**, or if I am someone who popped out whole from a Philip Roth story?

It has taken me decades to realize that I was born to write about *Fiddler on the Roof*. But ironically, *Fiddler* was so integral to the milieu in which I was raised that I have absolutely no memory of when I first saw it.

- I vividly remember going with my mother to see *Man of La Mancha* on Broadway. I cried. It was wonderful. That was probably sometime in 1966.

- I vividly remember being at MoMA and seeing Picasso's *Guernica* for the first time. I was awestruck. It was amazing. That was probably sometime in 1967.

- I vividly remember our trip to the Clairidge Theater in Montclair to see Barbra Streisand onscreen in *Funny Girl*. I loved it and I love it still. That was definitely in 1968.

But I have no memory of having seen *Fiddler on the Roof* when I was young—either onstage or onscreen—although I know, of course, that I did. And given how I live my life now that is an amazing fact.

So what **do** I remember about *Fiddler on the Roof*?

In May of 2000, just a little more than 14 years ago, Richard and I went to France with Juanita (his mom). It was her 75th birthday. My sister-in-law Kathryn wanted to have a big party in Florida, but Juanita said: "Why on earth should you all come here when we can pick someplace fun?" So off we went to France!

The first morning of the first day was spent at the Matisse Museum in Nice. Wow. Then after lunch we went over to the Marc Chagall Biblical Message Museum in Cimiez, high in the mountains above Nice. Have any of you ever been there? Good.

I… was… agog! I do not know how else to say it. And even talking to you about this now, even telling you about this day, I am getting chills up and down my spine.

The Marc Chagall Biblical Message Museum in Cimiez is filled with huge canvasses. You walk in, and the first thing that you see is a magnificent mandala. It lives in a painting called *Genesis*, and Chagall has placed Jesus Christ right in the middle of his mandala, and Chagall's Jesus is wearing a tallis as a loincloth!

I have now seen this image—and many others like it—at least a hundred times, but at that point it was new to me, and I just was stunned. This was not the Chagall of the flying lovers and the little flowers and all that "kitschy stuff." This was something totally different.

I had read books like *My Name is Asher Lev*, so I knew that "Jewish Art" was problematic. But here I was, looking at paintings made right after the Holocaust, and it was clear to me that the Jewish artist who had created them was seeking a way to cope with despair. Walking through the museum and looking at each painting in turn, I could hear Chagall demanding an answer from God: "Our Bible says You were **here** with Abraham and **here** with Jacob and **here** with Moses. And I even believe You were **here** with Jesus too. So where were You during the Holocaust?"

36

I was deeply, deeply moved. Three days later, I pleaded a headache and went back to the Marc Chagall Biblical Message Museum by myself, while Juanita and Richard went off with our tour group. I worked my way through a room of drawers filled with sketches and found a whole series of images of Jacob wrestling with the angel. The final one hangs on a wall in the museum, of course, but the sketches preserved in these drawers show how hard Chagall himself wrestled with Jacob's Angel. I had not expected any of this when I arrived in Nice. None of it. Not at all.

On my way out of the museum that first day, I bought a book about the artist by Andrew Kagan. The next day I got up really early in the morning. Richard was snoring away. I ordered room service, got my coffee, and headed out to the balcony with my book. I started to read... and then I got to page 48:

> In the allegory of music, a theme Chagall repeated in the animated *The Green Violinist*, appears once again his fiddler on the roof, that stock character preserved from the world of the *shtetl* by Chagall and Sholem Aleichem.

I look at the picture of the *Green Violinist* as if I am seeing it for the very first time, and I say out loud to all of Nice: "OMG! It's **the Fiddler**... on the Roof." (See page 57 for the full image.)

Let me digress for a moment. In that particular paragraph, Kagan is actually talking about the four murals—*Music, Dance, Drama* and *Literature*—that Chagall created for the State Jewish Chamber Theater in Moscow in 1920. The originals are now on exhibit in the State Tretyakov Gallery in Moscow, and have also been on exhibit in museums in New York, Paris, San Francisco, and other places as well. But at that time, way back in 2000, they had not been seen for decades. The four original murals had been hidden away in the former Soviet Union because people were afraid that if they fell into the wrong hands, they would be destroyed. So they were hidden away for decades until finally, after the Soviet Union collapsed, people were able to bring these treasures out safely. And now there is even a Chagall Museum in a country called Belarus. A Chagall Museum behind the Iron Curtain would have been unthinkable in 1964, but now—in 2014—this is all old news.

And yet, I am somewhat surprised to report that there is a bit of controversy about exactly which painting is **the** "Fiddler on the Roof." Just last week, a journalist from the *Washington Post* was writing about the event at Town Hall in Manhattan on June 9 celebrating *Fiddler's* 50th, Sheldon Harnick's 90th birthday, and the imminent centennial of the Folksbiene in 2015. How many of us were there at Town Hall on June 9? Hands up. Wow. Even in this little room, someone was there besides me? So sorry I didn't know to look for you.

On June 10, a journalist wrote about the Town Hall event for the *Washington Post*, and she added a link in her post to a Chagall painting called *Blue Violinist*. So I sent her a Facebook message: "Why did you pick that link? In 1964, that painting was in a private collection." No answer. And then there is the one called *Le Violoniste* from 1912. *Le Violoniste* has been owned by the Stedelijk Museum in Amsterdam for decades. Some people think that is "the one," but it isn't. **This is the one. This one—*The Green Violinist*—is THE "Fiddler on the Roof."** I could talk for at least an hour on this subject. In fact, I did speak for about an hour at Evanston Public Library in Illinois a few years back. But right now, you will just have to take my word for it…

Back to that morning—Saturday, May 20, 2000—I was thunderstruck. I said to myself: "How can this be news to me? This is something I have grown up with. This is something that has been part of my life for as long as I can remember."

And then, because I am primarily a film person, I started thinking about the movie and how there really is no Chagall in the movie version of *Fiddler on the Roof*… Norman Jewison was very determined to make his adaptation "realistic," and if you read his autobiography *This Terrible Business Has Been Good to Me*, Jewison writes a lot about his re-creation of the little synagogue and all these other things that he did to make his version of *Fiddler on the Roof* "authentic."

Me? I would claim that in making it "authentic," Jewison ruined part of the essence of *Fiddler on the Roof*, but ultimately that is for you to decide for yourself. At this point, just remember what I stated in my introduction: Conventional Wisdom claims that Jewison's version is "elaborately faithful." That is bunk. Whatever it is, it is **not** the same.

What about You?

Okay, so now I'm going to turn it back to you, and ask for a show of hands.

• Did you see the original Broadway production which ran from 1964 to 1972? If yes, raise your hand. Okay.

• Hold up your hand if you saw the 40th anniversary production which ran from 2004 to 2006, with either Alfred Molina or Harvey Fierstein as Tevye. Okay.

• Hold up your hand if you saw another stage performance after the film was released in 1971. Broadway revival? Community theater? School production? Almost everyone.

• Hold up your hand if you saw the 1971 film adaptation by Norman Jewison. In a theater? On VHS/DVD? Everybody.

• Bonus Points: Hold up your hand if you saw Maurice Schwartz's film version of *Tevye* from 1939. This is the Yiddish film written by, directed by, and starring Maurice Schwartz as Tevye. Nu? Why not? *Tevye* is now distributed by the National Center for Jewish Film. Ah… I see this one is a stretch.

• Now hold up your hand if you have seen a non-English version onstage in any other language. In Russian? In Hebrew? At Habima in Tel Aviv? Wow.

• And finally, is there anyone in this room who has never seen *Fiddler on the Roof* either onstage or onscreen? No? Hooray!

Why do I ask? A couple of years ago, I gave a lecture on Yente-the-Matchmaker at the Harold Washington Library Center in downtown Chicago, and I noticed a man in the audience who looked very perplexed. So I said to him: "Are you all right? Is everything okay?" And he said: "When are you going to talk about Barbra Streisand?" What could I say? So I said: "Whoops. Sorry. You're in the wrong lecture!" Now I always ask, even though it is almost always the case that everyone in my audience has seen *Fiddler on the Roof* at least once at some point in their lives, and most people have seen it several times in a variety of versions.

Looking back to 1916

Now I want to talk specifically about 1964 today, but before I can get there, I have to blitz very quickly through a preamble that begins in 1916. Nineteen-sixteen was the year that the last of Sholem Aleichem's eight Tevye stories was published, and it was also the year that Sholem Aleichem died. As we learned from Naomi Ragen's novel, *The Sisters Weiss* (which we discussed in our last Park Slope Hadassah Book Club meeting), there were already Jewish women writers on the literary scene—educated, intelligent, sometimes even scholarly women—who were writing, thinking, and acting as empowered individuals in 1916.

Did any of you see Michal Aviad's *The Women Pioneers* at the New York Jewish Film Festival in January? It is a terrific documentary about women from Russia and the former Soviet Union who made Aliyah in the 1910s and 1920s. By the time of Sholem Aleichem's death in 1916, very committed, politically active Jewish women had left Russia and gone to the Yishuv—the part of Palestine that was to become the State of Israel—and they were active members of Israel's earliest Kibbutz communities.

And of course—circling back to Barbra Streisand for a moment—we all know that "Yentl" is an example of someone who came to America at the turn of the 20th century to do exactly this, to realize the dream of creating herself as a new independent woman. We all know that Emma Goldman, who was born in Kovno—now Lithuania—was living here in New York in 1916, but was deported to the new Soviet Union after the Russian Revolution. We all know that Golda Meir, who was born in Kiev—now Ukraine—was living in Milwaukee in 1916. She made Aliyah in 1921. We all know this, right? Of course, right.

So when we are watching *Fiddler on the Roof*, we need to remember what we all know: the Russian Jewish community was very vibrant at the turn of the 20th century, and many women were active participants in the tumultuous upheaval.

But did you know that at the time of his death on May 13, 1916, Solomon Rabinowitz—the man we all know now by his pen name Sholem Aleichem—Solomon Rabinowitz had five "daughters"?

We know a lot about his family life because his fourth daughter Musa—who published under the name Marie Waife-Goldberg—wrote a book called *My Father, Sholom Aleichem* that she published in 1967 (well after *Fiddler on the Roof* had become a Broadway blockbuster). Nevertheless, much of the information that she provides in this book, information that has been available for almost 50 years now, has yet to make its way to Wikipedia. Nobody seems to know much about Solomon Rabinowitz's daughters. At best, they know that a writer named Bel Kaufman was his granddaughter…

So let me walk you really, really quickly through the Rabinowitz family tree, based on information that I have distilled from the pages of *My Father, Sholom Aleichem*.

The patriarch was Elimelech Loyeff. Elimelech Loyeff was the father of Olga Loyeff, the woman who became Olga Rabinowitz (aka "Madame Sholem Aleichem"). Elimelech Loyeff had a first wife, and this first wife had two sons named Israel and Yeshia (Joshua). Israel and Joshua both had one child each, and both were girls. Israel's daughter was named Manya, and Joshua's daughter was named Natasha. As far as I know, the name of wife #1 is lost to history. She gave birth to two sons, and then she died.

After wife #1—the wife with no name—died, Elimelech Loyeff married a woman named Rakhil (Rukhl) Yampolsky. Rukhl Yampolsky had one daughter named Olga, and this is the woman who married Solomon Rabinowitz. In America, she became "Mrs. Olga Rabinowitz," and her name is on all the Sholem Aleichem copyrights because she became the main trustee of his estate after he died. He died in 1916. She died in 1947.

To make a long story short, Solomon and Olga had six children (from oldest to youngest): Tissa, Lyala, Emma, Mischa, Musa, and Numa. (Lyala is their second daughter, and she was the mother of Bel Kaufman.) In total, Solomon and Olga had two sons named Mischa and Numa plus four daughters (Tissa, Lyala, Emma, and Musa). But, when Elimelech Loyeff died (which sadly happened after the deaths of his own two sons), Solomon Rabinowitz also became the legal guardian of the two girls—Manya and Natasha—who were technically his step-nieces at the time, and probably also his students before that.

RABINOWITZ FAMILY TREE

© Jan Lisa Huttner (2018)

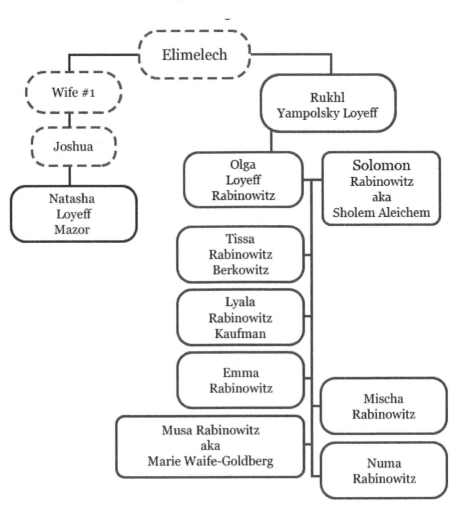

In czarist Russia circa 1885—the year that Elimelech Loyeff died—women could not inherit, and so all of Elimelech Loyeff's property went to his one remaining male heir, namely his son-in-law Solomon Rabinowitz (aka Sholem Aleichem). The fathers of these children—the sons of Elimelech Loyeff and his first wife—both got divorced and then died young, so the person who was actually raising these two little girls was Rukhl Yampolsky. After all, they were only slightly younger than her own daughter Olga. When Solomon Rabinowitz arrived on the Loyeff Estate in 1877, Olga was 15, Manya was 9, and Natasha was 5.

Complicated? I know. But here is what you need to know: Manya died soon after her grandfather (at age 19), but Natasha lived a long and full life as a member of Sholem Aleichem's "family circle." Legal terms like "ward" hardly do justice to the intimacy of their personal relationships. Olga was technically Natasha's aunt, but more likely, they grew up as two of three "sisters" who came of age in Rukhl Yampolsky's home. One thing, however, is beyond dispute: After Elimelech Loyeff died, Solomon Rabinowitz became the person legally responsible for Natasha's dowry. So Sholem Aleichem—the author who wrote eight stories about Tevye-the-Milkman—was also a man named Solomon Rabinowitz, and that man—Solomon Rabinowitz—was personally responsible for the dowries of five young women as they reached marriageable age… Ringing any bells?

So this puts a whole new light on what is going on in the Tevye stories. "I have five daughters!" Tevye announces at the start of every stage production of *Fiddler on the Roof.* "I have five daughters!!!" Furthermore, Natasha—who was, in effect, the eldest of Solomon Rabinowitz's own five daughters—married a man who was over 20 years older than she was.

No one to date has expressed much interest in the fact that Solomon Rabinowitz lived in a home filled with so many highly-educated daughters. Did this family dynamic influence what Solomon Rabinowitz chose to write about as Sholem Aleichem? Once again, I could talk for at least an hour on **this** subject too, but I won't. Right now—once again—you will just have to take my word for it. Today, we must flip right past all this and keep going.

For now, just think about what you already know about all the events that were happening in the world in those 22 years between 1894 and 1916. It was a period of tremendous change all around the world! And for women, it was, well—minimally—it was the dawn of the worldwide Women's Suffrage movement. And "Sholem Aleichem" and his wife and his daughters were all a part of it.

Looking back to 1939

So let us now do a little dip into 1939. Maurice Schwartz's Yiddish film *Tevye* was released in theaters in Warsaw and New York in the fall of 1939, at exactly the same moment in time that the Nazis were invading Poland. I have heard a lot of people say: "Oh, it is so much more authentic than *Fiddler on the Roof.*" It is **not** more authentic. That is simply wrong.

Schwartz's film is different than *Fiddler on the Roof* in many ways, but it is still an adaptation—an adaptation that takes its own liberties with the Tevye stories. This is a fact, not a critique. It is wonderful and I love it, but if you haven't seen it for yourself, then I must tell you that many problematic characters have been invented from scratch whereas many beloved characters—who are actually in the Tevye stories in black and white—have gone missing.

Another digression: The City Cinemas Village East—the little multiplex on Second Avenue and Twelfth Street in Manhattan—did you know that building once housed Maurice Schwartz's Yiddish Art Theater? All of these productions that Maurice Schwartz is so famous for today, including his stage production of *Tevye*, and his very famous Yiddish production *Shylock* "fartaytsht un farbesert" (which in English means Schwartz "translated and improved" William Shakespeare's play *The Merchant of Venice*), all of these productions had their premieres in this building that is still on the corner of Second Avenue and Twelfth Street.

It is such a wonderful place! If you go into theater one—the big one at the top of the main staircase—and look up, you will see that the beautiful chandelier hanging from the ceiling is in the shape of a six-point Jewish star. And there is a plaque just past the front door that says "Dedicated in 1926."

Maurice Schwartz's Yiddish Art Theater—one of a number of Yiddish theaters located on Second Avenue in the first half of the last century—

helped give rise to the description of Second Avenue as "Yiddish Broadway." I was living in Chicago when I wrote about *Tevye* for the *World Jewish Digest* in 2004, so when I came to New York to visit friends in 2008, I searched until I found it. Now that I live in Brooklyn, I go there all the time to talk to Maury's ghost.

Back to Tevye. The focus of Schwartz's version is on Chava's marriage to Fyedka, you know, the daughter who married the goy. And more than anything else, it captures the fact that it was filmed at the point when Jews in America were hearing about Kristallnacht and worried that something unprecedented was about to happen. Before that, no one wanted to believe it. They couldn't believe it. "We will ride this one out just like we've always done." But after Kristallnacht, there was a new feeling of heaviness and despair, and even so—as we all know now—that foreboding proved to be minor in comparison to what actually ended up happening. This is the context in which Maurice Schwartz released his adaptation in 1939. It is important to know all this when you watch it.

Looking back to 1964

So finally, finally, we get to the year that is our main topic today—1964—the year *Fiddler on the Roof* premiered on Broadway. And finally, finally, we get back to our first quote:

***Fiddler on the Roof*, born in the era when "fathers knew best."**

Really?

The first broadcast of *Father Knows Best* was October 3, 1954, during the first term of the Eisenhower Presidency. The final broadcast was May 23, 1960, a few months before John Fitzgerald Kennedy ushered in the New Frontier.

The Anderson Family! We all remember them, right? Of course, right! Jim and Margaret were such lovely people, right? Of course, right! But all this year, the American press has been covering 50th anniversary commemorative events, and the litany of names and dates reminds us that by 1964, the era of *Father Knows Best* was long over.

Here are a few milestone events from the early 1960s, and obviously these events are the ones I consider most relevant to the surprising and totally unanticipated success of *Fiddler on the Roof*.

February 19, 1963: Betty Friedan—born Betty Naomi Goldstein—publishes *The Feminine Mystique*. This book expands on themes first presented in a *Good Housekeeping* article Friedan published in August 1960 called **"Women Are People, Too."**

Remember what Perchik says to Tevye when they first meet in Act One, Scene 2 of *Fiddler on the Roof* ?

> **Tevye**: What do you do Perchik?
> **Perchik**: I'm a teacher. I teach children. Do you have any children?
> **Tevye**: Oh, I have five daughters.
> **Perchik**: **Five** daughters?
> **Tevye: Daughters.**
> **Perchik**: Well, **girls are people too.**

Tevye is fine with this answer. He offers Perchik food in exchange for lessons, and invites him home for Shabbat. Later—at the end of Act One—when Perchik pulls down the mechitzah separating the men from the women at Tzeitel's wedding and then starts dancing—in public!—with Hodel, Tevye signals to Golde and they start dancing too. In fact, from the moment Perchik arrives in Anatevka right up to the moment that Perchik leaves for Kiev early in Act Two—and even beyond when Tevye personally takes Hodel to the train station so she can join Perchik in Siberia—Stein makes it clear that Tevye is always on Perchik's side of every controversy and dispute.

And the Tevye/Perchik relationship starts when Joseph Stein—in his libretto—has Perchik use a phrase that clearly echoes the title of Betty Friedan's article "Women Are People, Too!" "Well, girls are people too!" Coincidence?

When I interviewed Stephanie Coontz about her book *A Strange Stirring: "The Feminine Mystique" and American Women at the Dawn of the 1960s* for the *JUF News*, she told me: "I had about 300 letters [in the Friedan archives] that I had to sort through to do my interviews, and I quickly realized a disproportionate number of the women who wrote to her were Jewish."

My gut tells me Sadie Singer Stein (the woman who was married to Joseph Stein when he was writing *Fiddler on the Roof*) knew all about Betty

Friedan, and most of the women in *Fiddler on the Roof*'s earliest audiences (most of whom were also "disproportionately" Jewish too) also knew all about Betty Friedan.

February 19, 1963: Martin Luther King Jr. gives his "I Have a Dream" speech from the steps of the Lincoln Memorial in Washington, D.C. Could any Jew alive that day—less than 20 years after the end of the Holocaust—fail to be moved by Dr. King's desire to live in a nation in which people are "judged by the content of their character"?

November 22, 1963: John Fitzgerald Kennedy is assassinated in Dallas, Texas. Jerome Robbins—having been invited to the Kennedy White House after he won the Best Director Oscar for *West Side Story*—shut everything down as soon as he heard and sent everyone on the *Fiddler on the Roof* team home to grieve.

February 9, 1964: The Beatles make their first appearance on the *The Ed Sullivan Show*. I was bouncing up and down on the sofa. Looking at me in disgust, my father said: "Settle down, young lady!" Years later, my father finally confessed that—at least with respect to The Beatles—he had not known best. The Boomers were booming and the "youthquake" was on.

March 27, 1964: An article about the murder of a woman named Kitty Genovese appears in the *New York Times*. The name "Kitty Genovese" was actually a private name that very few people knew when she was murdered on March 13. But now it is a name that conjures up an image of neighbors who stand by and watch while people they know face great brutality.

Who wrote this article for the *New York Times*? Martin Gansberg. Who wanted this article written? Metropolitan editor Abe Rosenthal. So two Jewish men—one of whom, Abe Rosenthal, had written a haunting article for the *New York Times* about a visit to Auschwitz in 1956—were the people who really made "Kitty Genovese" the name/the symbol that we know today. This is enormously significant.

Did any of you read Nicholas Lemann's big article in the *New Yorker* a couple of months ago, the one in which he talked about two new books on Kitty Genovese? Soon after, the *New Yorker* published a set of letters to the editor, and I actually called one of the writers (a man in Connecticut named John V. H. Dippel), and I did a phone interview. Why? Because in his letter, he pointed out how much the photo of Kitty Genovese in the *New York Times* article resembled photos of Millie Perkins as she had appeared in publicity shots for *The Diary of Anne Frank*. He was totally right. Maybe no one caught this at the time, but I now believe it made a huge subliminal impression.

August 4, 1964: Today is June 24, 2014. Fifty years ago on this date (June 24, 1964), many Americans—many of whom were Jewish-Americans—were in Mississippi for "Freedom Summer." James Earl Chaney, Andrew Goodman, and Michael "Mickey" Schwerner were already missing, but there was still hope. Three young men—one African American and two Jewish Americans—had disappeared. Their bodies were found on August 4.

In one of his notes, Jerome Robbins told Bert Convy—Broadway's first Perchik—that he should play Perchik as if he were leaving Anatevka to go to Mississippi…

August 24, 1964: Fannie Lou Hamer of the Mississippi Freedom Democratic Party demands to be seated at the Democratic National Convention in Atlantic City, New Jersey. The Credentials Committee refuses to seat the MFDP; Lyndon Johnson is nominated for a second term; and Hamer—like many other African American women leaders—is later obliterated from the history of the Civil Rights Movement.

October 1, 1964: Once again, it is a Jewish guy—a Jewish **student**—who is front and center. Jack Weinberg was arrested for "violating the University's new rules regarding student political activism," and this was the trigger event for the Berkeley Free Speech Movement.

November 4, 1964: LBJ wins a second term in a landslide election.

And here is how various events map out on the *Fiddler on the Roof* timeline:

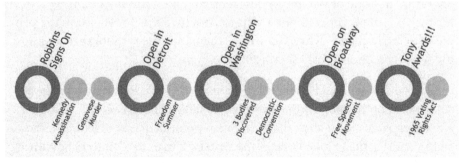

© Jan Lisa Huttner (2016)

In August of 1963, Jerome Robbins agrees to direct *Fiddler on the Roof*. Harnick, Stein, and Bock had been shopping it around. Nobody cared. Interestingly enough one of the complaints of the backers was: "What will you do when you run out of Hadassah Ladies?" So there you go, my dear Hadassah Ladies. Look how they underestimated us way back when.

Jerome Robbins signed on and suddenly everything was full speed ahead. Many people—most of them Jewish—were at the Fisher Theater in Detroit for the first set of pre-Broadway out-of-town performances when Chaney, Goodman, and Schwerner disappeared. Many people—again mostly Jewish people—were in Washington, D.C., for the second set of pre-Broadway out-of-town performances when the three bodies were discovered. The week after *Fiddler on the Roof* opened on Broadway, the Free Speech Movement erupted on the University of California's Berkeley campus.

June 13, 1965: The *Fiddler on the Roof* team won a record number of Tony Awards. In fact, they won in **every** category in which they were nominated **except** Set Design. How can that be? Those sets were so integral to the success of the original production. Set designer Boris Aronson filled his sets with references to Chagall. But in 1965, the Tony Award for Set Design went to *Baker Street*. *Baker Street*? Lost in the sands of time…

Alas, that is all I can say right now about 1964. We must jump ahead to our second quote:

Elaborately faithful and musically nearly complete.

Really?

This part of our discussion is centered on the character of Yente-the-Matchmaker. Some of you may remember that the original Yente was played by Bea Arthur. When you are listening to the Original Broadway Cast Recording and you hear this part right at the beginning—"The way he looks and the way she sees, it's a perfect match!"—that is Bea Arthur. And oh, by the way, those words are not on the film's soundtrack. I know some of you will doubt this, so when you get home, pop in your DVD, and look for yourself. Not in the movie, not there. Onstage? Yes. Onscreen? No.

This is just one example of dialogue we think is intrinsic to *Fiddler on the Roof*. The original cast album? Most of us have no doubt heard it a million times. So we probably hear those words when we are watching the film, even though they are no longer there.

In 1964, Bea Arthur was in her early forties. She was a huge woman with a booming voice. She was tall, even compared to the men. She had significant lines of dialogue and she even had her own song. That song—"The Rumor"—they did such a great job of it at Town Hall a couple of weeks ago. And at the end, they gave Jackie Hoffman the honor of spitting out Yente's venomous close: "And that's what comes of men and women dancing."

You might guess at this point that I could talk for well over an hour on the subject of Yente-the-Matchmaker too. My lecture on Yente-the-Matchmaker—"Yente, Yenta: How a Name Became a Noun"—is actually the most popular of all the lectures I have given on *Fiddler on the Roof.*

But for now, just think about this:

- You see a woman named Yente-the-Matchmaker onstage.
- She is in her early forties.
- She is huge (even compared to the male characters).
- She has a big, booming voice.
- She has important lines of dialogue.
- She has her own song.

And then you see the film. . .

- Yente-the-Matchmaker is now played by a woman who is in her mid-seventies.
- She is tiny (even compared to the other female characters).
- She has minimal dialogue.
- She has no song of her own.

And there is another subtle difference: Onstage—in 1964 as well as today— Yente-the-Matchmaker talks to everyone in Anatevka, the men and the women:

Yente: Avram, I have a wonderful match for your son.
Avram: Who is it?
Yente: Rukhl, the shoemaker's daughter.

Who is Yente talking to in this scene? Obviously she is talking to a male character named Avram. Now watch the film again, and you will see that Molly Picon—who plays Yente-the-Matchmaker onscreen—talks only to women.

This is a huge change. A few years back, I did an interview with a celebrated actress who was playing Yente in a Metro Chicago production. She said: "Yente is a businesswoman. She is the only woman onstage who speaks freely with all of the women **and** all of the men in Anatevka, because that is the nature of her job."

But this power—the power to speak with men as an equal—was stripped from Yente-the-Matchmaker in 1971. On film, Yent*e* has become what we now call "a yent*a,*" a gossip and a busybody who just yaks-yaks-yaks with other women. I guess there is nothing wrong with this in itself. Certainly there are some women who can be rightly described as "yentas." But is this "faithful" at all, let alone "elaborately" so? No. It is not.

So much for "elaborately faithful." Now let's look at "musically nearly complete." What else is missing onscreen besides Yente-the-Matchmaker's song "The Rumor"? Answer: Perchik-the-Revolutionary's song "Now I Have Everything."

In the movie, there is a scene that I derisively refer to as "outtakes from *Doctor Zhivago*." This scene replaces a wonderful duet in which Perchik-the-Revolutionary declares onstage that he has achieved the Freudian ideal: I have a love and a work. But Norman Jewison took away that song—"Now I Have Everything"—and he sent Perchik off to Kiev instead. This is, in fact, the only scene in the film version of *Fiddler on the Roof* that is not set in Anatevka. Perchik is running around with the other protesters in Kiev, and the scene looks just like the scene Uri Zhivago sees from his balcony in Saint Petersburg.

Please understand that I am not making a judgment call here. I am not claiming that one version is "better" than the other. But I do want you to see that these two Perchik characters are not the same. Onstage, Perchik has a love and a work. As he says, "Now I Have Everything." But onscreen, Perchik has become "Pasha Antipov"—the character in *Doctor Zhivago* who is played by Tom Courtenay—the character who marries Lara, but then leaves her so he can dedicate himself to The Revolution.

In conclusion, here are just a few of the momentous events that happened between 1965 and 1971:

- **January 20, 1965**: Lyndon Baines Johnson is inaugurated for his ill-fated second term.

- **June 13, 1965**: *Fiddler on the Roof* wins nine Tony Awards.

- **June 7, 1967**: The Israel Defense Forces (IDF) wrests Jerusalem from Jordanian control during the Six-Day War. This was an event of unparalleled importance for the Jewish people. It should come as no surprise that a *Fiddler on the Roof* that came after the Six-Day War, would be different from a *Fiddler on the Roof* that came before the Six-Day War. Jews had changed as a people in the interim.

- **August 28, 1968**: Protesters riot at the Democratic National Convention in Chicago.

- **May 4, 1970**: Newly inaugurated president Richard Nixon authorizes the bombing of Cambodia. Members of the Ohio National Guard shoot four students at Kent State University. Did you know that three of the four students killed at Kent State were Jewish?

- **August 26, 1971**: Bella Abzug leads the first Women's Equality Day parade in honor of the 50th anniversary of the 19th Amendment.

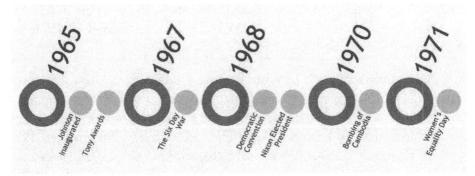

© Jan Lisa Huttner (2016)

Between 1965 and 1971, Martin Luther King, Malcolm X, and Bobby Kennedy were all assassinated. There were massive demonstrations in the USA against the war in Vietnam, which led to newly reinvigorated civil rights, feminist, and student movements. The United States was bitterly divided between those fighting for change and those fighting against it. All of these events—and more—made 1971 a fundamentally different time for Americans of every background (including Jewish Americans).

So now I throw the ball back to you. Ask yourself what you want your granddaughters to see—and what you want their daughters to see—on *Fiddler on the Roof*'s Diamond Anniversary in 2039. Do you want them to see the stage version of *Fiddler on the Roof* from 1964 with a powerful Yente and a virile Perchik? Or do you want them to see the screen version of *Fiddler on the Roof* from 1971 in which the importance of both characters has been considerably diminished?

We—the women of Hadassah—helped make *Fiddler on the Roof* a worldwide sensation in 1964, so I sincerely believe **we have the right and the responsibility** to weigh in on this question now!

Stempenyu the Fiddler (circa 1859)

Left panel: Sholem Aleichem (1888)
Center panel: Stempenyu
Right panel: Marc Chagall (1920)

SECTION 3

Stempenyu: From Berdichev to Broadway

This lecture was originally presented to the Chicago YIVO Society at the Evanston Public Library in Evanston, Illinois, on August 17, 2009. It was subsequently presented to Chicago Limmud at Oakton Community College in Skokie, Illinois, on February 14, 2010.

Date: Saturday, May 20, 2000
Place: A balcony on the 9th floor of Hotel Le Meridien in Nice
Time: Approximately 7AM

I had arrived in France on Thursday evening with my husband Richard and my mother-in-law Juanita (of blessed memory). We were there to celebrate Juanita's 75th birthday. ("Why should we have a party in Florida," she'd said, "when we have such a good excuse to go somewhere else?") I was a healthcare computer consultant exhausted by Y2K projects, and all I wanted was a stress-free vacation. After much research and debate, we picked a tour called The Riviera's Artistic Legacies.

Friday morning, we boarded a bus and headed off to our first stop: the Matisse Museum in Nice. After four delightful hours that included a delicious lunch, we arrived at the Marc Chagall National Biblical Message Museum in Cimiez. I walked through the door, and suddenly everything turned serious.

Abraham preparing Isaac for sacrifice! Jacob wrestling with the angel! Moses parting the Red Sea! And look: There's Jesus on the cross—wearing a tallis as a loincloth! I had walked in thinking that I already knew what I needed to know about Marc Chagall ("kitsch," nu?), but I fell headlong into these huge, dynamic canvases. Scholars call what happened to me on that Friday "aesthetic arrest."

When our guide started herding us back to the bus, I ran into the gift shop and quickly purchased one of their English-language picture books: *Marc Chagall* by Andrew Kagan.

Back on the bus, I listened quietly as the folks around me discussed the day: *Such vibrant colors! Such wonderful food!* But nothing I heard matched the buzz in my head. That is when I realized I was the only Jew in our group. We live in a world filled with Christian iconography, but I knew that I was seeing—really seeing—"biblical messages" from the brush of a Jewish artist for the very first time in my life, and Chagall's imagery had pierced something deep in my soul. I kept my thoughts to myself. This was no time to discuss weighty matters. We were in a rush! We had dinner reservations at the Hotel Negresco!

The next morning, I got up early, ordered breakfast, and took a quick shower. When room service arrived, I steered the waiter quietly past my sleeping husband and onto the balcony; after he left, I poured myself a cup of coffee and began reading. Chagall's *Green Violinist* appears opposite the title page in this particular book, **but I flipped right past him**. I read and read with growing fascination until I reached page 48:

> In the allegory of music, a theme Chagall repeated
> in the animated The Green Violinist, appears once
> again his fiddler on the roof, that stock character
> preserved from the world of the shtetl by Chagall
> and Sholem Aleichem.   (Kagan, Page 48 [*sic*])

I turned back and looked at the image of Chagall's *Green Violinist*. "Oh, my God," I said out loud. "It's **THE** fiddler on the roof."

"...his fiddler on the roof..." We all know him, right? He is on book jackets, catalogues and coloring books, CD and DVD covers, notecards and art stickers, gift books and magazine covers, and Hanukkah cards. And here he is on the very first *Fiddler on the Roof* Playbill cover:

Fiddler on the Roof

© Playbill, INC (1964)

But how well do we *really* know him?

Fiddler on the Roof had always been "there" in the background of my life, so much so that I cannot even tell you when or how any of it first embedded itself in my consciousness; all I can say for sure is that it was never prominent in any way. The Broadway embodiment of Sholem Aleichem's characters and

Marc Chagall's images was simply part of my cultural heritage, and since I was a serious-minded young lady with high intellectual aspirations, I barely gave it a second thought.

I was born in 1951, and I grew up in northern New Jersey, so I am sure that I saw *Fiddler on the Roof* on Broadway, but I have no memory of it. (On the other hand, I have vivid memories of the day my mother took me into "the city" to see *Man of La Mancha* in 1965.) I am also certain that I saw the film version of *Fiddler on the Roof* when it was released in 1971, but I have no memory of that day either. (On the other hand, I can provide specific details about the first time I saw *Funny Girl* in 1968.) It is quite likely that I saw Chagall's *Green Violinist* at the Guggenheim Museum, but all I remember now is the dramatic staircase. (On the other hand, I can picture a teenage me at MoMA standing in awe before Picasso's *Guernica*.)

There is only one certainty about my early encounters with *Fiddler on the Roof* that I can specify with absolute firmness. We owned a copy of the Original Broadway Cast Recording on a "long-playing record." After my father died, I took that well-worn vinyl LP home with me; it is sitting right now on a shelf in my office.

But I have just described to you the exact moment on Saturday, May 20, 2000 that I became obsessed with all things *Fiddler*. Something that I had always taken for granted suddenly became the focal point of deep mysteries, and my life turned inside out. Scholars call what happened to me that Saturday a "paradigm shift."

We flew home on Sunday, May 28. The next day was Memorial Day, and the day after that, I went back to work. When I told people that the trip to France had "changed my life," they were ready to listen, but I was tongue-tied. Even my husband, who certainly knew "something" had happened, would not have been able to tell you what—although he obviously knew that I was suddenly buying a lot of old books on Amazon (books about Chagall, books about Broadway, books by Sholem Aleichem). I learned on the Internet that other people also wondered why the popular musical about Tevye and his family was called *Fiddler on the Roof*. Was the title connected to the Chagall painting? If so, what was the significance of the connection? Mysteries multiplied and every new fact I learned raised a new set of questions.

On Tuesday, September 4, 2001, I quit my job. Lots of little things had happened to me between May 20, 2000 and September 4, 2001, and something very big happened to all of us exactly one week later on September 11, 2001. So I am not saying that I quit my job just to devote myself to *Fiddler on the Roof*, but clearly the fact that I am standing here today—lecturing on *Fiddler on the Roof*—is proof enough that my life really did change that day in Nice.

Now I will tell you about a man named Stempenyu, and why I believe— after nine years of research—that Stempenyu is "the missing link." But first I have a question for you.

Which Came First: The Chicken or the Egg?

In recent articles and books, various authors either strongly imply or argue outright that the ubiquity of this specific image—Chagall's *Green Violinist*—rests on the popularity of *Fiddler on the Roof* here in the United States. I disagree. Marc Chagall painted other musicians fiddling away on other rooftops, but most people are primarily interested in those other images now because they are **not** this one.

Just as Kagan says on page 48 of his book *Marc Chagall*, Chagall first produced **this** fiddler image on one of the four panels he created for Moscow's State Jewish Chamber Theatre in 1920. This painting—the *Music* panel—is now owned by the State Tretiakov Gallery in Moscow. The other three panels also displayed with it at the Tretiakov Gallery are titled *Dance*, *Drama*, and *Literature*. After he left Russia in 1922, Chagall recreated this image in 1924 and called it *Green Violinist*. This second version is the painting now owned by the Guggenheim Museum. And as far as I know, Chagall never recreated *Dance*, *Drama*, or *Literature*.

As I have already said above, I do not know when I first saw Chagall's *Green Violinist*—"the Guggenheim Fiddler"—but the first time I saw the *Music* panel—"the Moscow Fiddler"—was July 23, 2003. I know this for a fact because that was the day of the press party at the San Francisco Museum of Modern Art. I was there at SFMOMA because they were just about to show it to American audiences for the very first time, after decades spent literally buried behind the Iron Curtain.

(I flew to San Francisco—at my own expense—to cover the SFMOMA exhibit for the *Forward*. Obviously, by July of 2003, I had known for some time that I was "all in." So this is a good time to digress for a moment to express my everlasting gratitude to my husband Richard for his continued—and continuing—support and encouragement.)

Chagall not only painted this specific image twice, but he also wrote about it on the very last page of his autobiography *My Life*. These two facts suggest to me that this specific image had personal significance for Chagall himself decades before a "fiddler on the roof" was even a glimmer in the eye of any of the men who would one day create *Fiddler on the Roof*.

> These pages have the same meaning as a painted surface. If there were a hiding place in my pictures, I would slip into it… perhaps they would stick onto the back of one of my characters or maybe onto the trousers of **the musician in my mural**…? Who can tell what's written on his back? In the age of the RSFSR, I keep shouting: Can't you feel our electric scaffolding slipping under our feet? **And weren't our artistic premonitions right since we really are up in the air and suffer from one disease alone: the thirst for stability**. Those five years turn in my soul. I have grown thin. I'm even hungry. I long to see you again, B…, C…, P…, I am tired. And perhaps Europe will love me, and with her, my Russia.   (Chagall, Page 171 [*sic*])

After nine years of research, I now believe that *Fiddler on the Roof*—as **we** know it today—would not have been possible without Chagall's *Green Violinist*, and *Green Violinist*—as **we** know it today—would not have been possible without Sholem Aleichem's *Stempenyu*.

Who Was Stempenyu?

It is often the case that, once something is "found," it is hard to remember back to a time when it was "lost." In this specific case, now that Sholem Aleichem's novella *Stempenyu* is back in print again, I am here to tell you that I had a very hard time finding it back when I first started to look. But why was I looking for it in the first place?

By May 2003, my research on *Fiddler on the Roof* had led me to a wonderful book called *The Theatre Art of Boris Aronson* by Frank Rich with

Lisa Aronson (aka Mrs. Boris Aronson). I was sitting at a table in the Billy Rose Theatre Division at the New York Public Library for the Performing Arts, staring at this book and shaking because it contained the very information I had now been searching several years to find.

Finally, I went up to the desk clerk and tremulously asked: "Can you tell me how to find out if someone is still alive?" He said: "Who are you looking for?" I said: "Um… Frank Rich?" Well, he looked at me as if I were the dumbest person in the world. "Frank Rich is a columnist for the *New York Times*." "Oh," I said with a grimace, "I'm from Chicago."

The Rich/Aronson chapter on *Fiddler on the Roof* was enormously helpful, but then I noticed a tiny item on page 294 in the chronology section:

> STEMPENYU, THE FIDDLER by Sholom Aleichem
>
> Yiddish Art Theatre (Second Avenue Theatre)
>
> With Maurice Schwartz and Celia Adler
>
> Directed by Schwartz
>
> *set, costumes*

And thus, my search for Stempenyu began!

Soon after, I received a book from my Aunt Bernis. Bernis Hecht has been an active member of Brandeis University's National Women's Committee for decades, and she frequents used book sales in search of buried treasure. Bernis had tucked a note in the book, telling me she had found this Yiddish book at an estate sale… in Corpus Christi, Texas! When she saw it was by Sholem Aleichem, she bought it for me, assuming that I might like it.

Well, I knew just enough Yiddish at that point to sound out the table of contents: "Stem… pen… yu!"

I took the book from my Aunt Bernis to my Yiddish teacher—Nathaniel Stampfer—and together we searched the library at Spertus Institute for Jewish Studies, until we found an English version of *Stempenyu* in a collection of stories translated by Joachim Neugroschel that is now out of print.

By the time I had finished reading the prologue, I knew in my heart that I had found my "Rosetta Stone."

> Oh, what a man Stempenyu was! His talent was without beginning and without end. He would snatch up the fiddle, and drawing the bow across it in the most careless fashion, he would succeed in making it speak at once. It needed but a single movement of his elbow, and **the little fiddle was speaking to us all.** And how it spoke? In the most unmistakable accents! Really, with words that we all understood, in the plainest fashion, as if it had a tongue, and as if it were a real living, human being! **It would moan, it would wail, and weep over its sad fortune, as if it were a Jew.** And its cry was shrill and heartrending. It was as if every note found its way upward from out of the deepest depth of the soul.   (Berman, Page 6)

To the best of my knowledge, there is no proof positive that Marc Chagall ever read these words, but I believe—with my whole heart—that he did. And I think that you will too, once you have read this lovely story. One thing we do know for sure, however, is that Boris Aronson certainly knew *Stempenyu* because Boris Aronson designed the set and costumes for Maurice Schwartz's production of *Stempenyu* at the Yiddish Art Theatre.

Who Was Boris Aronson?

Boris Aronson was a theatrical genius who won five Tony awards for his design work on Cabaret, Company, Follies, Pacific Overtures, and Zorba. Boris Aronson was a man who knew Marc Chagall personally—both in Moscow and in Berlin—and he published one of the very first monographs about Chagall's work. It was published in 1924 in German, Russian, and Yiddish. I found a copy in Russian on Amazon, and I hired someone from the Department of Slavic Languages and Literatures at the University of Chicago to translate it for me.

But here are the only facts that **you** need to know about Boris Aronson:

• Aronson designed the set for *Stempenyu the Fiddler* in 1929.
• Aronson designed the sets for *Fiddler on the Roof* in 1964.

We know very little about Stempenyu, but we do know that he was definitely a real person. In her research on the novella, University of Michigan professor Anita Norich quotes a letter from Sholem Aleichem in which he explicitly says that Stempenyu was based on "a real figure, a violinist, from Berdichev."

In her memoir *My Father, Sholom Aleichem*, Sholem Aleichem's daughter Marie Waife-Goldberg writes:

> Take for example the incident of the tanner. This man, who lived in a nearby town, used to stay at the Rabinowitz Inn whenever he came to Pereyaslav to purchase hides for his tannery. One day he visited Grandfather Nahum with what seemed an excellent proposal for Sholom. His town desperately needed a Russian teacher. The people would take Sholom to their hearts and he would prosper there… But the town showed no awareness of its need of a Russian teacher. The teachers in the Hebrew schools felt themselves perfectly able to teach Russian and resented the intrusion of a new teacher. **Only in the house of Stempenyu, the klesmer (klesmer is the specific term for a musician who plays at weddings), did Sholom feel at home**. The family were virtually social outcasts and always in need of money—which the young tutor readily loaned, knowing it would never be returned—but it was a happy, jolly place, full of children, a home after Sholom's heart. Despite this haven, Sholom could hardly wait for the end of the semester, when he left, determined never again to be a teacher in a small town or seek his life's career in such a place.
>
> (Waife-Goldberg, Pages 52–53)

In his own memoir, *From the Fair*, Sholem Aleichem refers to this same incident; however, he calls the man in question "Abraham the Klezmer." Sholem Aleichem specifically says on page 211 that in his mind, Abraham was "a kind of Stempenyu…"

> Only in one house, Abraham the Klezmer's, did he feel he was among human beings. Abraham was an authentic artist, a

maestro who deserves to be depicted… He played so sweetly you could have melted listening to him. **He was a kind of Stempenyu… In real life he was a Stempenyu as well**. A strange sort. Poetic nature, a great lover of women and girls. (Leviant, Page 211)

In *The Book of Klezmer*, musicologist Yale Strom—who chose to illustrate his cover with a crop of Chagall's *Green Violinist*—writes:

> Then there was Stempenyu (1822-1879), who was immortalized by the great Yiddish writer Sholem Aleichem (1859-1916) in his novella *Stempenyu*. **The book, written in 1888, made him more famous than he already was.** Stempenyu was born with klezmer in his blood. He came from ten generations of klezmorim. His father Beri Bass played the bass, his grandfather Shmulik Trompeyt played the trumpet, his great-grandfather Fayvish played the tsimbl, and his great-great-grandfather Efrayim played the flute.
>
> (Strom, Page 116)

More important, though, is the use that Sholem Aleichem made of Stempenyu when he transformed a real man into a literary archetype. In the epilogue, after Stempenyu has lost Rochelle (a beautiful woman who "sings like a bird"), Sholem Aleichem writes:

> At that period, Stempenyu played as he never played before, and as he never played again. He reached the zenith of his power in those unhappy weeks and months immediately following the departure of Rochelle from the village, and the consequent shattering of all his bright hopes. For he had been more deeply touched by Rochelle than by anyone he had ever come across in this life. And, therefore, it would be safe to say that whoever did not hear him at this period can have no real idea of what his playing was like.
>
> And that's how it is always. We are filled with delight at the wondrous sweetness of the song which the little bird sings from its cage. The little bird is dreaming of green leaves, fresh flowers soaked with dew, balmy air, a burning sun, and a free world—a world without bars—a broad expanse of blue about which it may fly as it wishes. And, as it dreams, the little bird is overcome with the desire to sing—to pour out all the bitterness that is in its

heart. **And, so its singing is only another name for weeping, for expressing all the melting sorrows of its heart.** And, we who listen to it are filled with delight because of the sweetness of the melody. And, we are filled with sheer joy at the passionate tenderness of the little bird's notes. And, we imagine that they have come forth through feelings of pleasure in the bird's heart such as are in our hearts. But it is not so.

"She makes my heart ache with longing," said Stempenyu...

(Berman, Pages 191-192)

Poetic words, indeed, but we must put these words together with Sholem Aleichem's *Dedication*—"To my dearly beloved grandfather Reb Mendele Mocher Sephorim"—to fully appreciate their significance:

DEDICATION
TO MY DEARLY BELOVED GRANDFATHER
REB MENDELE MOCHER SEPHORIM

I know, dear grandfather—I feel how necessary it would be to purify Stempenyu through many waters. In your hands, the book would have taken on an altogether different appearance. It would have been a different book from what it is. You would have made of it a story about a story, a story within a story, and a story in itself as well.   (Berman, xiv)

...a story about a story, a story within a story,
and a story in itself as well...

Yes, in this case, "**the story in itself**" may well be "a Jewish romance" about a musician who falls in love with a beautiful young woman who has already been married off to someone else. But "**the story about a story**" is the story of an artist struggling to create a uniquely Jewish voice. And "**the story within a story**" is nothing less than the story of the Jewish people—trapped in the "cage" that was Russia at the end of the 19th century—"dreaming of a world without bars."

This artist—this artist struggling to create a uniquely Jewish voice—I believe that "this artist" was Sholem Aleichem himself, using the local memory of Stempenyu's reputation as a musician to create "Jewish Art" in words. But then, Marc Chagall—inspired by the novella *Stempenyu*—used the words of Sholem Aleichem to create "Jewish Art" in images. And finally Jerome Robbins (and his collaborators) combined these cultural treasures—the music, the words, the images—to create "Jewish Art" on Broadway.

Look again at Chagall's *Green Violinist.* What is that… in the bottom right corner?

© Dover (2000)

Can that be Rochelle… singing to Stempenyu… with Jacob's Ladder propped up against a barren Russian tree?

Menachem Mendel's Letter

My Sheineh Sheindel, white snow is falling.
There is no one. Everyone is gone. Understand.
Tevye is dead.
And dead is Mottel the Cantor's son.
Dead is dear uncle Pinye.

And on the snow rests **Stempenyu**, small and barefoot,
And, as always, still full of grace.
But the violin is mute. It has no more music.
For it has no one left to play for.

Israeli poet Natan Alterman first published "Mikhtav shel Menahem Mendel" ("Menachem Mendel's Letter") in early 1945, at the end of that blood-soaked winter, just before the Nazis conceded defeat and the Holocaust finally ended. But while I deeply respect the emotional state in which he must have written this poem, I sincerely believe that Alterman was wrong.

I believe that every time the curtain rises anywhere in the world on a new performance of *Fiddler on the Roof*, that sound we hear is Stempenyu's violin.

Open your heart and listen with me. He is playing for all of us now.

The little fiddle is speaking to us all…
In the most unmistakable accents…
with words that we all understood…
as if it were a Jew.

And its cry is shrill and heartrending…
and every note found its way upward.
from out of the deepest depth of the soul.

(Berman, Page 6)

Dueling Yentes

Left panel: Molly Picon onscreen (1971)
Right panel: Bea Arthur onstage (1964)

SECTION 4

Yente:
From Boiberek to Broadway

The original version of this lecture was presented to the Chicago YIVO Society (in collaboration with ORT Urban Women) at Wilmette Public Library in Wilmette, Illinois, and at the Harold Washington Library Center in Chicago on August 10, 2010. It was subsequently revised and presented to Congregation KAM Isaiah Israel in Chicago on December 14, 2010, to Hadassah's Zahavah Group at the Glenwood Oaks Restaurant in Glenwood, Illinois, on March 22, 2011, to Hadassah's Ketura Group at the Liberty Bank Auditorium in Lincolnwood, Illinois, on April 12, 2011, to the Adult Jewish Education Co-op of the Northwest Suburbs (AJEC) at Congregation Or Shalom in Vernon Hills, Illinois, on November 16, 2011, and at Temple Beth Emeth in Brooklyn, New York, on March 14, 2015.

PROLOGUE
Silent Meditation

Have you ever called someone "a Yenta"...
　　either to her face or behind her back?

If yes, when and in what context?
　　What does the word mean to you?

Has anyone ever called you "a Yenta" to your face...
　　or perhaps maybe you think you might
　　have been called "a Yenta" behind your back?

If yes, how does this make you feel?

Have you ever called a man "a Yenta"...
　　or heard a man referred to as "a Yenta"?

Store these questions in the back of your mind now and we'll return to them during the Q&A.

Mah nish tanah ha performance ha zeh?

Every time I set off to see a new production of *Fiddler on the Roof*, this is what I most want to know: *Mah nish tanah ha performance ha zeh*? How is **this** performance different from all other performances?

A lot of people think *Fiddler* is *Fiddler*, so they are not expecting **anything** to be different, and if we are talking about Norman Jewison's 1971 screen adaptation, then, of course, yes, you pop in the DVD and it is always the same.

But *Fiddler on the Roof* was not born in a multiplex in 1971; *Fiddler on the Roof* was born on Broadway in 1964. Almost 50 years later, it is still being performed, all around the world, on large stages and small ones, by school kids and professional companies. Every time a new production of *Fiddler on the Roof* is mounted, the creative team makes critical decisions behind the scenes.

In my life as a Jewish journalist, writing first for the *World Jewish Digest* and now for the *JUF News*, I have seen more than two dozen productions of *Fiddler on the Roof* in the past ten years alone. Most of these productions have been in Metro Chicago, from Evanston Light Opera and Marriott Lincolnshire in the north, to Drury Lane Oak Brook in the west, to the Theatre at the Center in Munster, Indiana, in the south. Downtown at the Oriental Theatre at Ford Center in the Loop, I have seen productions starring Theodore Bikel and Chaim Topol (two of the world's best-loved Tevyes).

As a kid, I know I saw *Fiddler on the Roof* on Broadway sometime in the 1960s, although I cannot remember anything about it now. However, I saw Broadway's controversial revival in 2004 **three** times (twice with Alfred Molina and once with Harvey Fierstein). I have also seen two Florida productions (one in Sarasota and one in West Palm Beach). And on my shelf, I have four CDs—three in English (starring Zero Mostel as Tevye in 1964, Chaim Topol as Tevye in 1971, and Alfred Molina as Tevye in 2004), as well as the all-Yiddish cast (starring Shmuel Rodenski as Tevye) that was recorded in Tel Aviv in 1965.

So, nu? What can be different? Oy, let me count the ways! Today, we are just going to focus on one character: Yente-the-Matchmaker. Sholem

Aleichem lovers know there is no Yente-the-Matchmaker in any of his eight original Tevye stories. In fact, she is the **only** major character specifically created for *Fiddler on the Roof*.

So who is Yente-the-Matchmaker? How has she been portrayed over the years? And what difference does any of this make anyway?

Background

Before we begin our discussion of Yente-the-Matchmaker, a few questions for you:

- Who here saw the **original** Broadway production of *Fiddler on the Roof* starring Zero Mostel as Tevye?
- Who here has seen the **film version** of *Fiddler on the Roof* starring Chaim Topol as Tevye?
- Who here has seen *Fiddler on the Roof* performed **on stage anywhere** in the past decade?
- Is there anyone here who has **NEVER** seen *Fiddler on the Roof* anywhere in any form?

Okay, good. Everyone here has seen *Fiddler on the Roof* at some time in some form. But here is a bit of background just in case you need a refresher:

The Broadway musical *Fiddler on the Roof* is based on a series of eight stories written by Solomon Rabinowitz between 1895 and 1916. Rabinowitz—best known by his pen name Sholem Aleichem—was born in Ukraine in 1859. When he died in New York in 1916, his death occasioned an outpouring of grief all across the Yiddish-speaking world, and thousands attended his funeral. Nevertheless, even though he tried to adapt several of his stories (including several of his eight Tevye stories), Rabinowitz was never able to succeed as a playwright.

As far as I know, the first adaption of the Tevye stories was an American silent film called *Broken Barriers* that was released in 1919. The Internet Movie Database (IMDb) also lists these:

- a German film called *Tevya und Seine Tochter* (*Tevye and His Seven Daughters*) from 1962;

- an Israeli film called *Tuvia v'Sheva Benotav* (*Tevye and His Seven Daughters*) from 1968;
- a Russian film called *Tevye Molochnik* (*Tevye the Milkman*) from 1985; and
- a second Russian film called *Izydi!* (*Get Thee Out!*) from 1991.

I know very little about any of these films, and as far as I know, no one I know personally has ever seen any of them.

The pre-*Fiddler* adaptation most readily available is Maurice Schwartz's film *Tevye*, which was originally released in 1939. In 2004, it was restored and re-released by the National Center for Jewish Film at Brandeis University. Thank you, NCJF! Schwartz based his *Tevye* on the popular stage production he created for his Yiddish Art Theatre on Second Avenue in Manhattan (starring Schwartz himself, of course, as Tevye).

Arnold Perl's play *Tevya and His Daughters* is also accessible in script form from the Dramatists Play Service. *Tevya and His Daughters* was performed Off Broadway for the first time in 1957. Howard Da Silva directed it, and Mike Kellin starred as Tevye. Note that I have never heard of anyone trying to revive it.

And no, no matchmakers appear anywhere in either *Tevye* or *Tevya and His Daughters*.

And now let us turn to *Fiddler on the Roof*

"A fiddler on the roof. Sounds crazy, no?" Well, maybe once, but not anymore. Performed on large stages and small ones, by professional companies, community groups, and school kids everywhere, the musical *Fiddler on the Roof*—now almost 50 years old—has proven itself to be one of Jewish American culture's all-time greatest hits.

However, as we approach *Fiddler on the Roof*'s Golden Anniversary, I want to look at familiar material with fresh eyes. My touchstone today is the ubiquitous word "yenta." I had used this word many, many times myself before I ever thought to question it. So I was surprised to learn that "yenta"—now accepted as Yinglish slang for "gossip, busybody"—is actually a relatively new word, a word that first entered our English language not as a noun but as a name. My contention today is that the transformation of the name "Yente" into the noun "yenta" reveals contemporary truths far beyond their original Jewish roots.

When *Fiddler on the Roof* premiered on Broadway, the character called Yente-the-Matchmaker was played by the imposing actress Bea Arthur. On opening night—September 22, 1964—Bea Arthur was a big, powerful woman with a booming voice and a huge stage presence. At the age of 42, this veteran character actress had finally found the vehicle that would propel her to stardom.

And yet, when Norman Jewison released his screen adaptation of *Fiddler on the Roof* in 1971, Yente-the-Matchmaker was played by the adorable pixie Molly Picon, a woman roughly twice Arthur's age and half her size. Most shocking of all, many of Yente's best lines were gone.

Alas, hardly anyone noticed! Even today, scholars continue to write that Jewison's *Fiddler on the Roof* is "**elaborately faithful (and musically nearly complete)**." In fact, these very words appear verbatim in the preface to *To Broadway, To Life! The Musical Theater of Bock and Harnick*, published by Oxford University Press in 2011.

I beg to differ.

The Yente-the-Matchmaker character was created by director Jerome Robbins and his original *Fiddler on the Roof* team. As played by Bea Arthur, she is a businesswoman who deals with everyone in town on an equal basis. But the character constructed by Norman Jewison's team— the Yente-the-Matchmaker played by Molly Picon—no longer interacts as an equal with the men of Anatevka.

Bea Arthur's memorable section of the Musical-Prologue has been deleted:

> Tell the truth, Avram, is your son so much to look at?
> The way she sees and the way he looks, it is a perfect match.
> (Stein, Page 5)

So has her Act Two song "The Rumor."

Stripped of her stature and pushed to the edge of the action, Molly Picon's Yente character has been relegated to the world of women, where she plays for cheap laughs as—you guessed it—a gossip and a busybody.

Why should anyone care today about how the name "Yente" made the leap from Yiddish into common American slang?

By taking *Fiddler on the Roof* out of the middlebrow ghetto—to which some would consign it—and treating it as seriously as one would treat a play by William Shakespeare, I intend to convince you that our ambivalence about strong female characters is just as real today as it was that night in 1964 when Bea Arthur first strode on stage wearing Yente-the-Matchmaker's pearls.

In what follows, I will fight for Yente-the-Matchmaker—and all the women subsequently dismissed as "yentas"—since her name became a noun.

Introducing Sholem Aleichem's Tevye Stories

The Broadway musical *Fiddler on the Roof* is based on a series of eight monologues written by Yiddish author Solomon Rabinowitz between 1895 and 1916. Today, these eight stories (all told in the first person by a character named "Tevye") are almost always considered one novel, and they are typically published together under the title *Tevye the Dairyman.*

Born in Ukraine in 1859, Rabinowitz is best-known by his pen name "Sholem Aleichem." In Yiddish, "Sholem Aleichem" literally means "peace be with you"—just like "Salam Aleykum" in Arabic—but it is typically translated as the colloquial equivalent of "Hello there!" Sholem Aleichem is now universally recognized as the greatest Yiddish writer in the Jewish canon.

Just as in *Tevye the Dairyman,* the major characters in *Fiddler on the Roof* are Tevye, his wife Golde, and their five daughters (from oldest to youngest): Tzeitel, Hodel, Chava, Shprintze, and Bielke. Rabinowitz originally gave Tevye and Golde seven daughters—a sixth named Taybele and one with no name—but that is a tale for another day.

The minor characters in *Fiddler on the Roof* are the suitors who come courting the three eldest daughters, and the matchmaker—Yente—who wants to arrange their marriages. These nine characters are then augmented by a chorus of neighbors living side-by-side in the village of Anatevka. Most of them are Jews, but some are Russian Orthodox Christians.

The microcosm/macrocosm plot of *Fiddler on the Roof* is built around the collision of two timelines. On the family level, three daughters—Tzeitel, Hodel, and Chava—have reached adulthood. So Golde, like most mothers, is preoccupied with their marriage prospects. On the community level, Jews are being forced out of Russia's "Pale of Settlement" through a brutal combination of pogroms and expulsion orders. So Tevye, even as he struggles to make a living, is always alert to signs of trouble in the wider world.

In the 19th century, the "Pale of Settlement"—on the western edge of Imperial Russia—held most of Europe's Jews. Since the breakup of the former Soviet Union, what was once the "Pale of Settlement" now spreads over portions of many countries which have borders with Russia, including Belarus, Lithuania, Moldova, Poland, and Ukraine. (Note however that this Jewish use of the word "pale" is not related to the English expression "beyond the pale" which has Irish origins.)

Yente-the-Matchmaker Onstage

Theater audiences first meet Yente-the-Matchmaker during the famous Musical-Prologue "Tradition." Of course, Joseph Stein's text just says "Tradition," but an exclamation point is always added when *Fiddler on the Roof* is actually performed—and it is "Tradition!" that frames Yente's story.

After introducing the Papas, the Mamas, the Sons, and the Daughters, Tevye says: "And in the circle of our little village, we've always had our special types. For instance, Yente, the matchmaker…" The spotlight finds Yente in the middle of a sales pitch:

> **Yente:** Avram, I have a perfect match for your son. A wonderful girl.
> **Avram:** Who is it?
> **Yente:** Ruchel, the shoemaker's daughter.
> **Avram:** Ruchel? But she can hardly see. She's almost blind.
> **Yente:** Tell the truth, Avram, is your son so much to look at? The way she sees and the way he looks, it's a perfect match.

Audiences typically respond to Yente's close with howling laughter.

Act One, Scene 1 of *Fiddler on the Roof* opens in the family kitchen where Golde is busily preparing for Shabbat. All five daughters are scurrying around completing chores and errands, when suddenly Shprintze (daughter #4) announces: "Mama, Yente's coming."

Golde immediately shoos them away so she can meet with Yente alone. "Golde darling," says Yente as she enters the kitchen, "I have such news for you." After some banter, Yente explains her mission: Lazar Wolf—Anatevka's butcher—wants to marry Golde's eldest daughter Tzeitel.

At first, Golde is thrilled. Yes, Lazar Wolf-the-Butcher is a middle-aged widower whereas Tzeitel is "not yet 20," but he is also one of the wealthiest men in town. Unfortunately, there is a problem: "Tevye doesn't like Lazar," says Golde with resignation.

Not to worry, Yente already knows this and she has a plan.

> **Yente:** Listen to me, Golde, send Tevye to him. Don't tell him what it's about. Let Lazar discuss it himself. He'll win him over. He's a good man, a wealthy man—true? Of course true! So you'll tell me how it went, and you don't have to thank me, Golde, because aside from my fee—which anyway Lazar will pay—it gives me satisfaction to make people happy—what better satisfaction is there? So goodbye, Golde, and you're welcome. (Stein, Page 15)

And thus, in a few brief moments of dialogue, Yente-the-Matchmaker reveals her nerves of steel: She deliberately instructs a wife to lie to her husband so that she, Yente, can make a profit from the deal. After Yente leaves, her girls ask questions, but Golde faithfully follows Yente's script. ("When I want you to know, I'll tell you.")

Hodel (daughter #2) and Chava (daughter #3) are giddy with anticipation, but Tzeitel (daughter #1) quickly sets them straight. In the much-loved but totally misunderstood song, "Matchmaker," Tzeitel adopts the pronoun "I" to indicate that she is **speaking as Yente**. Taking on Yente's voice, Tzeitel strips it bare.

> **Tzeitel:** Since when are you interested in a match, Chava? I thought you just had your eye on your books (Hodel *chuckles*). And you [turning to Hodel] have your eye on the rabbi's son.
> **Hodel:** Why not? We only have one rabbi and he only has one son. Why shouldn't I want the best?

Tzeitel: Because you're a girl from a poor family. So whatever Yente brings, you'll take. Right? Of course right. (*Sings.*)
Tzeitel [**as Yente**]: Hodel, oh Hodel, have **I** made a match for you! He's handsome, he's young! All right, he's sixty-two. But he's a nice man, a good catch—true? True. I promise you'll be happy. And even if you're not, there's more to life than that—don't ask me what.

Chava, **I** found him. Will you be a lucky bride! He's handsome, he's tall—that is, from side to side. But he's a nice man, a good catch, right? Right. You heard he has a temper. He'll beat you every night, but only when he's sober, so you're all right.

Did you think you'd get a prince? Well, I do the best I can. With no dowry, no money, no family background, be glad you got a man.
(Harnick, Pages 18–19)

Tzeitel's sisters wake up. They are convinced. They drop the romantic nonsense of the first stanzas ("Find me a find. Catch me a catch."), and join Tzeitel at the opposite end of the spectrum from where both started.

Chava: Matchmaker, Matchmaker, you know that I'm still very young. Please, take your time.
Hodel: Up to this minute I misunderstood that I could **get stuck** for good.
Chava and **Hodel**: Dear Yente, see that he's gentle. Remember, you were also a bride. It's not that I'm sentimental…
Chava, **Hodel**, and **Tzeitel**: It's just that I'm **terrified**!
Matchmaker, Matchmaker, plan me no plans, I'm in no rush.
Maybe I've learned **playing with matches a girl can get burned**…
(Harnick, Pages 19–20)

Tzeitel understands that Yente-the-Matchmaker is a businesswoman. Tzeitel understands that Yente's only goal is to make matches from which she will personally profit. Tzeitel understands that like any good saleswoman, Yente will say whatever she has to say to close a deal. Without even having been in the room, Tzeitel understands that Yente has convinced her mother to do something—not only to do something against Tzeitel's interests—but against Golde's own best judgment as well. By the end of a number that begins as a lyrical waltz, her sisters understand too.

79

Act Two, Scene 2 finds all three daughters transformed. Tzeitel has wriggled free from Lazar Wolf-the-Butcher, and she has married her beloved Motel-the-Tailor. Hodel has fallen in love with Perchik-the-Revolutionary. Chava has begun clandestine meetings with Fyedka-the-Russian. "So what can we do?" Tevye asks Golde. "It's a new world, a new world. Love."

Maybe so, but seething on the sidelines during Tzeitel's wedding, Yente has already demanded to know: "What happens to the matchmaker?" Should we expect Yente to "storm off" with Lazar Wolf at the end of Act One and let this "new world" simply unfold without her? Preposterous. More likely, Yente will look for new ways to insert herself, right? Of course right!

Learning that Hodel is planning to follow Perchik to Siberia, Yente seizes her moment in a number called "The Rumor." She directly challenges Tevye's patriarchal authority, making him an object of ridicule. Furthermore, she plants poisonous seeds of doubt about the cause of the pogrom that traumatized everyone at Tzeitel's wedding reception.

> **Yente:** Rifka, I have such news for you. **Remember Perchik, that crazy student?** Remember at the wedding, when Tzeitel married Motel and **Perchik started dancing** with Tevye's daughter Hodel? Well, I just learned that **Perchik's been arrested**, in Kiev.
> **Villagers:** No!
> **Yente:** Yes!
>
> **Woman One:** Shandel, Shandel! Wait till I tell you—Remember Perchik, that crazy student? Remember at the wedding. He danced with Tevye's Hodel? Well, I just heard that **Hodel's been arrested**, in Kiev.
> **Villagers:** No! Terrible, terrible!
>
> **Woman Two:** Mirila! Do you remember Perchik, that student, from Kiev? Remember how he acted when Tzeitel married Motel? Well, I just heard that **Motel's been arrested** for dancing at the wedding.
> **Villagers:** No!
> **Woman Two:** In Kiev!
>
> **Mendel:** Rabbi! Rabbi! Remember Perchik, with all his strange ideas? Remember Tzeitel's wedding where Tevye danced with Golde? Well I just

heard that **Tevye's been arrested** and Golde's gone to Kiev.
Villagers: No!
Mendel: God forbid.
Villagers: She didn't.
Mendel: She did.

Avram: Listen, everybody, terrible news—terrible. Remember Perchik, who started all the trouble? Well, I just heard, from someone who should know, that **Golde's has been arrested**, and Hodel's gone to Kiev. Motel studies dancing, Tevye's acting strange. Shprintze has the measles, and Bielke has the mumps.
Yente: And that's what comes from men and women dancing!
(Harnick, Pages 119–122)

    The unfolding dynamic of Act Two depends on Yente's powerful presence in this scene. Her goal is to preserve her own status and income, and her appeal to "tradition" is nakedly self-serving. The implication that Perchik "**started all the trouble**" (meaning Perchik caused the pogrom) because "**he danced with Tevye's Hodel**" is clearly absurd. It is just as absurd as Pastor John Hagee telling Terry Gross on the May 16, 2008, broadcast of NPR's Fresh Air that "New Orleans had a level of sin that was offensive to God…there was to be a homosexual parade there on the Monday that Katrina came." When disaster strikes, there are always people who want easy answers. The people who listened to Yente's rumor about Perchik would probably have listened to Pastor Hagee too.

    When Tevye learns that Chava has eloped with Fyedka, he finally erupts and will not be appeased. But would he have reacted so vehemently if Yente had not shamed him before all of his neighbors? Even though he knows better, Tevye also succumbs momentarily to the comforting illusion that embracing "tradition" might stave off a disaster that he already knows—in his bones—is imminent.

    Yente seizes the opportunity to pressure Golde into arranging matches for Shprintze and Bielke.

Yente: They'll be engaged, nothing to worry about later,
no looking around, their future all signed and sealed.

Golde: Which one for which one?
Yente: What's the difference? Take your pick.

(Stein, Page 137)

Suddenly the Constable arrives with an expulsion order: the Jews of Anatevka have three days to pack up and leave. In the chaos that ensues, only Yente-the-Matchmaker remains clear-headed. "Somehow or other, I'll get to the Holy Land," she tells Golde. "I'm going to the Holy Land to help our people increase and multiply. It's my mission."

Yente-the-Matchmaker—Yente-the-Businesswoman—is always looking for her next deal. She leaves the stage as determined as she entered it, invoking the matriarchs "Sarah, Rebecca, and Rachel" as her ancestors (rather than patriarchs Abraham, Isaac, and Jacob). Unlike Tevye and the members of his family, Yente-the-Matchmaker never changes or grows. Her character is consistent throughout—signed and sealed.

Ephraim-the-Matchmaker

In my introduction way back at the beginning, I said: "*Fiddler on the Roof* is based on eight stories," but Sholem Aleichem lovers know there is no one named Yente in any of his Tevye stories. Look closer, however, and there **is** a matchmaker. His name is Ephraim, and he makes his grand entrance midway through the "Hodel" story (which is the fourth "chapter" of the whole when *Tevye the Dairyman* is published as a novel).

> In a word, *va-ye-hi erev ya-ye-hi voy-ker* [there was evening, and there was morning]—one afternoon as **I was making my rounds of the Boiberek dachas**, someone hailed me in the street. I looked around to see who it was—why, it's Ephraim the Matchmaker! Ephraim the Matchmaker, you should know, is a Jew who makes matches.
>
> "Begging your pardon, Reb Tevye," he says, "but I'd like to have a word with you."
>
> "With pleasure," I say, reining in my horse. "I hope it's a good one."
>
> "Reb Tevye, you have a daughter," he says.
>
> "I have seven, God bless them," I say.
>
> "I know you do," he says. "So do I."

"In that case," I say, "we have fourteen between the two of us."

"All joking aside," he says, "what I want to talk to you about is this: being as you know a matchmaker, I have a match for you—and not just any match either, but **someone really exclusive, extraprime and superfine!**"

"Perhaps you can tell me," I say, "what's hiding under the label, because if it's a tailor, a shoemaker, or a schoolteacher, he can save himself the trouble and so can I. *Revakh ve-ha-tso-loh ya'amoyd la-yehudim mi-mo-koym akher*—thank you very kindly but I'll look for a son-in-law elsewhere. It says in the Talmud that… "

"Good Lord, Reb Tevye," he says, "are you starting in on the Talmud again? Before a body can talk with you, he has to spend a year boning up. The whole world is nothing but a page of Talmud to you. If I were you, I'd listen to the offer I'm about to make you, because it's going to take your breath away."

And with that he delivers himself of an after-dinner speech about the young man's credentials… "He's a young bachelor," he says. "**That is, he's not so young as all that**, but a bachelor he certainly is."

(Halkin, Pages 58–59)

By this point in Sholem Aleichem's original text, Tzeitel has long since evaded Lazar Wolf-the-Butcher and married Motel-the-Tailor without the involvement of any matchmakers whatsoever! (This happened in the prior story—number three—called "Modern Children.") And yes, Ephraim-the-Matchmaker has a match for Hodel, but he is already too late. Ephraim appears well after Tevye has already made a place for Perchik-the-Revolutionary in his home and in his heart ("my young friend began coming to my house every day"), so even as Ephraim is trying to convince Tevye to let him make the introductions, Hodel and Perchik are making marriage plans of their own.

Now compare these lines, and it is obvious that the creators of *Fiddler on the Roof* knew about Ephraim. How could they not, since they based the entire plot of their musical on the Tevye stories?

Tevye to Sholem Aleichem in the "Hodel" story:

And with that [Ephraim] delivers himself of an after-dinner speech about the young man's credentials. . . "He's a young bachelor," he says. "That is, he's **not so young** as all that, but a bachelor he certainly is."

Tzeitel [in Yente's voice] to Hodel in *Fiddler on the Roof*:

Hodel, oh Hodel,

Have I made a match for you!

He's handsome, he's young!

All right, **he's sixty-two**,

But he's a nice man, a good catch—true? True.

Coincidence?

Three stories later, Ephraim makes one more appearance in the penultimate story "Tevye Leaves for the Land of Israel." By this point Tzeitel, Hodel, and Chava have all married and moved on; Golde and Shprintze are dead; the other two daughters have mysteriously vanished; and Tevye is living alone with his youngest daughter Bielke. Ephraim wants to find Tevye a new wife, but he asks Ephraim to find a proper husband for Bielke instead. Ephraim agrees, and more complications ensue.

Yente-the-Poultrywoman

So the matchmaker in the Tevye stories is a man named Ephraim, but buried deep in the Rabinowitz corpus is a story called "Dos Tepl" ("The Little Pot"), dated 1901. As far as I know, it was first published in book form in a Yiddish collection of Sholem Aleichem stories called *Monologen* (*Monologues*). The narrator of "The Little Pot" is a widow named Yente who goes to see her rabbi with a serious Halakhic question that boils down to this: "My boarder has splashed some milk on my only meat pot. Can I still use it?" Obviously Yente wants the rabbi to say yes, and so, to that end, she tells him her full tale of woe.

Can I prove to you that anyone directly connected with *Fiddler on the Roof* ever read "The Little Pot" or had personal familiarity with the voice of Yente-the-Poultrywoman? No, I cannot. But when I compare the words of Sholem Aleichem with the words of Joseph Stein, the man who wrote "the book" for *Fiddler on the Roof*—aka the libretto—my brain is abuzz.

Yente to her rabbi in "The Little Pot":

> Of course, you understand, if my husband were still alive—
> oh me, oh my! And yet to tell the truth, I wasn't exactly licking
> honey when he was alive either. **He was never the bread-winner**,
> may he forgive me for saying this, all he did was sit and study; he
> sat over his holy books all day long, and I did the work…
>
> (Butwin, Page 180)

Yente to Golde in *Fiddler on the Roof*:

> Ever since my husband died I've been a poor widow, alone,
> nobody to talk to, nothing to say to anyone. It's no life. All I
> do at night is think of him, and even thinking of him gives me
> no pleasure, because you know, as well as I, he was not much
> of a person. **Never made a living**, everything he touched turned
> to mud, but better than nothing.   (Stein, Page 12)

No coincidence. Right? Of course, right!

A Bit of Etymology

Meanwhile, let us approach this question from the opposite direction. What if Joseph Stein knew nothing about Yente-the-Poultrywoman? Could Stein have had entirely different sources?

The name Yente actually has a very long and venerable history. Scholars have identified three women named Yente among Jewish victims slaughtered in Mainz, Germany, during the First Crusade in 1096! The root of Yente is the Old Italian word "gentile" meaning "genteel" or "refined," just like the root of the English words "gentry" and "gentleman." But after centuries of respectability, the name Yente began to turn pejorative in America, where it was considered an old-fashioned, rural name—much like Chastity and Prudence—by immigrants who wanted to be modern and urbane.

In the 1920s, humorist Jacob Adler—writing under the pen name B. Kovner—created a popular character named "Yente Telebende" for the *Forward*. Why did Adler pick this particular name? So far that is another mystery, but I would not be surprised to learn someday that Adler also had the voice of Yente-the-Poultrywoman ringing in his ears too.

Look up the name "Yente" today, however, and after specific references to *Fiddler on the Roof,* you will quickly be directed to the noun "yenta," common Yinglish slang for "vulgar/sentimental woman; gossip; busybody." Many very sincere people and ostensibly reliable sources tell me this use of "yenta" as a noun was common in 1964, but I have found no references to this noun in various dictionaries—either English or Yiddish—prior to 1960.

However, I have found two words that sound very similar to "yenta." The first is "yentshen," a Yiddish verb meaning "to groan or complain." The second is "yentz." When used as a verb, "yentz" means "to cheat; to fleece." When used as a noun, "yentz" means "one who cannot be trusted." The example in the 1960 edition of Wentworth's *Dictionary of American Slang* comes from 1952: "They tried to **yentz** me out of my end."

Before you ask, let me answer the question I know you have in your mind right now: No, the word "yenta" does not appear in any form—noun, name, or otherwise—in the 1960 edition of Wentworth's *Dictionary of American Slang.*

Perhaps Joseph Stein, who came from a Yiddish-speaking family, knew these words ("yentshen" and "yentz"). If he read the story "The Little Pot" during the drafting of *Fiddler on the Roof,* perhaps some magic alchemy occurred. This may sound farfetched, but in fact "The Little Pot" is one of the stories in the second book of Francis Butwin's two-volume edition of *The Collected Stories of Sholem Aleichem*—the book called *Tevye's Daughters* !

What if the phonetic combination of Yente-the-Poultrywoman's self-description (as written by Sholem Aleichem) coalesced in Joseph Stein's mind with the sounds of the words "yentshen" and "yentz," leading him to transform a man named Ephraim into a woman named Yente? Certainly Stein's Yente-the-Matchmaker does a lot of "**groaning and complaining**" in her private conversations with Golde, and when Tzeitel mocks Yente in "Matchmaker," she is definitely describing someone "**who cannot be trusted**."

Knowing of my obsession with this topic, my Chicago YIVO friend Alan Todres did a Google search on the nouns "yente" and "yenta." Alan's search (current as of March 2011) clearly indicates that the noun "yenta" was rarely used in English between the 1930s (the peak of Yente Telebende's popularity) and the 1960s. Usage begins to climb immediately after *Fiddler on the Roof*'s first Broadway performance in 1964, spiking after Norman Jewison's film version was released in 1971.

Does **this** look like a coincidence to you? My assertion is that the name "Yente" did not become the commonly used Yinglish noun "yenta" until **after** Norman Jewison turned Bea Arthur's Yente-the-Businesswoman into Molly Picon's Yente-the-Busybody. And that is exactly what this graph shows.

YENTE (DARK) ----> YENTA (LIGHT)

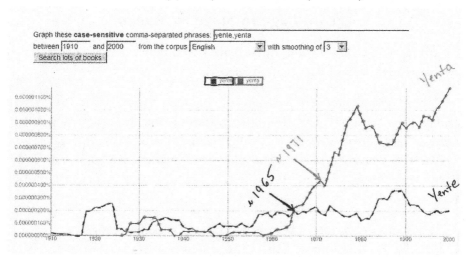

from Wikipedia (2011)

But me being me, I went one more step: I reached out to Henry Sapoznik (the person Google tells me has done more work on "Yente Telebende" than anyone else). Here is his reply to my question (Was Yente Telebende a "yenta"?) that I asked him during a phone call:

> From everything I can tell, certainly from the sound recordings… the one thing she is not in any of those performances—she's a lot of things—but **a gossip she is not**. So clearly this is something that happened after. The character, at least the way Kovner developed it both on the page and then there were two plays about Yente Telebende (including one which Boris Thomashefsky produced)…
>
> Where the character was broadly disseminated—even though it started on the page in the *Forward*—it was these thousands of

records that defined the character… Over time, I think what's happened is the popular perception of Yente from a woman who gave as good as she got—who was as sharp-tongued and maybe more so than her husband Mendel Telebende—it somehow got morphed from being a selfish sort of woman to being a gossip.

(Sapoznik, July 27, 2010)

From Page to Stage to Screen

To recap: I have told you today about two different literary characters—two women—both of whom are named Yente.

I have described a very well-known character named Yente-the-Matchmaker. This Yente—Yente-the-Matchmaker—is the character Joseph Stein created for *Fiddler on the Roof* in 1964. This Yente appears in *Fiddler on the Roof* in place of Ephraim, the male matchmaker who appears in two of Sholem Aleichem's eight Tevye stories, "Hodel" and "Tevye Leaves for the Land of Israel."

I have also described a relatively obscure character named "Yente-the-Poultrywoman." This Yente—Yente-the-Poultrywoman—is the narrator of a monologue called "The Little Pot" which Sholem Aleichem published in Yiddish in 1901. This Yente made her English debut in *Tevye's Daughters* (volume two of *The Collected Stories of Sholem Aleichem* published by Frances Butwin in 1949).

I have suggested through textual analysis that Joseph Stein (the man who wrote the libretto for *Fiddler on the Roof*) was aware of Yente-the-Poultrywoman when he created Yente-the-Matchmaker, but I do not know this for a fact. In all the many, many interviews that Joseph Stein did about *Fiddler on the Roof* from 1964 until his death at age 98 in October 2009, I have never seen this specific topic addressed. So as far as I know, no one ever asked Stein any relevant questions about Yente-the-Matchmaker.

My hope is that clues are buried in the personal papers Joseph Stein donated to the famous Billy Rose Theatre Division at the New York Public Library for the Performing Arts shortly before he died. These papers have yet to be catalogued and made available to the public, but I will keep trying, and should I find any answers, you can be sure I will let everyone know.

Finally, as I told you in my introduction, Yente-the-Matchmaker no longer sings in the film version of *Fiddler on the Roof.* Her section in the Musical-Prologue "Tradition" has been deleted, and so has her song "The Rumor." When Joseph Stein turned his libretto into a screenplay, Yente-the-Matchmaker also lost all her face-to-face interactions with the men of Anatevka.

Bea Arthur, Broadway's original Yente-the-Matchmaker, was born in 1922, and like Joseph Stein, she also died in 2009. In 1964, she was 42 years old, and just look at how tall this lady was! If you ever saw Bea Arthur as TV's *Maude* or as "Dorothy" on *The Golden Girls*, you will know for yourself what I have already said. She was a big powerful woman with a booming voice and a huge stage presence.

To everyone's surprise, the Broadway production of *Fiddler on the Roof* became an **enormous** hit. "There was evening and there was morning" (*va-ye-hi erev ya-ye-hi voy-ker*). And by the late 1960s planning for a film adaptation was well underway. I am not able to discuss all of the differences between the stage and screen versions of *Fiddler on the Roof* today (that is, in fact, the first question I began with when I decided to write a book about *Fiddler on the Roof* in 2001), but for now, let us begin by looking at who Norman Jewison cast as Yente-the-Matchmaker. He chose Molly Picon—**beloved** Molly Picon—who was born in 1898 and died in 1992, and who was 73 years old in 1971. Clearly, these two depictions of this one character are very different.

Now Hollywood is "big business," and I am sure many considerations went into this casting choice. For one thing, Molly Picon was the **only** member of the film's cast who was well-known in the Jewish American world. In 1971, Chaim Topol was only known for his role in *Sallah Shabati.* True, he had won a Golden Globe for Best Actor for that performance, but still. Suffice it to say that Chaim Topol—an Israeli actor who spoke English with a British accent—was not an obvious choice to play Tevye. Of the remaining cast members, only Paul Michael Glaser (who played Perchik) became a headliner. He played the Jewish member of the TV crime duo *Starsky & Hutch.*

So casting Molly Picon as Yente-the-Matchmaker made some commercial sense, but after that? One big question: Does Yente get to sing on screen? No! Yente's lines are eliminated from the Musical-Prologue "Tradition"—and her song "The Rumor" is gone! Yente's role onscreen is reduced to shtick on the sidelines.

One consequence is that Jewison's movie now affects our view of the stage production. Many directors choose to delete Yente's song "The Rumor" from Act Two in their own productions. Therefore, it is quite possible that many of you here today have never even heard it before. It simply is not performed all that much anymore.

"And that's what comes of men and women dancing!"

Take that line out of the production and it changes Yente's entire character. It does! In the 2004 Broadway revival honoring *Fiddler on the Roof*'s 40th anniversary, the most significant change was director David Leveaux's request that Sheldon Harnick and Jerry Bock write another song for Yente. Almost everything else in the 2004 production stayed the same. The new song Harnick and Bock wrote to replace "The Rumor" is called "Topsy-Turvy." "Topsy-Turvy," in the middle of Act Two, makes it very clear what Yente's true agenda is.

> **Yente**: It's all topsy-turvy: No? Yes!
> The world is a shambles, a mishmash, a mess.
> **Women**: We all have our troubles: Right? Right!
> **Yente**: And mine is my living; it changed overnight.
> And why? I'll tell you why. Young people.
> All of the sudden, everyone knows better than me.
> Who needs Yente?
> Why come to me when more and more they don't want marriage.
> It seems today they all insist on wedded bliss.
> A simple match is not for them. They'll only marry for love.
> **Women**: They want to be happy.
> **Yente**: They want to be happy. What kind of match is this?
> **All**: It's all topsy-turvy: Right? Right!
> The world is a mess, a muddle and a blight.
> **Yente**: The matchmaking business: finished, done.
> **Woman**: But still, count your blessings.
> **Yente**: I've counted. None!

Yente: "The matchmaking business: finished, done.
I've counted my blessings. None."

Yente is all about "the deal," and looking with respect at the dialogue Stein wrote for her in his libretto gives a whole new meaning to the issues surrounding the word "tradition" and the preservation of traditions in modern society.

A Tiny Bit of Shakespeare

According to Wikipedia, the verb "to gossip" first appears in Shakespeare, and then—as now—he used it primarily to define the behavior of women. But consider the words of Iago when he tells Othello that rumors are flying around about Desdemona (Othello's wife) and Cassio (his lieutenant).

> Therefore, as I am bound,
> Receive it from me. I speak not yet of proof.
> **Look to your wife**; observe her well with Cassio.
> (*Othello*, Act Three, Scene 3)

A quick online search finds Iago described with powerful words like "cynical and malicious," "pragmatic," "cunning in the extreme," "a Machiavellian schemer." But unlike all those other Shakespearean villains who attack their enemies with sharp knives and vials of poison, Iago's main weapon is gossip... just like Yente's. And yet, I have never heard anyone describe Iago as "**a gossip**." Have you?

And a Final Homage to Jerome Robbins

Let us circle back now to Geoffrey Block's claim in the foreword to Philip Lambert's book *To Broadway, To Life!* that Norman Jewison's screen adaptation of *Fiddler on the Roof* is "**elaborately faithful (and musically nearly complete)**."

Hopefully, I have convinced you that this description of Jewison's film ("elaborately faithful and musically nearly complete") is false, at least with respect to these two very different depictions of Yente-the-Matchmaker.

Who cares? Me.

My contention is that director Jerome Robbins—the primary force behind *Fiddler on the Roof* as we know it today on stage—wanted audiences to understand that "tradition" has less to do with faith than with social control.

When Perchik challenges the rabbi at Tzeitel's wedding ("It's no sin to dance at a wedding. Ask the Rabbi. Ask him."), the rabbi has no answer for him. ("Dancing—Well, it's not exactly forbidden, but… ") Almost none of the "traditions" in *Fiddler on the Roof* come from Mount Sinai. They have another source. They are culturally imposed.

In this way, Broadway's *Fiddler on the Roof* preserves the best of Sholem Aleichem. Recall that the narrator of "Dos Tepl" ("The Little Pot") is the widow Sholem Aleichem named Yente-the-Poultrywoman. She goes to see her rabbi with a serious Halakhic question, which—pardon the pun—boils down to this: My boarder splashed some watery milk on my only meat pot. Can I still use it?

What does her rabbi say after she tells him her full tale of woe? Nothing. The rabbi faints.

Why? The rabbi faints because face-to-face with Yente-the-Poultrywoman's mountain of sorrow, he cannot find the words to defend a rule that would require a poor widow to destroy her only meat pot just because it was accidentally splashed with someone else's watery milk. Sholem Aleichem allows the rabbi to stay silent; the author does not require his character to give voice to Halakhic laws deprived of compassion.

There is something fundamental that drew Jerome Robbins to Sholem Aleichem: Robbins recognized someone who rejected the comforts of "tradition" (as he did), someone who was also repelled by the constraints others would impose on him in the name of religion. As artists, they both celebrated the unique voices of individual human hearts. Neither one would accept limits to his own artistic autonomy, just as neither one would accept a life partner chosen for him by someone else.

Jerome Robbins was a phenomenally successful man who lived life as an active bisexual and never married. Now ask yourself this: In his heart of hearts, did Jerome Robbins really wish he could turn back the clock, return to Anatevka, and have Yente make him a match? Did he want his future all "signed and sealed" by a matchmaker? Preposterous! So much for "nostalgia."

Is *Fiddler on the Roof* a "sentimental" musical, as most critics—most of whom are still men—claim? Only if you shut Yente up, double her age, shrink her down, rob her of her music, and turn her into a joke. We would never let this happen to Iago, but it seems strong, powerful female characters still fill us with fear. Therefore, if we want to honor the Golden Anniversary of *Fiddler on the Roof*, we must restore Yente-the-Matchmaker to her rightful role in the drama and begin treating her with respect.

©2016 Huttner/Rosenzweig

Far from the Home I Love

Left panel: "This is Mine" Act One, Scene 3
Right panel: "But Papa" Act Two, Scene 3

SECTION 5

Hodel:
From Sofievka to Siberia

This lecture was originally presented to the Chicago YIVO Society (in collaboration with ORT Urban Women) at Northbrook Public Library in Northbrook, Illinois, and the Harold Washington Library Center in Chicago, Illinois, on August 18, 2011.

Who is the main character in *Fiddler on the Roof*?

I will not blame you if you say "Tevye," but today I will make the case that the main character in *Fiddler on the Roof* is actually Hodel. Yes, I am talking about Tevye's second daughter Hodel—the one who marries Perchik-the-Revolutionary—and no, I am not kidding.

True, Hodel is not a character with a whole lot of stage time, but Hodel has the predominant female voice on the Original Broadway Cast Recording from 1964, and as we listen to her songs together today, I think you will hear for yourself that Hodel's lyrics are the ones that carry many of the most important messages in *Fiddler on the Roof.*

Before we begin, I want to stress that we will only be discussing the stage version of *Fiddler on the Roof* today. All of the musical snippets that you will hear come from this 1964 recording. As I explained in last year's lecture on Yente-the-Matchmaker, Norman Jewison's 1971 film adaptation—beloved though it may be—takes many liberties, especially with respect to how its female characters are depicted.

Therefore, despite what you may have heard from others, Jewison's film is not "elaborately faithful and musically nearly complete." This assessment— even though it is based on a direct quote from a book published last year by Oxford University Press—is simply wrong. Norman Jewison's film version of *Fiddler on the Roof* is its own thing, and I will not refer to it again in the body of today's lecture (although I will be open to questions about it in the Q&A).

My focus today will be on Jerome Robbins's original production of *Fiddler on the Roof*, which debuted almost 50 years ago. The first Broadway performance was on September 22, 1964. I will play snippets of all of Hodel's songs today, and trace her character arc from her first appearance (as one of the daughters in the chorus) to her last moments onstage... in a deserted train station... where she stands alone with Tevye... singing her good-byes to him and to us.

Then we will drop back in time to Sholem Aleichem's original Tevye stories to see how the master himself crafted some of these very same plot points. Did the *Fiddler* team get it all wrong? This is definitely Conventional Wisdom, but I vehemently disagree. Today I will argue that the *Fiddler* team actually got closer to the core of Solomon Rabinowitz's art than most people—including well-known scholars and critics—realize.

A bit of background for those of you coming to hear me speak for the first time: Do you all know that "Sholem Aleichem" is a pen name? "Sholem Aleichem" in Yiddish is very similar to "Salam Aleikhum" in Arabic. Both expressions literally mean "Peace be with you." But in Yiddish, "Sholem Aleichem" is also used more colloquially to mean "Hello there."

Some scholars speculate that Solomon Rabinowitz—the man—chose this pen name because he was writing articles and stories that appeared regularly but sporadically, so he wanted his readers to recognize him. "Hello there. It's me. Remember that story you read last week? You liked it, right? So, nu: Here I am again. I'm back. Hello there."

Bottom line: When someone refers to this author as "Aleichem" or "Mr. Aleichem," they are totally missing the point. And any index that contains references to "Aleichem, Sholem" is inherently unreliable. Me? I always refer to the man as Solomon Rabinowitz or Rabinowitz, and I always refer to the author as Sholem Aleichem.

Midway through my lecture, Hodel will reach the point in both dramas —in the musical *Fiddler on the Roof* as well as in the "novel" *Tevye the Dairyman*—where she waits with Tevye for a train that will take her east, all the way from Anatevka to Siberia. On stage, "east" will be to her left. That is a bit of a visual joke because Hodel is heading to Siberia to marry a Communist revolutionary. "Exit stage left." Ha! Ha! Ha! And at that point, I hope you will remember that the title of this lecture is "Hodel: From Sofievka to Siberia." And I hope you will say to yourself: "Hodel: From Sofievka to Siberia? Jan has talked a lot about Siberia today, but where the heck is Sofievka?"

Unlike Anatevka, Sofievka is a real place. When Solomon Rabinowitz was a young man, Sofievka was part of Russia. Today, Sofievka is found on maps of a country called Ukraine. Regardless, once I have told you all about Sofievka and the importance of this place in the life of Solomon Rabinowitz, I sincerely believe that the next time you see *Fiddler on the Roof*, you will see it in a whole new way.

Let us begin where *Fiddler on the Roof* begins, with **Tevye**:

> A fiddler on the roof. Sounds crazy, no? But in our little village of Anatevka, you might say every one of us is a fiddler on the roof, trying to scratch out a pleasant, simple tune without breaking his neck. It isn't easy. You may ask, why do we stay up there if it's so dangerous? **We stay because Anatevka is our home.** And how do we keep our balance? That I can tell you in one word— Tradition! (Stein, Page 2)

What follows is the Musical-Prologue "Tradition," in which Tevye introduces the villagers of Anatevka (beginning with members of what we would now call "the nuclear family"): the Papas, the Mamas, the Sons, and the Daughters.

Somewhere in the crowd of daughters, **Hodel** sings:

And who does Mama teach
To mend and tend and fix,
Preparing me to marry
Whoever Papa picks?

All: The daughters, the daughters—Tradition.
Tevye: I have five daughters!
All: The daughters, the daughters—Tradition.

Hodel has yet to be individuated. At this point, Hodel is just one of the girls dancing around when the daughters—as a category—are introduced on stage. She has not even been identified as one of Tevye's daughters yet.

97

But I have seen so many productions of *Fiddler on the Roof* in the past decade that I typically play a little game with myself. Once everyone is dancing around on stage during the Musical-Prologue, I guess who is who on the basis of size, bearing, and costume. And with all due modesty, I must say that I am now very good at this game!

Hodel's first words as Hodel (that is, the first words attributed to a person named Hodel who is a unique character) come in Act One, Scene 1 during the number "Matchmaker."

> **Hodel**: Matchmaker, Matchmaker,
> Make me a match,
> Find me a find.
> Catch me a catch.
> Matchmaker, Matchmaker,
> Look through your book
> And make me a perfect match.

Her sister Chava (Tevye's third daughter) sings the next part:

> **Chava**: Matchmaker, Matchmaker,
> I'll bring the veil,
> You bring the groom,
> Slender and pale.
> Bring me a ring for I'm longing to be
> The envy of all I see.

> **Hodel: For Papa,**
> **Make him a scholar.**

> **Chava**: For Mama,
> Make him rich as a king.

> **Chava** *and* **Hodel**: For me, well,
> I wouldn't holler
> If he were as handsome as anything.
> (Harnick, Pages 17-18)

So in her very first words to us "as Hodel"—meaning as a specific character—what is her "I want" statement? "For Papa, make him a scholar."

And from these very first words, we (in the audience) now know two of Hodel's characteristics as a unique individual:

- She is tightly bound to her father's point of view.
- She knows what her father wants for his daughters, that is, she knows Tevye wants his daughters to marry scholars.

Note that even Tevye's wife Golde knows this. At the beginning of Act One, Scene 1, when Yente-the-Matchmaker first suggests matching Tzeitel with Lazar Wolf-the-Butcher, Golde's immediate response is: "Tevye wants a learned man." (Stein, Page 15)

The music at the beginning of the "Matchmaker" number is a dreamy, lyrical waltz. But do not be fooled. If you heard my lecture last year on Yente-the-Matchmaker, then you know the truth about what happens next.

In the second part of the number, Tzeitel—Tevye's eldest daughter— breaks into her sisters' reverie, impersonates Yente-the-Matchmaker, and begins to mock her. By the third part of the number, Tzeitel has convinced her two younger sisters (Hodel and Chava), and their emotional tone has completely flipped.

> **Chava**: Matchmaker, Matchmaker,
> You know that I'm
> Still very young.
> Please, take your time.

> **Hodel**: Up to this minute
> I misunderstood
> That **I could get stuck for good.**

> **Chava** *and* **Hodel**: Dear Yente,
> See that he's gentle.
> Remember,
> You were also a bride.
> It's not that
> I'm sentimental.

> **Chava, Hodel** *and* **Tzeitel**:
> It's just that I'm terrified!

Matchmaker, Matchmaker,
Plan me no plans,
I'm in no rush.
Maybe I've learned
Playing with matches
A girl can get burned…
(Harnick, Pages 19–20)

The result? By the end of this very first number, the concept of "Tradition" has suddenly been challenged, and the roles that were assigned to everyone in the Musical-Prologue have already been upended.

Tzeitel has seen through Yente's plan to pair people based solely on her own self-interest. Now Tzeitel is warning her sisters: "Playing with matches, a girl can get **burned**." Hodel hears Tzeitel, she understands, and her romantic balloon pops: "Up to this minute, I misunderstood that I could get **stuck** for good."

So this is the beginning of Hodel's arc as a psychological individual in *Fiddler on the Roof*: Hodel knows that her father Tevye wants her to marry a scholar, but she also knows that her mother Golde is aligned with Yente-the-Matchmaker. Once Tzeitel has convinced her that Yente is not to be trusted, Hodel knows she must be careful, otherwise she will "get stuck for good."

What will happen next?!?

Now let me drop back for just a moment and ask about you.

How many people in this audience have seen *Fiddler on the Roof* onstage sometime in the last ten years? And how many people have seen *Fiddler on the Roof* onstage anywhere at any time in their lives? Okay. And how many people have only seen the film version of *Fiddler on the Roof*? Aha. If you are in this last category—people who have only seen *Fiddler on the Roof* onscreen—then **you** should expect some surprises today.

Now back to Hodel.

On the first step of this character's journey, we watch as she questions her assumptions about her future. Persuaded by their eldest sister Tzeitel, Hodel and Chava agree that they will look for their own marriage partners; they will defy the traditional "whoever Papa picks" constraint.

All lovers of *Fiddler on the Roof* know exactly what happens next: Perchik-the-Revolutionary (a student at the university in Kiev) arrives in Anatevka, and Tevye invites him to join the family's Shabbat dinner. Meanwhile Tzeitel wriggles free from Yente-the-Matchmaker's deal with Lazar Wolf-the-Butcher (a widower who is older than her father) by convincing Tevye to bless her pledge to marry Motel-the-Tailor. ("Tzeitel and Motel, they asked me, they begged me," says Tevye in Act Two, Scene 1.)

Soon Tzeitel and Motel are standing under a chuppah (a wedding canopy) with the rabbi. All of the women are on one side of the chuppah; all of the men are on the other side of the chuppah.

> **Tevye**: Is this the little girl I carried?
> Is this the little boy at play?
>
> **Golde**: I don't remember growing older.
> When did they?
>
> **Men**: Sunrise, sunset,
> Sunrise, sunset.
> Swiftly flow the days…
>
> **Women**: Sunrise, sunset,
> Sunrise, sunset,
> Swiftly fly the years…   (Stein, Pages 89-90)

The chorus for the men is separate from the chorus for the women. There is no overlap. And then, at the far edge of the crowd, we hear Perchik's voice followed by Hodel's voice.

Perchik: They look so natural together.
Hodel: Just like two newlyweds should be.
Perchik *and* **Hodel: Is there a canopy in store for me?**

All: Sunrise, sunset,
Sunrise, sunset,
Swiftly fly the years.
One season following another,
Laden with happiness and tears.

(Harnick, Pages 89–90)

Close your eyes now and visualize this scene with me. We can see Perchik on the left edge of the left side singing with all the men. We can see Hodel on the right edge of the right side singing with all the women. They cannot hear each other, but as we watch them sing, we know they are already hearing each other's thoughts, because they answer in unison: "Is there a canopy in store for me?"

Perchik sings: "They [Tzeitel and Motel] look so natural together." And Hodel responds to him from the other side of the stage: "Just like two newlyweds should be." And we—in the audience—hear the first union of a male and a female voice when they sing (together): "Is there a canopy in store for me?"

Their voices, when they sing together, bring forth the overlapping of all the men and women, singing as one in the final stanza: "One season following another, laden with happiness and tears." Do you all hear that?

And then the party begins, and what does Perchik do? Perchik pulls down the mechitzah—the barrier that is separating the men from the women— Perchik pulls down the mechitzah!

Perchik: It's no sin [to dance at a wedding]. Ask the rabbi. Ask him.
(*They all gather around the rabbi.*)
Tevye: Well, Rabbi?
Rabbi: (*Thumbs through a book, finds the place.*) Dancing—Well, it's not exactly forbidden, but...
Tevye: There, you see? It's not forbidden.
Perchik: (*To Hodel*) And it's no sin. Now will someone dance with me?
(*Hodel rises to dance.*)
Golde: Hodel!

Hodel: It's only a dance, Mama.
Perchik: Play! (*Perchik and Hodel dance.*)
(Stein, Pages 98–99)

At first everyone is terrified… but then—bit by bit—everyone begins to dance… even the rabbi. Tevye and Golde start to dance, and then Motel and Tzeitel join in, and soon everyone is dancing and the mechitzah—the barrier separating the men from the women—is gone!

Yente-the-Matchmaker storms offstage with Lazar Wolf-the-Butcher. (Those are Joseph Stein's exact words in the libretto: "They all dance, except for Lazar and Yente, who **storm** off.")

Tzeitel is now the wife of Motel-the-Tailor, and there is no going back. And that is the end of Act One… minus, of course, a friendly little neighborhood pogrom.

✡ ✡ ✡ ✡ ✡

At the beginning of Act Two, Perchik asks Hodel to marry him, but first he announces that he must leave Anatevka and head off to parts unknown.

> **Perchik**: Before I go (*he hesitates, then summons up courage*), there is a certain question I wish to discuss with you… A political question… The question of marriage… The relationship between a man and a woman known as marriage is based on mutual beliefs, a common attitude and philosophy towards society… this relationship has positive social values. It reflects unity and solidarity… And I personally am in favor of it. Do you understand? (Stein, Pages 106-107)

Yes, Hodel understands, and yes, Hodel agrees. And when they start to sing, we (in the audience) hear their voices overlap—as shown in the words in bold below—as they finish each other's sentences.

> **Perchik**: I used to wonder,
> Could there be a wife
> To share such a difficult, **wand'ring kind of life.**
> **Hodel: I was only** out of sight,
> Waiting right here.
> **Perchik**: Who knows tomorrow

Where our **home will be?**
Hodel: I'll be with you and that's
Home enough for me.
Perchik: Everything is right at hand.
Hodel *and* **Perchik: Simple and clear.**
Perchik: I have something that I would die for,
Someone I can live for, too.
Yes, now I have everything—
Not only everything,
I have a little bit more—
Besides having everything,
I know what everything's for.
(Harnick, Pages 108–109)

If you have never seen *Fiddler on the Roof* on the stage, that is, if you have only seen the movie, then this may be the first time you have ever heard this sensual song.

Why? Because this is one of two songs that Norman Jewison decided to cut out of his onscreen adaptation. Nevertheless, it is one of the most important songs in the stage version.

Once again—just like in "Sunrise, Sunset"—Hodel and Perchik hear each other and respond to one another, and we hear the overlap of the male and female voices in the way in which they finish each other's sentences.

Musically, the creators of *Fiddler on the Roof* are clearly telling us that this is genuine love between two equals "based on mutual beliefs and a common attitude and philosophy towards society," with "positive social values," that "reflects unity and solidarity." These two people are intimately connected at the deepest level—and just like a Chagall painting—Hodel and Perchik soar right up to the heavens.

Listen to the very end of the song. Can you hear how the pitch of Perchik's voice ascends? When you look at this song on a lyric sheet, you can see that Perchik's voice rises with elation and exhilaration.

Musically, when a song ends with a higher note progression, the composer's intent is to signify passion.

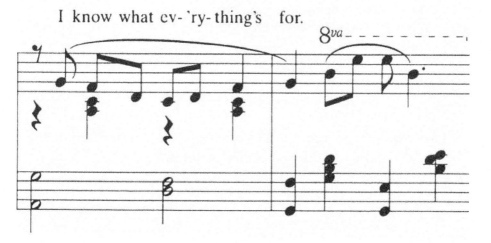

I know what ev-'ry-thing's for.

In my first lecture for the Chicago YIVO Society—Stempenyu: From Berdichev to Broadway—I talked about the paintings in which Marc and Bella Chagall fly high above the city of Vitebsk. Hodel and Perchik, like Marc and Bella, are entwined in erotic, passionate, eidetic love.

"Then I take it you approve?" asks Perchik. And just like Hodel, the creators of *Fiddler on the Roof* nod in assent. Yes, they understand and, yes, they approve.

But just in case we (in the audience) still do not get the point about the elation and exhilaration of romantic love, the creators of *Fiddler on the Roof* provide a counterpoint.

Tevye: Do you love me?
Golde: I'm your wife.
Tevye: I know—
But do you love me?
Golde: Do I love him?
For twenty-five years I've lived with him,
Fought with him, starved with him.
Twenty-five years my bed is his.
If that's not love, what is?

Tevye: Then you love me?
Golde: I **suppose** I do.
Tevye: And I **suppose** I love you, too.
Tevye *and* **Golde**: It doesn't change a thing,
But even so,
After twenty-five years,
It's nice to know.
(Harnick, Pages 116–118)

Lovely song, but notice that the Tevye/Golde duet is the mirror image of the Perchik/Hodel duet that comes right before it.

Instead of "Everything's for"—up Up UP—we have "It's nice to know"—DOWN DOwn down—two songs which appear on the lyrics sheets as mirror images of one another.

What we actually hear in "Do You Love Me?" is a beautiful but very bittersweet song about two people who have never felt the exhilaration of romantic love. Romantic love has never been a part of their lives, so Tevye and Golde literally have no clue what it is or how it feels.

Yes, 25 years after the day they met and married ("The first time I met you was on our wedding day…"), Tevye and Golde agree that they have managed to forge a successful partnership… But that is not the same thing at all, and we (in the audience) know it from the notes of resignation in their music.

✡ ✡ ✡ ✡ ✡

A couple of months pass. Perchik has disappeared. No one knows where he is. Finally, Hodel gets a letter. Perchik was arrested in Kiev. He has been sent to Siberia.

Hodel tells her beloved father Tevye that she intends to go to Siberia to join Perchik. Tevye takes her to the train station…

> **Hodel**: Oh, what a melancholy choice this is,
> Wanting **home**, wanting him,
> Closing my heart to every hope but his,
> Leaving the **home** I love.
>
> There where my heart has settled long ago
> I must go, I must go.
> Who could imagine I'd be wand'ring so
> Far from the **home** I love?
>
> **Yet, there with my love, I'm home.**
> (Harnick, Page 124)

I am asking you now to recognize that "home" is the thematic engine of *Fiddler on the Roof*. Here is the dynamic arc of the plot of *Fiddler on the Roof*:

> **Tevye** [to Audience]: "We stay because Anatevka is our **home**."
> **Hodel** [to Perchik]: "I'll be with you and that's **home** enough for me."
> **Hodel** [to Tevye]: "There with my love [Perchik] I'm **home**."

Once again, essential elements of *Fiddler on the Roof* mirror one another. On the one hand, the constraints of "Tradition" grow ever weaker for these characters. On the other hand, the question "where is home?" becomes increasingly urgent.

Hodel, by invoking three Wandering Jews named Abraham, Joseph, and Moses, gives Tevye an irrefutable argument. Tevye has no rebuttal because he knows full well that God once said to Abraham: "Go forth from your native land and from your father's house to the land that I will show you." Tevye knows God sent Joseph to Egypt in chains, and he knows God sent Moses back across the Sinai to lead the Jewish people to the Promised Land.

Having already conceded that God Himself made the match between Hodel and Perchik ("Did Adam and Eve have a matchmaker? Yes, they did. Then it seems these two have the same matchmaker."), all Tevye can do now is look to God and say: "Take care of her. See that she dresses warm."

Let us be very clear here: No one is forcing Hodel to leave Anatevka. No one onstage knows yet that there will soon be an edict from the Czar affecting Tevye, his family, and the entire Jewish community, an edict that expels them from Anatevka and scatters them all to parts unknown.

Hodel is going on her own steam, of her own free will, with her own desires, thoughts, intentions, and goals. Why? "There with my love I'm **home**." I have seen some performances in which Tevye whispers his last words like prayers, whereas in other performances Tevye barks them out like imperatives: "Take care of her!"

Hodel exits stage left. Off she goes—to Siberia—and then the drama proceeds…

But to me, this scene at the train station is the climax of *Fiddler on the Roof.* All the rest is denouement.

> **Tevye**: Give him my regards, this Moses of yours…
> **Hodel**: Papa, God alone knows when we shall see each other again.
> **Tevye**: Then we will leave it in His hands… (*looks to heaven*).
> Take care of her. See that she dresses warm.   (Stein, Pages 124–125)

✡ ✡ ✡ ✡ ✡

Now let us look at Hodel's arc in Sholem Aleichem's original Tevye stories.

The Tevye stories are actually eight separate stories that were written over a span of almost 20 years. Today, since *Fiddler on the Roof* turned the name Tevye into such a worldwide commercial juggernaut, they are typically collected and published together as one "novel" called *Tevye the Dairyman.*

Some scholars argue that *Tevye the Dairyman* is one of the greatest novelistic achievements in literary history. Someone in real time is writing about the passage of time in a literary form that has integrity as a novel; yet in reality, these were eight separate stories published (as I have already said) over a span of almost 20 years! That is remarkable!

Looking at *Tevye the Dairyman* as a novel, Hodel—Tevye's second daughter—makes minor appearances in the first three chapters; she plays a central role in the fourth chapter (the one called "Hodel"); and she sends letters back to her family (so readers know her fate) as the remaining four chapters unfold.

In *Fiddler on the Roof*, Tevye has five and only five daughters, but Hodel is still his second child, the one born after Tzeitel and before Chava. I will not stop to address this now, but some of you probably know that the original stories mention seven daughters, and there are films from Germany and Israel which include all of them. In English translation, both films are called *Tevye and His Seven Daughters*.

But in *Fiddler on the Roof*, there are five daughters. From oldest to youngest, they are: Tzeitel, Hodel, Chava, Shprintze, and Bielke. Sholem Aleichem also includes a daughter named Teibl (who never gets her own story and is just mentioned in passing), and a seventh daughter (who never even gets a name, let alone a story of her own). We know absolutely nothing about either of them, not even where they are in the birth order.

If you like, we can talk more about all of this in the Q&A, but for now, let us move on.

Sholem Aleichem tells us quite explicitly that although Tevye loves all his daughters deeply, Hodel has a special place in his heart. In "Tevye Leaves for the Land of Israel" (the seventh story out of eight), Tevye—narrating his own story—says this to Sholem Aleichem:

> I'll tell you the honest truth: I myself am no weeping willow. The last good cry I remember having, in fact, was when I found my poor Golde dead on the floor, and before that, when my Hodl left me standing in the station, all alone like a fool with my horse. There may have been a few other times when my eyes were a wee bit wet, but that's all; on the whole, it's not like me to blubber.
> (Halkin, Page 112)

In a musical, when the creators want to signal that a certain moment has high drama and emotion, they insert a song. That is the role **music** plays in a **musical**. That is why the musical as an art form is different from a play; it has a musical element. It is the job of the creators to take the most emotional moments in the text and, through music, amplify these emotions even more.

So who was it that selected this particular moment—the moment in which Hodel sings "Far From the Home I Love" at the train station—as a moment which required such a dramatic song? My contention is that it was Sholem Aleichem. It was Sholem Aleichem who put these words in Tevye's mouth.

Count for yourself and you will see nine blunt words above devoted to Golde's death ("I found my poor Golde dead on the floor"), versus sixteen plaintive words devoted to Hodel's departure ("my Hodl left me standing in the station, all alone like a fool with my horse").

And so, the creators of *Fiddler on the Roof* gave Hodel a song of her own ("Far From the Home I Love") to honor this very specific and highly intimate moment.

(Note that these words come from the penultimate story, "Tevye Leaves for the Land of Israel." This seventh chapter in Sholem Aleichem's "novel"—written in 1909—takes place after Golde's death, whereas Golde is very much alive at the end of *Fiddler on the Roof*.)

Although Tevye has brief conversations in *Fiddler on the Roof* with both Tzeitel and Chava, Hodel is the only daughter who gets a full scene alone with her father. When Tevye takes Hodel to the train station in the middle of Act Two, he knows that Perchik has been arrested, but he does not know why. Once they arrive at the train station, Hodel must explain why she is leaving Anatevka to join Perchik in Siberia. Words alone will not suffice. To make her case at the train station, Hodel needs music.

I do not have time today to tell you all the subtle differences between the characters and incidents in the two different versions—*Tevye the Dairyman* versus *Fiddler on the Roof*—but for our purposes, I think I can do no better today than to just read what Sholem Aleichem himself had to say about Hodel's departure for Siberia.

(Keep in mind that this is a quote from a monologue. Tevye is talking to the character "Sholem Aleichem:" he is reporting on his conversation with Hodel, and his reaction after she leaves Anatevka.)

Hodel: "I am going to follow him there."

Tevye: She seemed to be speaking with pride as if he, Perchik, had done some great deed which deserved a medal made from a pound of iron. What could I say? And so I replied as usual with a commentary: "I see, my daughter, that you have made your decision. As it says in the Holy Torah, 'Therefore a man shall leave his father and mother.' Because of Perchik, you are abandoning your parents and going off to a place you don't know, somewhere—as I once read in a storybook—over a desert beyond a frozen sea, where Alexander of Macedonia sailed and was lost on a distant island among wild savages.

And she answered me: "With *him,* it doesn't matter. I will go anywhere with him, even to the ends of the earth."

I tried to explain with logic, as usual, how foolish that was, then she explained to me with her logic, which I will never understand. So I told her a parable about a hen that hatched ducklings. As soon as the ducklings were able to stand on their legs, they jumped into the water and swam away while the poor hen stood there clucking. "What do you have to say to that, my dear daughter?"

"What can I say? It's certainly a pity for the hen. But because the hen stood there clucking, is that a reason the ducklings shouldn't swim?"

Do you appreciate those words? Tevye's daughter spoke to the point. (Halkin, Pages 65–67)

In the novel, this conversation takes place the night before they go to the train station. Then, the next day, when they get to the train station, Tevye says to Hodel:

"Please give him my regards, your Alexander of Macedonia. Tell him that I am relying on him as an honorable man not to mistreat my daughter and to make sure she writes an occasional letter to an old father."

And as I spoke, didn't she suddenly throw her arms around my neck and start to cry? "Let us say goodbye," she said. "Be well, Papa. God alone knows when we shall see each other again."

Well that was too much for me. I could no longer control myself. I remembered this same Hodel when she was still a baby and I held her in my arms, in my arms.

Forgive me, Pani Sholem Aleichem. She's right here, right here, deep, deep. I cannot begin to say it. You know what, Pani? Let's better speak of something happier. What do you hear about the cholera in Odessa?   (Halkin, Pages 68–69)

I note with some frustration that although this bit of "laughter through tears" is widely quoted in lectures about Sholem Aleichem ("Let's better speak of something happier. What do you hear about the cholera in Odessa?"), I have never once heard it identified as a reference to Tevye's reaction to the loss of his daughter Hodel.

"Fartaytsht un farbesert!" That is what Maurice Schwartz used to say about his Yiddish productions of *King Lear* and *The Merchant of Venice*. Shakespeare! "Translated and improved!" Here too, my claim is that in this pivotal moment, *Fiddler on the Roof* **is** Sholem Aleichem, "translated and improved" through the magic of music.

Who gets the musical moment? By invoking one of the most respected paradigms in musical theater, *Fiddler on the Roof*'s creators have signaled that Hodel is the central female character in their production. Hodel not only does more singing than any other female character in *Fiddler on the Roof*, she is, in fact, the only female character in *Fiddler on the Roof* who gets her own solo.

✡ ✡ ✡ ✡ ✡

Fiddler on the Roof is often accused of softening Sholem Aleichem's hard edges. Most of the (mostly) male critics are particularly outraged by the "happy endings" of the multiple romances. They point out, accurately enough, that in "Get Thee Out!"—Sholem Aleichem's final Tevye story— the people leaving with Tevye are Tzeitel (who is now a widow), Tzeitel's two young children (who are nameless), and Chava (who has returned home just in time to join in their exile).

How long has it been since Chava married Fyedka, and where has she been in the interim? Sholem Aleichem provides no clues. In fact, he only gives Chava one single word of dialogue, the word "Papa." What little we know comes through Tzeitel:

> From the first minute she found out we were being sent away, she decided they would send all of us, she too along with us. Wherever we go—so Chava herself said—she will go. Our exile is her exile. (Shevrin, Page 126)

This is what we know—and this all that we know—from what Sholem Aleichem tells us in his Tevye stories. But some people think they know better…

Yiddish Theatre scholars can now document that prior to his death in 1916, Sholem Aleichem tried to interest prominent New York producers in a theatrical version of his Tevye stories. His adaptation of his own stories from page to stage was focused solely on Tevye's relationship with Chava. This is the treatment that eventually reached fruition decades later in Maurice Schwartz's 1939 film *Tevye*.

So, what should we—a full century after Sholem Aleichem's death— make of the fact that in Schwartz's 1939 film *Tevye*, Chava returns home begging for forgiveness after years of abuse by her husband's family? Me? I just don't see the relevance.

Life in 1964 was not the same as life today. No one on the *Fiddler on the Roof* team could reach out to the National Center for Jewish Film in 1964 and ask to have a *Tevye* DVD sent overnight via Federal Express. It is very unlikely that anyone other than Boris Aronson even knew about Schwartz's 1939 film, and even Aronson would not have seen it for years by that point.

Are we really going to penalize the *Fiddler on the Roof* team for not using scenes that were part of a Yiddish film from 1939, especially when there was probably no opportunity to watch it even if they had known to look for it? In 1964, it was hard enough just to find Sholem Aleichem's Tevye stories because the books that contained English translations of them were long out of print.

Furthermore, as all of the cover art on albums and books and posters proudly proclaim, the 1964 Robbins version of *Fiddler on the Roof* was explicitly "based on Sholom Aleichem's **stories**." And as in "Get Thee Out!,"

Chava decides that the exile of her family is "her exile" too. The only difference is that in *Fiddler on the Roof*, we don't have to wonder where Fyedka is or if he is even still alive. Chava makes this decision with Fyedka's full support and participation.

> **Chava**: We are also leaving this place. We are going to Cracow.
> **Fyedka**: We cannot stay among people who can do such things to others.
>
> (Stein, Page 150)

As the curtain falls on *Fiddler on the Roof*, we sit suspended in the audience—our hearts in our throats—hoping against hope that Tevye (accompanied by Golde, Shprintze and Bielke) will eventually arrive in America, just as we want Tzeitel, Motel, and their baby to make it to Warsaw, and we want Chava and Fyedka to make it to Cracow. Meanwhile, we pray that Hodel and Perchik will manage to survive together in Siberia and continue their arduous work there. One way or the other, all three of Tevye's daughters know that they should keep sending letters in care of Uncle Abram.

"God alone knows when we shall see each other again."

"Then we will leave it in His hands."

From my point of view, there is nothing "soft" about the ending of *Fiddler on the Roof*, especially when we consider the basic elements of Solomon Rabinowitz's own biography, most especially the details of his marriage to the woman history now knows by her Russian name, "Olga." "I have five daughters," brays Tevye when the daughters introduce themselves in the opening moments of the Musical-Prologue, and—"miracle of miracles"—Solomon and Olga Rabinowitz did too.

With so much interest in this man since his death in 1916, there has been amazingly little examination of Solomon Rabinowitz's family life. Okay, so there is not much in Wikipedia, but look in the Jewish Virtual Library, look in YIVO's huge *Encyclopedia of Jews in Eastern Europe*, ask Jeeves the question "How many children did Sholem Aleichem have?" and you get... well... nothing.

Perhaps people assume that with such a huge outpouring of literary treasures, Rabinowitz didn't have time for much else. But the reality is quite the opposite. Based on what I have pieced together from *My Father, Sholom Aleichem,* by his daughter Marie Waife-Goldberg, Solomon Rabinowitz and his wife Olga had six children and two wards. So let me tell you a bit about them just as quickly as I can.

Solomon Rabinowitz—Sholem Aleichem—was born into a relatively prosperous family. His father was a scholar and his mother basically ran the business. They had a large number of children; some have said as many as 11 or 12. Mama Rabinowitz—Chaya Esther—was raising them all, while Papa Rabinowitz—Reb Nochem Vevik—did his thing. And then Papa Rabinowitz made some bad business decisions and the family was suddenly bankrupt. They were forced to leave their home, and soon after that, Mama Rabinowitz died.

On page 102 of his autobiography, *From the Fair,* Sholem Aleichem tells us quite clearly that his mother died of cholera soon after his Bar Mitzvah. Since he was born in 1859, that means Chaya Esther died sometime in the summer of 1872. Unable to care for his many children alone, Reb Nochem Vevik dispersed them, sending them off to different relatives. Then he remarried, and bit by bit he started calling his children back home. But his second wife—who is always called "Stepmother" and never given a name of her own—was not pleased, and as soon as she could, she forced them out again.

And so, at the very young age of 16 or so, Solomon was basically alone in the world. He made his living as a teacher, a marginal living at best. *From the Fair,* which he was still working on when he died in 1916, contains stories of his various adventures, most of which are heartbreaking.

Then one day Solomon is at an inn where he meets another young man, a bit older than himself, named Joshua Loyeff. (In her book *My Father, Sholom Aleichem,* Marie Waife-Goldberg spells his name "Yeshia," Yeshia Loyeff.) Joshua, described in *From the Fair* as "an angel in human guise," is the son of a very wealthy man named Elimelech Loyeff. After talking to this educated, intelligent, and clearly destitute young man, Joshua decides that his father Elimelech should meet Solomon too.

Solomon meets Elimelech; Elimelech inspects him "as if he were a fish in the market," and then Elimelech hires him for two concurrent jobs. Solomon is to work part-time as a tutor for Elimelech's teenage daughter Olga (Joshua's stepsister), and in the evenings he is to serve as a private secretary (doing correspondence and other clerical tasks for Elimelech to support the management of his estate).

Who was on the estate when Solomon Rabinowitz arrived in Sofievka? This gets a bit complicated, so please bear with me.

Elimelech had a first wife, but I have been unable to find a name for her anywhere. The first wife had two sons: Joshua and his older brother Israel. Both sons had married, fathered one daughter, and then divorced. Like their mother-in-law, these wives disappeared into history without receiving names from Rabinowitz (or, as far as I know, from anyone else).

After his first wife died, Elimelech—like Reb Nochem Vivek— married again. The name of his second wife was Rukhl Yampolsky. (In her book *My Father, Sholom Aleichem*, Marie Waife-Goldberg spells her name "Rakhil," Rakhil Yampolsky Loyeff.) In the fullness of time, Rukhl gave birth to a daughter named Olga.

So when Solomon Rabinowitz arrived in Sofievka, the people in residence were:

- Elimelech Loyeff (the patriarch)
- Rukhl Loyeff (his second wife)
- Israel Loyeff and his daughter Manya
- Joshua Loyeff and his daughter Natasha
- Olga Loyeff (daughter of Rukhl)

In other words, Solomon—at that time a young man of 18—was to be a teacher in a home with three girls:

- Olga (age 15)
- Manya (age 9)
- Natasha (age 5)

LOYEFF FAMILY TREE
© Jan Lisa Huttner (2018)

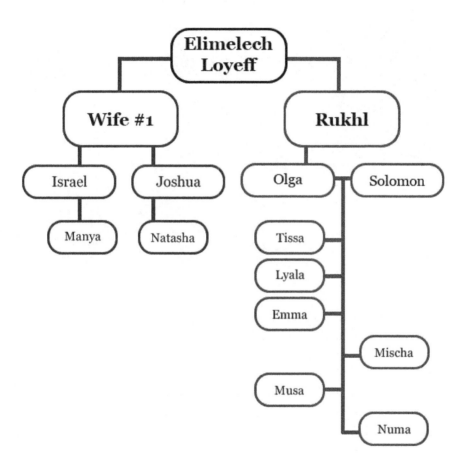

Here is a photo of Perchik teaching Bible stories to Bielke and Shprintze under Hodel's watchful eye. The real Solomon Rabinowitz—Sholem Aleichem—seems to have stumbled into the exact same configuration found in Act One, Scene 6 of *Fiddler on the Roof.* Can this be a coincidence?

© Oceanside High School, NY (circa 2000)

Since Joshua and his older brother Israel are rarely to be found at home, Olga and Solomon end up spending a great deal of time together. Need I say that they soon find themselves falling in love? Eventually, Olga's parents catch on and they are not happy. Of course Elimelech likes this young man, but he never considered Solomon a potential son-in-law; he always considered him an employee. So Elimelech forces Solomon out of the house, and Solomon is soon alone and on his own again… And then—miraculously—Olga and Solomon get married.

Solomon himself provides no explanation for this happy resolution. What details we have come from his daughter Marie's book *My Father, Sholom Aleichem,* which was published in 1968, (four years after *Fiddler on the Roof* opened on Broadway and three years after it swept the 1965 Tony Awards).

Solomon Rabinowitz—Sholem Aleichem—died in 1916, but Olga Rabinowitz—Madame Sholem Aleichem—died in 1942. Marie was very close to her mother Olga, and she reports that Olga repeatedly told her it was up to her to write the story of "life with father." And yet the story Marie tells likely depends far more on Olga's private recollections than anything published by or about her father. For example, Marie reports that her father Solomon—Sholem Aleichem—always spoke glowingly of her grandfather Elimelech Loyeff. But when she asks her mother, Olga says: "My father was a tyrant." So we must take it from there…

The fact that they found each other again and were finally reunited cannot be because Solomon fought for Olga. He was intentionally denied access to her, and he seems to have accepted Elimelech Loyeff's banishment with his tail between his legs. So it had to be Olga who took steps to go after him. Certainly my heart tells me this is what happened. Regardless, one way or the other, they became man and wife in 1883.

Sadly, by the time Olga and Solomon married, both Israel and Joshua were dead, leaving the two girls under the care of their grandfather (Elimelech Loyeff) and his second wife (Rukhl Yampolsky). Technically, Rukhl was their step-grandmother and Olga was their step-aunt, but as I have already said, these three girls were very close in age. In 1877—when Solomon arrived in Sofievka—Olga was 15, Manya was 9, and Natasha was 5. Six years later—when Olga and Solomon married in 1883—Olga was 21, Manya was 15, and Natasha was 11. So once again we must listen to our hearts, and my heart tells me that these three girls—who had always lived on the estate together under the care of Rukhl Yampolsky—were raised as sisters.

And then, more sadness: Elimelech Loyeff (who was a very wealthy man) died in 1885. According to Russian property laws, women could not inherit, so Elimelech Loyeff's vast fortune went to Solomon Rabinowitz, and Manya and Natasha (both now teenagers) became his legal wards. If I am right about the emotions in play at this moment, then a handsome young man who had been transformed by love from teacher into brother-in-law, now managed all the financial resources of a family that no longer had any men in it other than him.

Since Olga and Solomon had had their first child—a daughter named Ernestina ("Tissa")—in 1884, the new patriarch (age 25) suddenly found himself with six female dependents under his wing: his wife, his mother-in-law, his daughter, and his two sisters-in-law (aka "wards"). Talk about truth being stranger than fiction!

And the family kept growing… with ever more female members. Lyala was born in 1887, and Emma was born in 1888. Despite the death of Manya in 1887 at age 19, the Rabinowitz family was thriving… and then—as those of you who know the details of Sholem Aleichem's biography will certainly remember—he blew it all away. In 1890, he lost Elimelech's fortune in a stock market crash! Once again, Solomon Rabinowitz was totally destitute. He had no money left, and he fled Russia to escape his creditors.

What to do? Rukhl Yampolsky pawned all her treasures and Natasha (now 18) offered up her dowry. Whatever funds they had left, they gave to him. Olga called her husband back home, reassuring him that his debts had been covered. Sofievka became the dream of a lost paradise.

They moved to Odessa, then back to Kiev. Olga went to school and became a dentist. Olga continued to have children (including two sons) even while working, and Rukhl Yampolsky—known to the children as "Babushka"—ran the household. In fact, the family lived in Kiev because Olga had protected status. Some of you may already know that, at that time, most Jews were required to live within the Pale of Settlement. Jews needed special permission to live in major cities; most of the Russian Empire was off limits. The Rabinowitz family was able to live in Kiev because Olga—as a dentist—had professional status.

We know all of this because their fourth daughter Musa—the daughter known to us now as Marie Waife-Goldberg—wrote it all down in her book *My Father, Sholom Aleichem*.

Believe it or not, I only found out about all of this myself quite recently. After years of research on *Fiddler on the Roof*, it suddenly occurred to me to ask a very simple question: I wonder if Solomon Rabinowitz had any daughters? I asked myself this question, and then I went looking for an answer, and for a moment, when I actually found the answer, I honestly felt as if I were hallucinating.

Look at this chart with me, and we will do the count together (from oldest to youngest): Natasha, Tissa, Lyala, Emma, and Musa. Five!

RABINOWITZ FAMILY TREE

© Jan Lisa Huttner (2018)

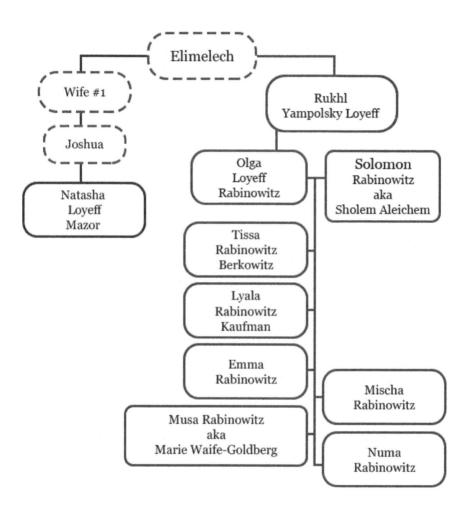

I kept saying to my husband Richard: "Can this really be right?!?" I kept thinking I must be wrong. If I were right about this, then surely someone would have noticed. But in fact, no one seems to have noticed… and that fact… in itself… speaks volumes!

In 1895, Sholem Aleichem wrote a story about a man named Tevye who has seven daughters. By the time of his death—in 1916—he had written eight stories about Tevye, but he has only told us the fates of five of these seven daughters. One gets a name (in a passing reference), but not a story. The other one gets neither a name nor a story. They both seem to have vanished from his mind. Then, almost 50 years later—in 1964—the creators of *Fiddler on the Roof* bring an adaptation of these stories to Broadway, and they give Tevye exactly five daughters (and no more).

And how many daughters did the real Solomon Rabinowitz have? Well, he had four daughters and one ward, meaning he was responsible for five dowries. And to the best of my knowledge, no one has ever noticed this "coincidence" before.

Furthermore, after Natasha gave Solomon her dowry, she ended up marrying a man who was more than 20 years her senior. Even if I tried, I would never be able to make all this up. But I am not making any of this up. Marie Waife-Goldberg wrote it all down for us in her book *My Father, Sholom Aleichem* (published in 1968 and still in print).

And one more thing: The woman known to history as Olga Rabinowitz, can you guess what her Jewish name was?

Here is the answer—I kid you not—on page 65 of her daughter's book: "Grandfather Elimelech and Babushka had only one child, my mother, who was born in 1864 and whose Jewish name was Hodel."

So who is the main character in *Fiddler on the Roof*? I sincerely believe the main character in *Fiddler on the Roof* is Hodel. This is her song:

> **Hodel** [to Tevye]: How can I hope to make you understand
> Why I do what I do,
> Why I must travel to a distant land
> Far from the home I love?

Once I was happily content to be
As I was, where I was,
Close to the people who are close to me
Here in the home I love.

Who could see that a man would come
Who would change the shape of my dreams?
Helpless, now, I stand with him
Watching older dreams grow dim.

Oh, what a melancholy choice this is,
Wanting home, wanting him,
Closing my heart to every hope but his,
Leaving the home I love.

There where my heart has settled long ago
I must go, I must go.
Who could imagine I'd be wand'ring so
Far from the home I love?
Yet, there with my love, I'm home.
                    (Harnick, Pages 123–124)

And this is my conclusion:

An author now known to us as Sholem Aleichem used details from his own life to create indelible characters, and somehow the team that adapted his stories and turned them into *Fiddler on the Roof* understood this material well enough to craft one of the best-loved musicals in theater history.

Two very real people named Solomon and Olga (Hodel) Rabinowitz found their "home" in one another, and through all their wanderings—which were considerable—they nurtured five "daughters" (as well as two sons) and left as their legacy a literary masterpiece that changed the Jewish world forever.

©2016 Huttner/Rosenzweig

My Republic

Top row on left: Chaya Esther and Nachum Rabinowitz
Top row on right: Elimelech and Rachel Yampolsky Loyeff

Middle row: Natasha Loyeff Mazor, Tissa Rabinowitz Berkowitz,
Lyala Rabinowitz Kaufman, Emma Rabinowitz,
and Musa Rabinowitz (Marie Waife-Goldberg)

Bottom row from left: Misha Rabinowitz, Solomon Rabinowitz (Sholem
Aleichem), Olga Loyeff Rabinowitz, and Numa Rabinowitz.

Tevye's Daughters:
From Chawton to Broadway

This lecture was originally presented to the Chicago YIVO Society (in collabora-
tion with ORT Urban Women) at Northbrook Public Library in Northbrook, Il-
linois, and the Harold Washington Library Center in Chicago on August 8, 2012.

My name is Jan Huttner, and it is really a great pleasure to welcome you
here tonight to the Harold Washington Library Center for the fourth of my
series of lectures on *Fiddler on the Roof*. We are preparing ourselves for the
50th anniversary of the first Broadway performance of *Fiddler on the Roof,*
which will be celebrated a couple of years from now on September 22, 2014.

I have now dedicated more than a decade of my life to trying to understand what I call the "sources and synergies" of *Fiddler on the Roof*. What
do we know for sure about *Fiddler on the Roof*? That is, what do we know
in our heads? And what do we know in our hearts, even though these
things may be more in the realm of speculation? These are the two big questions we will be discussing tonight.

I am giving tonight's lecture as a participant in the Chicago YIVO
Society's 2012 Summer Festival of Yiddish Culture, an annual set of programs—now in its 15th year—held in collaboration with many of the li-
braries in the Metro Chicago Public Library system. In fact, I was at Northbrook Public Library earlier today, doing this presentation for the first time.
So you are the beneficiaries of this afternoon's Q&A session.

The Chicago YIVO Society is the largest regional chapter of the YIVO
Institute originally established in Vilnius, Lithuania, in 1925. YIVO is an
acronym for the Yiddish name "Yidisher Visnshaftlekher Institut." The YIVO
archives were presciently moved from Vilnius to Manhattan in the late 1930s,
preserving this great treasure trove of Ashkenazi Jewish culture from Eastern
Europe. I am very, very proud to have been a member of the Board of the
Chicago YIVO Society for the past several years. Some of you already know

that I am now in the process of moving to Brooklyn—where my husband Richard has just taken a new position at SUNY Downstate Medical Center—and that is why tonight's handouts have a little map of Brooklyn on the back.

We are not sure yet if this is a permanent move or merely temporary. We think it is permanent, but who knows? What is most important with respect to tonight's presentation is that some time after Labor Day, I will be in Brooklyn. And you can bet that I will make it a high priority—after cooking dinner for Richard, of course—I will make it a high priority to get to the archives at the New York Public Library for the Performing Arts at Lincoln Center to get definitive answers to some of the topics that I will speculate about tonight. So let us begin.

Tonight's lecture is called "Tevye's Daughters: From Chawton to Broadway." First, a show of hands. Raise your hand if you have **never** seen *Fiddler on the Roof* anywhere, in any form, at any point in your life, either on the stage or on the screen. Phew. We can start with the assumption that we have all seen *Fiddler on the Roof.*

A couple of years ago I did a lecture right upstairs in the Reader's Room on the seventh floor (the room with the busts of Saul Bellow and Gwendolyn Brooks). This was my lecture on Yente-the-Matchmaker, and there was a young man in the audience who looked very confused. Finally I stopped and asked: "Is everything okay?" His reply: "Umm, when are you going to start talking about Barbra Streisand?" Oops! When everyone stopped laughing, I said, as kindly as I could: "So sorry. Barbra isn't coming tonight. This lecture is about a character in *Fiddler on the Roof* named Yente, not the movie *Yentl.*" Poor guy. But now I always ask upfront, just to make sure we are all in sync before I begin.

Question: If I showed you a map of the world right now, who here could point to Chawton? Just my friend Sandy? Sandy probably knew where Chawton was well before she knew who I was. But I am glad to know that even the Google-obsessed among you waited, because Chawton is a "big reveal." So please be patient. I promise you, by the time you leave here, you will all know where Chawton is, and you will also know why I think Chawton is such a surprisingly significant place in a lecture about *Fiddler on the Roof.*

One final question before we begin: Who here tonight has heard one or more of my prior lectures on *Fiddler on the Roof*? As I have already said, this is the fourth in a series. My goal is to present as much new material as possible tonight, so you do not need to know anything about what I said in prior lectures. Nevertheless, the more you know, the more context you will have. That is obvious. And we can certainly pull different threads together during the Q&A.

This lecture begins with a quote from Amanda Walgrove's January 13 post on the website *Tablet: A New Read on Jewish Life*. The date is important because January 13, 2012, was just a few days after the beginning of the second season of *Downton Abbey*. (Although it had already been shown in the United Kingdom in September 2011, season two of *Downton Abbey* made its American debut on the PBS program Masterpiece Classics on January 8, 2012.) Hold up your hand if you have never seen an episode of *Downton Abbey*. Okay, most of you are familiar with *Downton Abbey*.

Now here is the quote from *Tablet*:

> The patriarchs of the 1960's musical *Fiddler on the Roof* and of the posh British television series *Downton Abbey* share a **very deep and most unlikely** kinship.

And then, a few days later, a similar quote from Emily Nussbaum appeared in the January 23, 2012, issue of the *New Yorker* magazine:

> I prefer to think of *Downton* as an **experimental take** on *Fiddler on the Roof.* Just think of the Earl of Grantham as Tevye with his three rebel daughters, plus a much better roof. L'chaim, m'lord.

If you are a *Downton Abbey* fan, you will likely find this very clever. If you are not, you will just have to take our word for it. Joking aside, the balls, the gowns, the servants, and the whole panoply of life at *Downton Abbey*—can we reduce them all to an "experimental take" on *Fiddler on the Roof*? Is it really just "a much better roof" that separates Tevye from Lord Grantham? Is this, in fact, an "unlikely kinship"?

No. Not at all. Prepare yourself for some surprising news. I believe there are some very real connections between *Downton Abbey* and *Fiddler on the*

Roof, much deeper than I suspect either Nussbaum or Walgrove ever imagined when they penned their clever bons mots.

The text of *Fiddler on the Roof* is based on eight stories written by Yiddish author Solomon Rabinowitz, best-known now by his pen name Sholem Aleichem. Scholars speculate that Rabinowitz chose this name—Sholem Aleichem—because he was writing short pieces that came out frequently in weekly newspapers. Often a new story would come out just before Shabbat and a family would read it as a Shabbat story when they were all together on Saturday. So this was an early example of what we now call "branding." Rabinowitz was basically using this pen name—Sholem Aleichem—to say: "Hey, hello there! Remember me? You liked my story last week, so try this new one." It worked! People loved him! Solomon Rabinowitz was a man of many talents.

These eight stories by Sholem Aleichem are all monologues told in the voice of a man named Tevye. They were written over the course of almost 20 years, and they trace the trajectory of events that were happening to Jews living in the Russian "Pale of Settlement" real time. Changes in the real world over the course of those 20 years are reflected in the pages of these eight stories. Today—since the premiere of *Fiddler on the Roof* on Broadway in 1964—these eight stories are typically published as one "novel" called *Tevye the Dairyman* (at least in English versions).

Tevye the Dairyman—a novel with eight chapters—holds a very unique place in the history of world literature today, because it actually traces the changes that occurred from the time that Solomon Rabinowitz was a young man—recently married—until just before he died. He was born in a place now found on the map of a country called Ukraine, but like many Jews from Eastern Europe, he died in New York. Those of you who saw Joseph Dorman's recent documentary *Sholem Aleichem: Laughter in the Darkness*, know all about this. And those of you who have read Sholem Aleichem's "Tevye" stories know that in the original, Tevye has seven daughters.

But on the Original Broadway Cast Recording of *Fiddler on the Roof* released in 1964, Tevye famously tells us: "I have five daughters!"

> **The Daughters**: And who does Mama teach to mend and tend and fix, preparing me to marry whoever Papa picks?

All: The daughters, the daughters...

Tevye: I have five daughters!

All: Tradition. The daughters, the daughters. Tradition.

This is where our mystery begins: How do we get from Sholem Aleichem's original seven daughters to *Fiddler on the Roof*'s five daughters to *Downton Abbey*'s three daughters?

So let me ask a very simple question: Did anyone else have five daughters? Answer: Yes! Mr. and Mrs. Bennet of Longbourn—an estate in Hertfordshire just north of London—they had five daughters: Jane, Elizabeth, Mary, Kitty, and Lydia.

First Impressions

Mr. Bennet has five daughters in *Pride and Prejudice*; Tevye has five daughters in *Fiddler on the Roof*; and furthermore, there is a missing link!

How many of you already know that a musical adaptation of *Pride and Prejudice* once played on Broadway? Is this a shock to you? Hold on!

In 1959, a musical called *First Impressions* premiered on Broadway. It was a musical comedy adapted by Abe Burrows, best-known today as the creator of the big hit *Guys and Dolls*, as well as *How to Succeed in Business without Really Trying*. Not bad to be the creator of *Guys and Dolls*, right? Of course, right. The reference is clearly stated: "From Helen Jerome's dramatization of Jane Austen's novel *Pride and Prejudice*, with music and lyrics by Robert Goldman, Glenn Paxton, and George Weiss" (three people who, alas, were never heard of on Broadway again).

Some background: Jane Austen wrote a novel about the Bennet family. It was her first novel. She called it *First Impressions*. She could not get anyone to publish it. Then she wrote a second novel called *Sense and Sensibility*.

Sense and Sensibility—which **was** published—became very popular. So after *Sense and Sensibility* was published and became popular, the publishers of *Sense and Sensibility* came back to Jane Austen and said: "You know that first book *First Impressions*? Give it a new name that sounds more like *Sense and Sensibility*, and game on." I am speaking in 21st-century lingo now, but like Solomon Rabinowitz, Jane Austen clearly had a knack for branding. At the beginning of the 19th century, a novel called *First Impressions* went nowhere, but with the title *Pride and Prejudice*, it became one of the greatest classics in

Western literature. Poor Abe Burrows. Twentieth-century critics damned his musical in part because they hated the title. "Why did you call it *First Impressions*?" Abe Burrows said: "Well, that is what it was originally called."

The lead actors in *First Impressions* were Polly Bergen in the role of "Lizzie," Farley Granger in the role of "Mr. Darcy," and Hermione Gingold in the role of "Mrs. Bennet." Are you laughing yet? This is all true! How many of you have a mental image of Polly Bergen? She was a very, very beautiful woman. And Farley Granger? He was a very, very handsome man. And Hermione Gingold? She was the star of the show!

For Jane Austen fans, the idea that someone would create a musical comedy around the character of Mrs. Bennet is just extraordinary, but this will not be the first time tonight that "truth is stranger than fiction."

Immediately after the overture (which, unlike the "Tradition!" number that opens *Fiddler on the Roof*, is in fact a very conventional musical overture), Mrs. Bennet sings a song called "Five Daughters." I kid you not. It is a long song, so here are a couple of snippets for you (taken from the hard copy of the libretto):

> Five daughters
> How did it happen?
> How could I have managed
> To produce five of a kind?
>
> Five treasures
> Petticoated treasures
> If I see another stitch of lace
> I'll lose my mind.
>
> I don't deny
> That my girls are precious pearls.
> It's not that I'm not proud of them
> It's just there's such a crowd of them.
>
> Five problems
> Unmarried problems
> Maiden after maiden

That's the way this family runs.
Maiden after maiden…
Why didn't we have sons?
Mrs. Bennet rattles on about all her problems, concluding with this:

Five maidens
Waiting to be mated
Jane's too shy, too easily hurt
Lydia's just a frivolous flirt
Kitty's always tagging along
Mary sings that horrible song
Lizzie
And Lizzie…

(*Spoken.*) Dear Lord
We need extra help with Lizzie…
So much needs to be done
And if you possibly can
Please keep her mouth closed.
Thank you.

(*Sung.*) Daughters help a home to thrive
And I've got Five!
(Jerome & Burrows, Page 13)

Now please notice two of this song's attributes. First of all, who is she addressing here in her spoken recitatif? God. Mrs. Bennet is speaking directly to God (which is astonishing if you can anticipate what I will tell you next). She is directly addressing God, and asking God to please tell Lizzie to keep her mouth shut.

Those of you who know the plot of *Pride and Prejudice*, you will know that these are very much the characters we meet when we read *Pride and Prejudice* (or when we see any of the various big screen and small screen adaptations). Jane is shy; Lydia is a frivolous flirt; and Kitty is a tag-along. The horrible song that Mary sings causes poor Mr. Darcy to plug up his ears.

And yet, to me, the most interesting aspect of this song is that Mrs. Bennet is literally addressing God Himself in her spoken recitatif.

In this terrific Al Hirschfeld illustration below, we see Mrs. Bennet (played by the indefatigable Hermione Gingold) on the left, with Mr. Darcy (played by Farley Granger), Lizzie (played by Polly Bergen), and Mr. Wickham (played by James Mitchell).

© Al Hirschfeld (1959)

Now, let us listen to Mrs. Bennet's big number (which occurs about two-thirds of the way through Act Two).

My poor, poor family... my little dears
How we've suffered and struggled through the lean, lean years
But I know

The hand of Providence will one day turn the tide
And I will be granted
That wonderful dream
I've always kept inside.

A house in town
A house in town
Just a tiny **MMM** spectacular
House in town
Nothing very much
Just a smashing house in town.

(*Repeat stanza.*)

I can see it now...

And Mrs. Bennet continues to fantasize about her new house in town...
But there is something that I want you to notice. The first time I heard
it, honestly, I fell off my chair. Notice the vocalizations indicated by the
MMM? For all of you who have spent years listening to people kvetch
about how nobody could deedle-dum like Zero Mostel, here we have (just
a couple of years before *Fiddler on the Roof*'s premiere) similar vocalizations
made by Mrs. Bennet. And then the pièce de résistance:

There'll be dancing
There'll be drinking
There'll be caviar
By the ton.

Ach du lieber
What a triumph
And the evening's
Just begun.

Excitement is growing
The tension is mounting
The glorious moment is here
(*Spoken.*)

A hush falls over the crowd.
A delicate fanfare, oh not too loud, not too soft.
All eyes will turn to see
There, **poised at the top of the stairs**... me.

Gad, she's beautiful! (Jerome & Burrows, Page 68)

What do we have here? In 1959, we hear Mrs. Bennet talking to God; we hear Mrs. Bennet doing vocalizations; and we hear Mrs. Bennet dreaming about showing herself off at the top of a huge staircase. "Gad, she's beautiful!"

Then, a few years later, in 1964, we hear Tevye talking to God; we hear Tevye doing vocalizations; and we hear Tevye dreaming about "one long staircase just going up and one even longer coming down and one more going nowhere just for show." Coincidence?

But nobody knows about *First Impressions* anymore. It has completely disappeared from memory. Poof!

Why was *First Impressions* such a flop? Let me speculate. First of all, although Hermione Gingold was a star right after *Gigi* (for which she won the Golden Globe in the Best Supporting Actress category in 1958), building an adaptation of *Pride and Prejudice* around the character of Mrs. Bennet is just nuts. The Jane Austen contingent—I know some of you are here tonight—can weigh in on this question during the Q&A, but the very idea of it melts my mind. Equally important: Polly Bergen could barely sing. While she was a very, very beautiful lady, her voice is so bad that it is painful to listen to her on the original cast album of *First Impressions* now.

Farley Granger (the actor who played Mr. Darcy) published a 2007 memoir, *Include Me Out: My Life from Goldwyn to Broadway*, in which he claims that Polly Bergen was an absolute disaster as Lizzie Bennet. On page 199, he even mocks her:

> ... on opening night, she quite clearly and loudly sang "A Poifect Evening"... the conductor was looking up in shock and there were a couple of titters from the audience.

According to Granger, as soon as Bergen read the reviews, she suddenly claimed to be too ill to continue. On page 200, he tells us that once the

134

stand-in took over as Lizzie, everything went much better ("…everything clicked, and the audience response was terrific…"), but it was already too late. ("We closed at the end of two and a half months.")

Hermione Gingold also wrote a memoir called *How to Grow Old Disgracefully*. She published it in 1989, but sorry to report, it has nothing juicy in it about *First Impressions*. As far as I know, Polly Bergen has yet to write a memoir of her own, so we may never know her take on any of this.

However, even though *First Impressions* has been largely forgotten, it casts a shadow over the history of Broadway. To me, it is very important to remember that it came out during the run of *My Fair Lady* (which ran from March 1956 to September 1962). I think the producers were after the same kind of thing, namely, a high-toned adaptation of a British classic. My guess is that the success of *My Fair Lady* made investors eager to find something like it, and that helps to explain the origin of this particular piece of work.

So *First Impressions* was chasing *My Fair Lady*, but equally important, look what was chasing *First Impressions*.

Gypsy premiered in May 1959, and it ran on Broadway until March 1961. So look at the dates here: *Gypsy* opened on May 21, 1959, and *First Impressions* closed on May 30, 1959. Coincidence? I doubt it.

Ask yourself this: however good Hermione Gingold might have been, if you had the money, would you have gone to see her in *First Impressions*, or Ethel Merman in *Gypsy*? Merman's reviews were extraordinary, and *Gypsy* is now considered one of the greatest musicals in Broadway history. Caught between the end of the *My Fair Lady* run and the beginning of the *Gypsy* run, poor *First Impressions* never had a chance.

Now for our purposes, here is the critical question: Did the *Fiddler on the Roof* team know about *First Impressions*?

Frankly, even though my gut tells me that we all know the answer must be yes, I cannot give you a definite answer. However, I ask you to remember who created *First Impressions*. All of them were well-established Broadway figures at that point in time. The book for *First Impressions* was written by Abe Burrows (best known today for *Guys and Dolls*), and the producer was Jule Styne (best known before *First Impressions* for the *Bells Are Ringing* and best known today for *Funny Girl*). The people on the *Fiddler on the Roof* team were also Broadway "players." Jerome Robbins was extremely well known, and Sheldon Harnick and Jerry Bock had already won multiple awards for *Fiorello!*

Here is my bottom line: With less than five years separating the last night of *First Impressions* from the first night of *Fiddler on the Roof*, it is highly unlikely that the *Fiddler on the Roof* team had **no knowledge whatsoever** of *First Impressions*. Since all of these people were consummate professionals, we must leave it at that for now.

Parsha Pinchas

Mr. and Mrs. Bennet had five daughters. Do we know of anyone else who also had five daughters?

How many of you know your weekly Torah portions? I see it has been a long time for most of us, so let me do a brief refresher. At some point in the past, our ancestors divided the Torah (known in English as The Five Books of Moses) into sections to be read aloud, one each week. We refer to these sections as the weekly portion, or in Hebrew, by the plural "parshot." In this case, this particular parsha is named after a man named Pinchas who was a descendant of Aaron. (In English, his name is Phineas.)

At the end of the Book of Numbers (which is the fourth of The Five Books of Moses), the children of Israel have finally reached the end of their 40 years of wandering. Encamped at the edge of the Promised Land, they stop to have an elaborate discussion about who should get what once they take possession of Israel according to God's promise. This comes at the end of the Book of Numbers, right before the start of the Book of Deuteronomy.

We learn the details in Parsha Pinchas. The patriarch Jacob had 12 sons, and his favorite son—Joseph—had two sons of his own (Ephraim and Manasseh). Moses tells the people that the land of Israel is to be apportioned to the male descendants of these sons. Suddenly new voices emerge from the descendants of Manasseh in the line of Joseph.

"Now Zelophehad, son of Hepher, had no sons, only daughters. . . Give us a holding among our father's kinsmen." And Moses not only listens to these women, he takes their case directly to God!

And here is a beautiful sculpture of Zelophehad's daughters—Mahlah, No'ah, Hoglah, Milcah, and Tirzah—done by an artist named Judith Klausner.

© Judith Klausner (2010)

Mahlah, No'ah, Hoglah, Milcah, and Tirzah—the daughters of Zelophehad—go to the Tent of Meeting, and they say to Moses and the Elders: "Let not our father's name be lost to his clan just because he had no son."

Moses brought their case before the Lord; and the Lord said
to Moses, "**The plea of Zelophehad's daughters is just**. You
should give them a hereditary holding among their father's
kinsmen, transfer their father's share to them. Further speak to
the Israelite people as follows, 'If a man dies without leaving a
son, you shall transfer his property to his daughter.' This shall
be the law of procedure for the Israelites in accordance with the
Lord's command to Moses.   (Num. 27: 5–11)

Picture me falling off my chair the first time I read this. Then, after I pick
myself up, I start searching Google… And sure enough, I discover a couple of
obscure posts by Jane Austen aficionados pointing out the parallels between
the plot of *Pride and Prejudice* and the story of Zelophehad's Daughters.

Once again, for our purposes, here is the important question: Did Jane
Austen know the story of Zelophehad's Daughters?

Jane Austen's father was a minister, so she was very well educated for a
woman of her time, and she certainly knew her Bible. Let us remember where
the story of Zelophehad's Daughters is to be found. It is not buried someplace obscure, where many people might miss it. The story of Zelophehad's
Daughters is at the end of the Book of Numbers, right before the opening
lines of the Book of Deuteronomy. A well-educated person who knew what
Jane Austen would have called the "Old Testament" would surely have known
about this. And if Jane Austen knew the story of Zelophehad's Daughters,
then surely Sholem Aleichem did too. Right? Of course, right.

Perhaps you are thinking: "Oh, come on, Jan. You can connect anything with anything. What about King Lear? Didn't he have daughters
too?" Yes, he did. But the trajectory of *King Lear* is very different. Perhaps
some of you heard the presentation I did last year on Hodel? In that presentation, I actually made the radical assertion that Hodel—not Tevye—is the
main character in *Fiddler on the Roof*. I have my reasons, but tonight you
will just have to take my word for it.

Chawton

So where is Chawton? Chawton is southwest of London. This is the place
Jane Austen once lived, the place where she wrote the majority of her wonderful novels. All of her papers are now housed there in the Chawton House

Library (in the large mansion that once belonged to her brother). Has anyone been there? Lucky you.

✪ ✪ ✪ ✪ ✪

We have a singer here tonight. For the Jane Austen fans among you, let me locate the song she will sing. Lizzie is at Netherfield (Mr. Bingley's estate). Jane is ill and Lizzie has come to Netherfield to help care for her. Caroline (Mr. Bingley's evil sister) insists that Lizzie play the piano. She thinks Lizzie will embarrass herself, but quite the contrary. Lizzie plays and sings beautifully, and Mr. Darcy—who had previously mocked her—is smitten. So this is a really critical moment, and before we consign *First Impressions* to the dust heap of theatrical history, let us listen to Lizzie's big number.

> The road of love
> The road of love
> Is often a troublesome journey
> As winding, wand'ring as the road
> From Uxbridge to Tunbridge to Selsey by the sea.
>
> But love will find out the way
> Love will find out the way
> Though winding and wand'ring the road may be
> Love will find out the way.
>
> To reach the heart
> To reach the heart
> Is often a worrisome journey
> As twisting, turning as the road
> From Uxbridge to Tunbridge to Selsey by the sea.
>
> But love will find out the way
> Love will find out the way
> Though winding and wand'ring the road may be
> Love will find out the way.
>
> (Jerome & Burrows, Page 42)

Three Scenes from the Life of Jerome Robbins

As described by Amanda Vaill in her 2006 biography
Somewhere: The Life of Jerome Robbins.

SECTION 7

Jerome Robbins:
From Rozhanka to Broadway

This lecture was originally presented to the Chicago YIVO Society (in collaboration with ORT Urban Women) at the Harold Washington Library Center in Chicago, Illinois, on August 13, 2013. It was also presented at Evanston Public Library in Evanston, Illinois, on August 15, 2013.

Welcome to tonight's lecture, "Jerome Robbins: From Rozhanka to Broadway." It is so great to be here in Chicago again, and to see so many familiar and much-loved faces in the audience. New York is great—of course New York is great—but I have missed you all so much! Like Sholem Aleichem, I have become a Wandering Jew.

The good news is that my move to Brooklyn has enabled me to spend "quality time" engrossed in the Jerome Robbins Papers at the New York Public Library for the Performing Arts at Lincoln Center, so that should make tonight's lecture a real win-win for all of us.

As many of you already know, this is my fifth annual lecture on *Fiddler on the Roof* for the Chicago YIVO Society's Summer Festival of Yiddish Culture, so it would help me to know which other lectures you have heard. Here is a list. As I read the titles, please raise your hand if you heard this lecture:

• 2009 **Stempenyu: From Berdichev to Broadway** (in which I discover Stempenyu—the Klezmer musician—and explain why I see him as the subject of Marc Chagall's famous painting *Green Violinist*);

• 2010 **Yente: From Boiberik to Broadway** (in which I discuss Yente-the-Matchmaker and how the Ashkenazi name "Yente" became the Yinglish noun "yenta"). This is the lecture I have done most frequently, not just for ORT and YIVO, but also for several Metro Chicago congregations and Hadassah groups.

- 2011 **Hodel: From Sofievka to Siberia** (in which I make the seemingly outrageous claim that the main character in *Fiddler on the Roof* is Hodel—Tevye's second daughter—the daughter who marries Perchik-the-Revolutionary);

- 2012 **Tevye's Daughters: From Chawton to Broadway** (in which I explain why five is the **right** number of daughters for *Fiddler on the Roof*, even though Sholem Aleichem originally gave Tevye seven daughters in *Tevye the Dairyman*).

Now, how many of you are coming to one of my lectures for the very first time? No worries. I promise you all that no prior knowledge of my work on *Fiddler on the Roof* is required; most of the material I will present tonight will be new and unique to this lecture.

Now let us begin.

This is from the cover of the Original Broadway Cast Recording of *Fiddler on the Roof* from 1964. Who is "The Fiddler" and how did he get on **this** roof?

This is the cover of the 40th anniversary commemorative DVD of Norman Jewison's 1971 film version of *Fiddler on the Roof*. How did "The Fiddler" get on **this** roof?

This is the cover of the most recent paperback edition of Sholem Aleichem's *Tevye the Dairyman*, translated by Aliza Shevrin and published in 2010. How did "The Fiddler" get on **this** roof?

This is the cover of Joseph Dorman's 2011 documentary *Sholem Aleichem: Laughing in the Darkness*, released on DVD in 2013. How did "The Fiddler" get on **this** roof?

Clearly, it is very hard to talk about Sholem Aleichem in the 21st century without mentioning *Fiddler on the Roof*, even though—as many of you know—Sholem Aleichem's last Tevye story was published in 1916 (almost 50 years before *Fiddler on the Roof* made its Broadway debut).

Sholem Aleichem's eight Tevye stories were published between 1895 and 1916. Today they are typically published as one "novel" called *Tevye the*

Dairyman, even though the eight separate stories were published over a span of 20-plus years. The final story, "Lekh-Lekho," was published in 1916, which was the same year that Solomon Rabinowitz—the man whose pen name was Sholem Aleichem—died. He left behind a huge number of essays, novels, and stories, so the eight stories we now call the Tevye stories were a mere drop in this overflowing bucket.

Before 1964, individual stories appeared in various collections, but the Tevye stories were not published as a set of eight (at least not in English) until after 1964. But now we routinely talk about the eight Tevye stories as one "novel," and the people in the marketing department always find a way to invoke *Fiddler on the Roof.* That's how significant "The Fiddler" imagery is in 2013.

The first time I asked myself this question—How did "The Fiddler" get on the roof?—was way back on May 20, 2000. I was on vacation; I was just a tourist toddling around France. I went to the Marc Chagall Biblical Message Museum in Nice and suddenly my life turned inside out. Growing up in Northern New Jersey in the orbit of Manhattan tastemakers, I had been convinced that Marc Chagall's work was mere kitsch. But after spending a few hours at the Marc Chagall Biblical Message Museum in Nice, I knew that I was wrong. Clearly there was more to Marc Chagall's work than I had ever realized. More than a decade later, after 13 years of devoted effort, I finally believe that I know the answer to this question—How did "The Fiddler" get on the roof?—and I also know that there is one person who, more than any other, deserves credit for the ubiquity of *Fiddler on the Roof*'s now iconic imagery.

When I ask you to guess who, I expect to hear you call out Sholem Aleichem, Zero Mostel, or Chaim Topol. Some of you who are *Fiddler on the Roof* aficionados might even name Sheldon Harnick, the man who wrote the lyrics to all the songs in *Fiddler on the Roof* and is now "the last man standing" (so to speak). Not only is Harnick the only member of the original creative team who is still alive, he is also a master raconteur. Harnick hails from Chicago, so every time he comes here (for example, when Timeline Theater did their fabulous production of *Fiorello!* a couple of years ago), he does terrific interviews with local media personalities. But I think even Sheldon Harnick would agree that the answer to **my** question—How did "The Fiddler" get on the roof?—is this: When all is said and done, it was Jerome Robbins who put "The Fiddler" on the roof.

The man we now know as "Jerome Robbins" was born in the Jewish Maternity Hospital on the Lower East Side of Manhattan on October 11, 1918. Both of his parents were immigrants from Eastern Europe. His father—Hershel Rabinowitz—arrived in the USA in 1905 at the age of 18 and promptly renamed himself Harry. On the other hand, his mother—Lena Rips—had arrived in the USA as an infant, so she was thoroughly acculturated. She even attended college for two years before she married Harry in 1911.

Little Gershon Rabinowitz—that was his name, Gershon Rabinowitz—grew up in Weehawken, New Jersey, right across the Hudson River from Manhattan; in fact, he lived due west of the spot where Jerome Robbins Place can now be found at Lincoln Center.

Gershon Rabinowitz (a Rabinowitz, yes, but no relation to the family of Solomon Rabinowitz aka Sholem Aleichem) was artistically precocious, playing piano recitals in public at a very early age and gravitating to dance as an adolescent. The son's talent and temperament made the father extremely anxious, and history was to prove Harry Rabinowitz prescient.

By the late '30s, Gershon Rabinowitz—already known on Broadway as a chorus line gypsy named "Jerry Robbins"—was also winning recognition as a politically progressive choreographer of ballets about labor unions and other left-wing causes. By the early '40s, he was a soloist with the American Ballet Theatre.

Skip ahead to 1962 when Sheldon Harnick, Jerry Bock, and Joseph Stein began trying to interest people such as producer Harold Prince in a new script called *To Life* (which Amanda Vaill in her biography of Robbins calls a very "upbeat" title). Harnick and Bock had won both a Tony Award and a Pulitzer Prize for *Fiorello!* And Joseph Stein had been nominated for a Tony Award for *Take Me Along*. So these men were no slouches. On the contrary, they were well-known and accomplished: lyricist, composer, and librettist. But the doors all slammed shut anyway. No one expressed much interest in *To Life*.

By this time, Jerry Robbins—who now used the more dignified first name Jerome—had also amassed numerous awards and honors, including a Tony in the Choreography category for *West Side Story* onstage in 1958 and an Oscar in the Best Director category for *West Side Story* onscreen in 1962. By 1963, the prestigious list of Broadway shows with which Jerome Robbins had already been associated by this point just melts the mind.

Here is a sample of shows from the Internet Broadway Database (IBDB. com) in alphabetical order: *A Funny Thing Happened on the Way to the Forum, A Tree Grows in Brooklyn, Bells are Ringing, Call Me Madam, Funny Girl, Gypsy, Mother Courage and Her Children, On the Town, Peter Pan, Silk Stockings, The King and I, The Pajama Game*, and *Wonderful Town*. Robbins's efforts were essential to the success of each of these beloved shows. He played a variety of roles behind the scenes, most typically as choreographer, director, and/or "show doctor." ("Show doctors" may not get public credit, but everyone in the cast feels their presence nonetheless.)

Like most members of the Baby Boom generation, I grew up loving Mary Martin as Peter Pan on television. I never associated *Peter Pan* with Jerome Robbins, but in fact, that television production was based on a Broadway musical—with Mary Martin as Peter—choreographed by Jerome Robbins. "I'm flying!!!" All of this happened before Jerome Robbins met with Harnick, Stein, and Bock about what was to become *Fiddler on the Roof.*

In the summer of 1963, after Robbins had finished work as the "show doctor" on *Funny Girl*—for which everyone except a grateful Barbra Streisand gave directorial credit to Garson Kanin—Harnick, Stein and Bock arranged a meeting with Robbins. A few days later on August 29, 1963, Robbins sent a telegram to Ruth Mitchell—who had been his stage manager for five prior productions—inviting her to join him on *Fiddler on the Roof.* The telegram from Robbins to Mitchell—now preserved for posterity in the Jerome Robbins Papers at the New York Public Library for the Performing Arts at Lincoln Center—says this:

> I am going to do a musical of Sholem Aleichem
> stories with Harnick and Bock   Stop   I am in love with it
> Stop   It is our people [*sic*]

But before making a formal commitment, Robbins demanded an extraordinary level of recognition, not just in the credits—where his name was not only to be the **same size** as the authors' name, but also **set off in a box** with the words "Entire Production Directed and Choreographed by Jerome Robbins"—but also financially. Robbins negotiated a 20 percent royalty for himself, to be taken from the author portion of the earnings. That is, in fact, the money that has endowed the Jerome Robbins Dance Collection at the New York Public Library (which Robbins dedicated to his mother Lena).

Was it worth it? Was it worth it?!? Many years later, when Amanda Vaill interviewed Joseph Stein for her book *Somewhere: The Life of Jerome Robbins*, Stein (who many of you know wrote the text—aka "the book" aka the libretto—for *Fiddler on the Roof*) said: "Jerry always drove a very hard bargain, but he deserved his credit. If we hadn't had him, it would have been a different show."

Indeed! Hiring Boris Aronson to create a visual tableau based on Marc Chagall's imagery? This idea came directly from Jerome Robbins. So without Robbins, there would literally be no fiddler and there would be no roof. But note that Robbins only brought Aronson onto the team after Chagall sent Robbins a telegram on September 7, 1963, saying he was unable to do the set design himself. Three words: **Regrette trop occupé.** This is French for "Sorry, I'm too busy." Now, look at the dates, and it is immediately clear that Chagall was one of the first people Robbins reached out to once he agreed to direct this new musical that was now carrying the working title *Tevye*.

Way back in 2003, when I wrote an article for the *Forward* on Chagall, Aronson, and "The Fiddler," I did not know this. And, in fact, when I recently reread Amanda Vaill's biography of Robbins with this reference to Chagall, I was dumbstruck. My first instinct was to chastise myself: Why didn't I know this before? But then I cut myself some slack. Duh! I began publishing pieces on *Fiddler on the Roof* in 2002 and 2003, before any of this information was easily accessible. For example, Vaill's book *Somewhere* was published in 2006.

Because there are so many misstatements in the literature about Chagall's supposed abhorrence of *Fiddler on the Roof*, not to mention open questions about how the famous final title—*Fiddler on the Roof*—got attached to a musical previously known first as *To Life* and then *Tevye*, these three words—**regrette trop occupé**—are really important to know.

I have permission from the Jerome Robbins Foundation to show you two documents tonight. This first document has no date, but it is attached to some other documents in a set of file folders dated 1963. So let's use these folders as a timestamp.

Picture me at the New York Public Library for the Performing Arts at Lincoln Center... a block away from Jerome Robbins Place. After a decade of work on *Fiddler on the Roof*, I am touching this document for the very first time. Robbins is thinking aloud, and I am here to listen:

> In searching for a comparative vision, the paintings and trans-figurations of Chagall come closest. In his fantasy atmosphere, particulars; in his free & nonrealistic choice of colors & form; in his child's fantasy evocations & artist's sophistication & elegance, his evocations of the time, life & richness of shtetl life which becomes so riveting, exciting, & stimulating. He [now some cross-outs here] has translated & elevated the material above the limited appeal of those who recognize its sources, & revealed and made endeared it to all people everywhere. This is also our job. (Robbins, LAPLC)

So right from the very beginning—in September 1963—as soon as he accepted the assignment, Jerome Robbins was already bringing the visual conception of Marc Chagall into his production, and taking as his own mission the need to do the very same: "**elevate**" appeal "**above those who recognize its sources**," reveal and endear it "**to all people everywhere. This is also our job**."

Can you imagine how I felt when I found this piece of paper? Wow!

Looking back, it seems incredible to me that so much happened between August 29, 1963 (the day Robbins sent Ruth Mitchell the telegram that I am paraphrasing here as "I'm in") and September 22, 1964 (the night of *Fiddler on the Roof*'s Broadway premiere). When the folks at the Fisher Theater in Detroit saw the very first out-of-town performance of *Fiddler on the Roof* on July 27, 1964, they got a song—a duet in Act Two—with Motel and Tzeitel singing "Dear Sweet Sewing Machine." I have the lyrics for it, and folks, its absence is no great loss. But the audience at the Fisher Theater in Detroit did not get "Do You Love Me?"—a song that Harnick and Bock wrote later at Robbins's request—now considered one of the high points of the show.

So maybe we should not be too hard on that poor guy I have so maligned over the years, the man known only known by his initials. He—TEW—was the critic from *Variety* who saw the first Detroit performance and concluded, and this is a quote: "There are no memorable songs in this musical." Austin Pendleton—Broadway's first Motel-the-Tailor—told Amanda Vaill that the mood in Detroit was grim:

> The cast, dispirited by their reception, became enervated by Jerry's
> endless blocking changes and merciless prodding, and rumors
> began to swirl. "It was all over town [by which Pendelton meant
> New York] that the show was a disaster."　　　　(Vaill, Page 369)

And Pendleton knew this because his agent was calling him and urging him to escape. He was instructed to get on the next plane leaving Detroit and do something else; the buzz was this musical *Fiddler on the Roof* was never going to make it on Broadway.

But as we all know, when *Fiddler on the Roof* finally did open in New York two months later—after continuing the run in Detroit and then going on to tryouts in Washington, DC—it quickly became one of the most successful shows in Broadway history. In 1972, *Fiddler on the Roof* broke the prior record and became the longest running show on Broadway. Finally *Chorus Line* overtook it, but for more than ten years *Fiddler on the Roof* was the longest running show in the history of Broadway.

Now Walter Mirisch (the executive producer of the screen adaptation of *West Side Story*, which won ten Oscars—including Best Picture—in 1962) was in New York a few weeks after that opening night on Broadway. So Joseph Stein arranged tickets for him, and after seeing it, Mirisch immediately urged United Artists to buy the screen rights. They hesitated, but several years later—once everyone was convinced that *Fiddler on the Roof* had legs—United Artists finally agreed.

By that point, Walter Mirisch had established a working relationship with Norman Jewison on three hits: *The Russians Are Coming, The Russians Are Coming* (in 1966); *In the Heat of the Night* (in 1967); and *The Thomas Crown Affair* (in 1968). So should we be surprised that once again Walter Mirisch turned to Norman Jewison? No. But most Broadway aficionados will not tell you this, preferring instead to embellish apocryphal tales and juicy gossip: "The suits at United Artists thought from his name that Jewison was

Jewish…" So what? By that time Walter Mirisch and Norman Jewison had a well-established working relationship, and Walter Mirisch had every confidence that Norman Jewison knew how to manage a budget (something that was never one of Jerome Robbins's considerable strengths).

Many people were surprised when they heard that Norman Jewison was set to direct the screen adaptation of *Fiddler on the Roof.* Hadn't Jerome Robbins won a Best Director Oscar for his work on *West Side Story?* But people-in-the-know knew the truth: Mirisch had actually fired Robbins, and banished him from the set of *West Side Story.* Robbins—who was fussy and persnickety—had gone way over budget, so **no way** would Walter Mirisch ask Jerome Robbins to direct a screen version of *Fiddler on the Roof.*

Did Walter Mirisch make the right decision when he eliminated Jerome Robbins from the *Fiddler on the Roof* team and hired Norman Jewison to direct? Who will ever know?!? Me, I never deal in counterfactuals. When Richard Altman, who was Jerome Robbins's assistant on the original Broadway production, was doing research for his book *The Making of a Musical: Fiddler on the Roof,* Walter Mirisch told him:

> I am aware of the immense contribution Jerry Robbins made to *Fiddler* on the stage, but would he have any more to contribute to it as a film? (Altman & Kaufman, Page 182)

Altman lets this remark speak for itself, maybe because by this time Altman (like many members of the original creative team, including Bock, Harnick, and Stein) was working for Mirisch. Altman was in a rush to get *The Making of a Musical* out before the movie premiered. I have been through all of the Mervyn Kaufman Papers—Kaufman was co-author of *The Making of a Musical*—at the New York Public Library for the Performing Arts at Lincoln Center, so I know this for a fact. Their book was part of the publicity campaign for the film, so some of the statements that Altman makes about the stage production should be taken in context and with a grain of salt.

In his 2001 biography *Dance with Demons: The Life of Jerome Robbins,* Greg Lawrence writes:

> Actor Barry Primus, who was a good friend and frequent collaborator of Robbins, recalled that Robbins engaged in some discussions about directing *Fiddler* onscreen, but his ideas fell on deaf ears, if they were entertained at all.

Primus said [now this is Lawrence quoting Primus]: "*Fiddler* fell apart because Jerry wanted to start the script from zero. He wanted to start with nothing. He had this idea which was to start with an album of pictures and then go backwards."

(Lawrence, Page 350)

In other words, Robbins was already working on a radically different concept of how to present *Fiddler on the Roof* onscreen, and again—you can make up your own mind about this—I think a lot of people now watching *West Side Story* as a film would agree that the pieces of *West Side Story* that hold up the best onscreen are the dances that Jerome Robbins directed. On the other hand—50 years later—some pieces of *West Side Story* do not hold up quite so well onscreen. Many of the straight dramatic scenes directed by Robert Wise feel dated now. So who can say what Robbins might have done if he had had the chance to adapt *Fiddler on the Roof* for the big screen?

I have no intention of denigrating the work of Norman Jewison tonight. That said, I do want to convince you that even though the two versions obviously share many common elements, *Fiddler on the Roof* onstage and *Fiddler on the Roof* onscreen differ in critically important ways. And yet, I cannot end this section of my talk without pointing out that in 1962, *West Side Story* received 11 Oscar nominations and won 10 Oscars, including Best Picture and Best Director (an award which was **shared**—for the first time in Oscar history—by Robbins and Wise). Which Oscar did *West Side Story* lose? It lost Best Adapted Screenplay, which went to *Judgment at Nuremberg*.

Ten years later, in 1972, *Fiddler on the Roof* received eight Oscar nominations, but it only won three Oscars. Furthermore, all three were in relatively minor categories: Best Cinematography, Best Sound, and Best Music Scoring Adaptation. For the record, the big winner in 1972 was *The French Connection*. But lest you conclude from this fact that the Era of Big Musicals was over, I remind you that the big winner the very next year was *Cabaret*. *Cabaret* went head-to-head with *The Godfather* and emerged with eight Oscars in 1973, including Best Director. Yes! Bob Fosse beat Francis Ford Coppola in 1973!

Digression: *The Invention of Tradition*

In 1983, Jewish historian Eric Hobsbawm—the author of many books with heavy titles such as *Nations and Nationalism Since 1780*—released an influential collection of essays called *The Invention of Tradition*. Here is the description of this book on Amazon:

> Many of the traditions which we think of as very ancient in their origins were not in fact sanctioned by long use over the centuries but were invented comparatively recently.

So what is an example of an invented tradition? Scottish tartans.

Look closely at the cover of his book *The Invention of Tradition*. The men who went into battle with William Wallace (the real guy Mel Gibson played in *Braveheart*), none of these guys were actually wearing kilts and tartans in the 13th century. The kilts and tartans are a historical anachronism. Scottish tartans—as we know them today—were not the handiwork of ancient Celtic clans.

Scottish tartans became popular during the reign of Queen Victoria, around the same time that the Royal Family started going back and forth to the Scottish Highlands. Routinely heading up to Balmoral Castle for vacation was not practical before there was a railroad to take the Royal Family from London to Scotland. Before the railroad, it was very difficult to travel so far north over land. So the whole business of Scottish tartans and the related items that Hobsbawm traces in his book—the kilts and the tartans and paraphernalia like shoulder clips with a thistle motif—people started buying all this kitsch around 150 years ago, after the purchase of Balmoral Castle in 1852.

In his conclusion, Hobsbawm ties together the invention of national "traditions" and the rise of nation-states as national movements that deliberately included some parts of the population and explicitly excluded others. In the late 19th century, tartans were used by the English hierarchy to make people in Scotland feel better about being British. The English needed manpower to run an empire they called the "British Empire." So there could be no further talk about being English versus Scottish versus Welsh. The new line was: "We are all British!" And one of the ways that the Queen's men accomplished this feat was through the creation of traditions. Let us honor Scottish "tradition" by having a regiment in the British Army that marches in kilts while they play their bagpipes. Stanley Berkeley's famous painting *Gordons and Greys to the Front* (which depicts a scene from the Battle of Waterloo in 1815) was actually created in 1898.

From the Jewish perspective, I think that Theodor Herzl—were he here today—would make a similar argument about the Dreyfus Trial, that the Dreyfus Trial invoked anti-Semitic tropes to make people in France feel better about being "French." They did this by identifying an "other" who was not French, namely all the Jews who were living in France and were citizens of France, but were not **really French** like the "real French" were French.

Did any of you hear the segment on NPR the other day about Vercingetorix? There is a big national movement in France now to resurrect a general from Gaul named Vercingetorix who fought against Julius ("All Gaul is divided into three parts") Caesar. Vercingetorix is now celebrated by some as the first "French" hero because he went up against Julius Caesar for the honor of "France" in 52 BCE. Celebrating a French hero named Vercingetorix in the 21st century is definitely an invented "tradition."

Today, I am asking you to think anew about the question of "tradition." When "tradition" is invoked in the Musical-Prologue to *Fiddler on the Roof*, we need to remember all those kilts in *Braveheart* and retain a bit of skepticism.

In *Fiddler on the Roof*, we learn about Jewish tradition in the Musical-Prologue "Tradition," which is known as "Tradition!"

> **The Daughters**: And who does Mama teach to mend and tend and fix, preparing me to marry whoever Papa picks?
> **All**: The daughters! The daughters!
> **Tevye**: I have five daughters!!!
> **All**: Tradition! The daughters! The daughters! Tradition!

Ever since *Fiddler on the Roof* became a big hit, we have been led to believe that **this** was actual Jewish tradition in the shtetl: Mama raised the daughters, and then they—the daughters—all married "whoever Papa picked."

Walter Mirisch hires Norman Jewison (who, as I have already told you, is not Jewish) to direct the film adaptation of *Fiddler on the Roof*. Norman Jewison is from Canada, so not only is he not Jewish, he is not American either. When he made *Fiddler on the Roof*, Norman Jewison was a peacenik who was actively protesting the Vietnam War. Jewison actually left the USA at one point due to his disgust with American activities in Vietnam. Norman

Jewison was Canadian, so he did not want to be associated with the Vietnam War in any way.

Me? I think some of the decisions Jewison made in the process of adapting *Fiddler on the Roof* from stage to screen are directly related to his feelings about Vietnam. I won't be talking about this specific subject anymore tonight, but you can certainly ask me to say more during the Q&A.

Meanwhile, back to *Fiddler on the Roof*...

Here is a piece of Conventional Wisdom about *Fiddler on the Roof*, as it appears in the foreword to an Oxford University Press publication from 2011 called *To Broadway, To Life! The Musical Theater of Bock and Harnick*:

> ...over the next four decades the new Broadway sensation would be followed by an **elaborately faithful (and musically nearly complete)** film in 1971, three Broadway revivals (1976, 1990, and 2004), and... (Lambert, Page viii)

Please focus on this word "nearly." Nearly means almost, but not quite. So what has changed? Let us start with the matchmaker. In 1964, Yente-the-Matchmaker was played by Bea Arthur. Close your eyes for just a second and pull up a mental image of Bea Arthur. She was a huge woman with a loud booming voice. In 1964, she was 42 years old, and as I said back in my lecture on Yente, she was "tall, even compared to the men!"

Bea Arthur's Yente also had some significant pieces of dialogue—although not as much as she wanted of course—and she even had her own song called "The Rumor." And as you can tell from these lines from the Musical-Prologue "Tradition," she interacted with the men in Anatevka as well as the women:

> **Tevye:** In the circle of our little village, we've always had our many special types, for instance, Yente-the-Matchmaker.
> **Yente:** Avram, I have a perfect match for your son, a wonderful girl.
> **Avram:** Who is it?
> **Yente:** Ruchel, the shoemaker's daughter.
> **Avram:** Ruchel? She can hardly see. She's almost blind.
> **Yente:** Tell the truth, Avram, is your son so much to look at? The way she sees and the way he looks, it's a perfect match! (Stein, Page 5)

"The way she sees and the way he looks, it's a perfect match." This is Yente doing a deal, right? Of course, right. And who is she talking to? She is talking to Avram, right? Of course, right. So this is how Jerome Robbins chose to introduce the character of Yente-the-Matchmaker in 1964: Yente-the-Matchmaker is introduced onstage in the middle of doing a deal with a man named Avram.

Now those of us who have seen *Fiddler on the Roof* on the stage and/or those of us who have the original cast album on vinyl—which many people of my generation still do—we know these words so well that we just assume they are in the movie. Surprise! I know you will be skeptical when I say this, so go home and check it out for yourself. If you hear these words ("Avram, I have a perfect match for your son...") either on the DVD or on the soundtrack, do let me know right away.

It is not as if Chaim Topol himself didn't know these words; they are clearly there on the London cast album from 1967. Topol as Tevye says: "And in the circle of our little village, we've always had our special types, for instance, Yente-the-Matchmaker!" And then Yente—played in the original London production by Cynthia Grenville—says: "Avram, I have a perfect match for your son."

While we're on the subject, Jewison made two additional changes to the Musical-Prologue "Tradition." Tevye no longer brays "I have five daughters!" when the daughters are first introduced. And instead of saying "And who does Mama teach to mend and tend and fix, preparing **me** to marry whoever Papa picks?"—as they do on the 1964 original cast album—the daughters now say "And who does Mama teach to mend and tend and fix, preparing **her** to marry whoever Papa picks?" I grant you this is a subtle point, but I think this switch from first person to third person is highly indicative. For now, just add these to the list of changes Norman Jewison made, justifying my claim that "nearly means almost, but not quite."

Norman Jewison cast Molly Picon as Yente-the-Matchmaker onscreen in 1971. Molly Picon is tiny, even compared to the women. Furthermore, she has minimal dialogue and her conversations never include men. In her onscreen negotiations, Yente-the-Matchmaker talks only to women; Yente no longer talks directly (that is, face-to-face) with any of the men of Anatevka. And her song "The Rumor" is gone.

So is this the same character? If you halve her size, and you double her age, and you take away most of her dialogue, and you eliminate her one musical number (in a musical!), is she still **the same**? Answer: No. Although she is still there on the screen, Yente-the-Matchmaker is definitely diminished.

Unfortunately, I cannot go through a complete discussion of this one point with you tonight. Those of you who have heard my lecture "Yente/Yenta: How a Name Became a Noun" know that I could actually talk about this specific subject for hours, and obviously I cannot do that tonight. But for me, these are no longer subtle points; cumulatively, these are huge differences.

Onstage, Yente-the-Matchmaker is a businesswoman whose ability to make a living depends on a cool head and a sharp tongue. When Tzeitel impersonates Yente in the number "Matchmaker," she clearly wants her naïve younger sisters to appreciate just how dangerous Yente really is. ("He's handsome, he's young! Alright he's sixty-two… He's handsome, he's tall—that is from side-to-side…")

Yente is filled with rage at Tzeitel's wedding.

> **Golde**: I had a sign. My own grandmother came to me from the grave.
> **Yente**: What sign? What grandmother? My grandfather came to me from the grave and told me her grandmother was a big liar.

(The stage directions specify that Yente "**storms off**" with Lazar Wolf when the dancing begins.)

Onscreen, however, Yente is in the crowd holding up a candle, her eyes wet with tears. In "Yente/Yenta: How a Name Became a Noun," I go as far as to compare Robbins's Yente with Iago (the villain of Shakespeare's *Othello*). Onscreen, however, Jewison's Yente is just a sentimental old gossip.

The second song Norman Jewison eliminated was "Now I Have Everything," the first song in Act Two. So let's look at the lyrics:

> **Perchik**: I used to tell myself
> that I had everything,
> but that was only half true.

I had an aim in life and that was everything,
but now I even have you.
(Harnick & Bock, Pages 108-109)

Those of you who have never seen *Fiddler on the Roof* on the stage may
be unfamiliar with these lyrics because they are not in Norman Jewison's
film version of *Fiddler on the Roof.* So here is some background for those of
you hearing this song for the first time.

Perchik is a student who arrives from Kiev at the beginning of Act One.
Hodel is Tevye's second daughter. Hodel and Perchik fall in love. Unlike
Tzeitel and Motel, they do not ask for Tevye's "permission." When they decide to get married at the beginning of Act Two, they tell Tevye their plan,
and then they ask for his blessing.

The Perchik who arrived in Anatevka was filled with revolutionary
fervor. But once in Anatevka, he finds himself anew as a man in love. When
he says "besides having everything, I know what everything's for," Perchik
is, in fact, giving voice to a Freudian precept first reported by Erik Erikson
in his best-selling book *Childhood and Society* (published in 1950):

> Freud was once asked what he thought a normal person should be
> able to do well. The questioner probably expected a complicated
> answer. But Freud, in the curt way of his old days, is reported to
> have said: "Lieben und arbeiten" (to love and to work)...
> Thus we may ponder, but we cannot improve on "the professor's"
> formula.   (Erikson, Pages 264–265)

Indeed this statement is so succinct that it has become axiomatic, even
if there is no other evidence that Freud himself ever said it. But perhaps
Sigmund Freud was actually quoting Leo Tolstoy who (according to biographer Henri Troyat) wrote much the same in a letter to Valerya Arsenyev
when he was courting her way back in 1856:

> One can live magnificently in this world, if one knows how to
> work and how to love, to work for the person one loves and to
> love one's work.   (Troyat, Page 152)

According to these sages, then, a full human life requires both love and
work, and this is what Perchik means when he says: "Besides having every-

thing [namely his work as a revolutionary], I know what everything's for," because he has also found love.

To my amazement, I learned in the Jerome Robbins Papers at the New York Public Library for the Performing Arts that the song "Now I Have Everything" was originally written for Motel-the-Tailor. The songsheet sits in a box clearly labeled "Motel June 1964." Sheldon Harnick and Jerry Bock had already written two different songs for Perchik and Hodel, but neither one satisfied Robbins. At this point (in June 1964), they had yet to write "Wonder of Wonders, Miracle of Miracles," the much-loved song we all now associate with Motel-the-Tailor.

So what happened? Just like "Dear Sweet Sewing Machine" (a song Harnick and Bock wrote for Tzeitel and Motel that Robbins eventually deleted), these early Perchik/Hodel songs had very pedestrian lyrics. By all accounts, Robbins kept pushing and pushing until—to use Motel's words—he had "a perfect fit."

The version of "Now I Have Everything" that I played before was from the Original Broadway Cast Recording starring Bert Convy as Perchik and Julia Migenes as Hodel. Now let us listen to the same song from the 2004 Broadway revival...

This is the coda to "Now I Have Everything" sung by Robert Petkoff as Perchik. His Hodel was Laura Michelle Kelly.

> **Hodel**: And when will we be married, Perchik?
> **Perchik**: I will send for you as soon as I can. It will be a hard life...
> **Hodel**: But it will be less hard if we live it together.
> **Perchik**: Yes. Besides having everything, I know what everything's for.

What I want you to hear is how the notes go **up** when Petkoff sings the words "I know what everything's for..."

Now listen again to what is playing underneath his soaring voice as he sings *Besides having everything, I know what everything's for.* It is the "Matchmaker-Matchmaker" melody. Can you all hear it?

When Perchik and Hodel tell Tevye that they do not need his **permission**—but they do want his **blessing**—Tevye has the second of his three onstage soliloquies. He is furious. How can Hodel tell him she is going to marry Perchik with or without his permission? Everyone agreed at the beginning (in the Musical-Prologue "Tradition"), that daughters marry "whoever Papa picks."

Tevye's soliloquies (addressed to the audience) are really dialogues with God. Tevye is looking up—beyond the theater's balcony—when, suddenly, he says:

> Did Adam and Eve have a matchmaker? Yes, they did.
> And it seems these two have the same one.

Tevye gives his blessing to the marriage of Hodel and Perchik because he realizes that God has already given His permission. Hodel and Perchik are in love—soaring, ecstatic, romantic love—and now both Perchik **and** Hodel have "a love and a work." Hodel doesn't just plan to marry Perchik, she intends to join The Revolution. This is what Hodel means when she tells Tevye that she will help Perchik do "the greatest work a man can do." She will not wait at home; she will stand with him, side-by-side. Hodel makes a promise to Perchik: "[This hard life] will be less hard if we live it **together**."

And yet, Norman Jewison chose to eliminate these two songs—"The Rumor" and "Now I Have Everything"—from his adaptation. Worse yet, he replaced "Now I Have Everything" with a scene of Perchik in Kiev, which looks to my eyes like footage borrowed from *Doctor Zhivago*. I recently saw *Doctor Zhivago* (which was originally released in 1965), on a huge screen at the Brooklyn Academy of Music, and trust me on this, Jewison's Perchik would fit in just fine. I can see him in my mind's eye, marching alongside "Pasha Antipov" (Tom Courtenay) and the rest of the leftwing Russian intellectuals. One thing we know about Pasha, though: Pasha does **not** have a love and a work. How anyone can marry "Lara"—luminously played by Julie Christie—and not love her is beyond me, but there it is. "Uri Zhivago" (Omar Sharif) loves Lara, but her husband Pasha—soon to become known by his nom de guerre "General Strelnikov"—has no room in his heart for love. Pasha is all about the work.

✡ ✡ ✡ ✡ ✡

Now back to *Fiddler on the Roof*: I accept that Norman Jewison made these changes, and I frankly do not care why. I have no doubt he had his reasons. For me, the only important question is this: What difference does it make? Even if it is **not** "musically nearly complete," is Norman Jewison's version of *Fiddler on the Roof* onscreen still "**elaborately faithful**" to Jerome Robbins's version of *Fiddler on the Roof* onstage?

Answer: No. *Fiddler on the Roof* onscreen is simply **not the same** as *Fiddler on the Roof* onstage. The cumulative effect of Norman Jewison's many changes—some of them tiny but significant in context—is to diminish the female characters, minimize the element of romantic love, and reduce the margin for individual autonomy in *Fiddler on the Roof.* But why?

Connubial bliss is especially well-documented in the two core relationships that gave rise to this great Broadway musical called *Fiddler on the Roof.* Author Solomon Rabinowitz (aka Sholem Aleichem) and painter Marc Chagall are men who are known by readers everywhere to have had both "a love and a work." If "tradition" as represented in the opening stanza of the original prologue ["preparing **me** to marry whoever Papa picks"] were really binding, if that truly was the way it was back in the day, then Olga Loyeff would never have become Olga Rabinowitz, and Bella Rosenfeld would never have become Bella Chagall. Both of these strong-minded women were from wealthy families, and we can be very sure that neither of them married a man picked for her by her Papa.

In the case of Solomon Rabinowitz, we know from the biography *My Father, Sholom Aleichem*—which was written by their daughter Marie Waife-Goldberg—that Olga's father Elimelech Loyeff did everything in his power to separate the young lovers. But Olga defied her Papa and she eloped with Solomon anyway. No permission. No blessing.

But even more damning to the case that there was a "tradition" of matchmaking is the minimal role that matchmaking plays in the actual Tevye stories. Perhaps you think there was someone named Yente in one or more of Sholem Aleichem's Tevye stories, and that this Yente character was engaged by Lazar Wolf to facilitate a match with Tzeitel? Sorry, folks, you will not find her because she is not there.

As I have pointed out in prior lectures, there is no matchmaker in "Today's Children" (which is the third story in the Tevye series, meaning the third chapter when the eight stories are read as one novel). In "Today's Children," Lazar Wolf-the-Butcher asks Tevye's wife Golde to have Tevye come meet with him so the two men can make an arrangement man-to-man. But when Tzeitel protests, Tevye reassures her:

> "If you say no, it's no. No one will force you, God forbid. We only meant it for the best, for your own good," I said. "But if that's not what your heart tells you, what can we do? Most likely," I said, "it wasn't meant to be." (Shevrin, Page 45)

In "Today's Children," just like in *Fiddler on the Roof*, Tzeitel wants to marry Motel-the-Tailor because she loves him. And just like in *Fiddler on the Roof*, Tevye learns the details, not from Tzeitel but from Motel: "I love your daughter and your daughter loves me, and it's been more than a year since we gave each other our pledge to marry."

In both cases, once Motel smooths his feathers a bit, Tevye agrees to the match. As Tevye tells Sholem Aleichem: "The very next day we held the engagement party and soon afterwards the wedding" (Shevrin, Page 52).

Furthermore, there is no Yente character anywhere in **any** of the Tevye stories. (You can be sure that this fact is discussed at length in my lecture "Yente/Yenta: How a Name Became a Noun.")

In the next story, the story called "Hodel" (which is story number four in the Tevye series, meaning the fourth chapter when the eight stories are read as one novel), a matchmaker named Ephraim—a man, not a woman—approaches Tevye with a prospective mate for Hodel, but he is too late. Hodel has already fallen in love with Perchik.

Three stories later in "Tevye Leaves for the Land of Israel" (which is story number seven in the Tevye series, meaning the penultimate chapter when the eight stories are read as one novel), Golde has died, so Ephraim comes to Tevye looking to fix him up with a new wife. Tevye, however, is worried about Bielke—his youngest daughter—because she has devoted herself to caring for him, and he knows this is no life for her. So he asks Ephraim to make a match for Bielke.

But as those of you who have read the original stories already know, this marriage is a disaster. Bielke never has a chance to experience the joy of romantic love—like her three older sisters—but she doesn't get financial security either. Podhotsur (the man Bielke marries) turns out to be a war profiteer.

160

Bielke is stuck forever with a cheater who quickly goes bankrupt. He is the Bernie Madoff of his day, making Bielke the "Blue Jasmine" of her day. And that is what comes of matchmaking in Sholem Aleichem's Tevye stories!

I also encourage you to see the Russian film *Jewish Luck* from 1925. It is a Yiddish version of Sholem Aleichem's *Menakhem Mendl* stories starring Solomon Mikhoels—a famous Russian-Jewish actor in his day—as a "luftmensch" (which is Yiddish for airhead). In the film's most memorable sequence, Menakhem Mendl plans to make a bundle as a matchmaker. He has an elaborate dream in which he loads an endless series of young women in full bridal regalia onto a ship bound for Argentina.

This scene may be very funny onscreen, but in reality, this is how all too many Jewish women from Eastern Europe ended up living out their lives as prostitutes in Latin America. Nathan Englander's novel *The Ministry of Special Cases* is an eloquent source of information on this painful topic, as is *Bodies and Souls: The Tragic Plight of Three Jewish Women Forced into Prostitution in the Americas* by Isabel Vincent (an investigative reporter now living in Brazil).

A swindler like Menakhem Mendl shows up one day claiming to be a matchmaker, but instead of making matches, his real purpose is to sell women into slavery. So was his creator—Sholem Aleichem—really an advocate of the "tradition" of matchmaking? Maybe, but if so, I have found no evidence of it in any of his stories.

Finally, there is an anthropological text called *Life is With People: The Culture of the Shtetl*, which was used as a source book by the *Fiddler on the Roof* team during their research phase. I have also found several volumes of YIVO archive material in Jerome Robbins's files, so I know for a fact that his approach to preparation was zealous. The authors of *Life is With People*, Mark Zborowski and Elizabeth Herzog, explicitly state that matchmakers were primarily employed by people who were rich, either in cash money or in yikhus (which is Yiddish for status or "pedigree").

The details of such a transaction are well-spelled out in Barbra Streisand's wonderful film *Yentl.* Say you are the poor daughter of a very famous rabbi and a rich guy in town wants your prestigious name in his family's future gene pool. Then a matchmaker comes to your parents to make a match. On the other hand, if you are a rich man who has a daughter, then you hire a matchmaker to find a scholar (like in *Yentl*), ensuring that your grandchildren will inherit yikhus from the prestige of their father. But—and this is a quote from *Life is With People*—poor people like Tevye's daughters had "the **privilege** of marrying for love."

In other words, if you did not have money, and you did not have yikhus, then a matchmaker had no use for you. In this case, you had the "privilege"—again this word comes directly from an anthropological text—you had "the privilege of marrying for love."

But now ask yourself this: In this whole panoply of players, starting with Solomon Rabinowitz (aka Sholem Aleichem) and Marc Chagall, and then the whole *Fiddler on the Roof* team—Sheldon Harnick, Joseph Stein, and Jerry Bock plus Boris Aronson and even Zero Mostel—who is the one person in this whole panoply of players who did not have the "privilege" of marrying for love? Answer: Jerome Robbins.

And now all summer, every time I hear people on Fox News going on about "traditional marriage," I see Jerome Robbins rising up in my mind's eye like Fruma Sarah (something Nora Ephron once said about Lillian Hellman), screaming: "DOMA?!? Give me a break!!!"

Please take this seriously, folks. *Fiddler on the Roof* made its debut on the world stage in 1964. The Stonewall Riots began in June 1969, so *Fiddler on the Roof* opened five years earlier, in the pre-Stonewall Era. Jerome Robbins had a lot of issues with his homosexuality. He was engaged to a woman at one point, and the parents on both sides tried very hard to get them to the altar. But Jerome Robbins was a gay man living before it was acceptable to be bisexual, and he was not allowed the privilege—in 1964— the **privilege** of marrying a person (in this case, a man) of his own choice.

I began my research on *Fiddler on the Roof* in 2000. I became a professional film critic in 2003, so I have spent many hours since 2003 writing about adaptations, mostly from page-to-screen but often from stage-to-screen (and sometimes even vice versa). Of course, I expect every version to be different, because the set for every performance venue is unique, and every artistic modality has its own rules.

Specifically with respect to *Fiddler on the Roof*, I have also written about the dozen plus stage productions I have seen in the past decade. Barely a year goes by without a new production staged somewhere in Metro Chicago. Our last local *Fiddler on the Roof* was at the Paramount Theatre in Aurora. That was in March. I never get bored; I love them all precisely because I appreciate the subtle decisions made by each creative team.

Back to Perchik's song "Now I Have Everything." At the end, his notes go "up" in pitch.

Besides having everything, I know what everything's for.

On the original cast album, the very next song is "Do You Love Me?" which is now one of the best loved songs in *Fiddler on the Roof.* No one at the Fisher Theater in Detroit heard "Do You Love Me?" in June 1964. It was added later.

At the end of "Do You Love Me?" when Tevye and Golde are singing their final lines together, their notes go "down" in pitch.

It doesn't change a thing, but even so,
After 25 years, it's nice to know.

Listen closely and you can hear that these two songs are complementary. They run along parallel lines, and the meaning of each one is made clear by its relationship to the other. In the first song, two people are marrying for love, and the song ends in the exhilaration of romantic love. We know this because the notes go up.

The counterpoint is an arranged marriage. In this case, two people met on the day of their wedding. (Tevye: "The first time I met you was on our wedding day.") They got married and it worked out pretty well for them. But in 25 years, neither of them has ever known the exhilaration of romantic love. We know this because the notes go down. When Tevye and Golde say "If that's not love, what is?" it is clear that neither of them has a clue.

News flash! Romantic love is not a new concept in Western culture! And yet many critics—especially male critics—excoriate the creators of *Fiddler on the Roof* for supposedly imposing romantic love on the plot when Sholem

Aleichem (the author they supposedly revere) never intended it to be there. This, despite the fact that the worst marriage in his eight Tevye stories is the one explicitly arranged by a matchmaker. This, despite the fact that he himself had a genuinely romantic personal story.

Romantic love is not a new phenomenon. Troubadours began singing about romantic love in the High Middle Ages, and Western literature has been on the side of the lovers since the first time Peter Abelard met Héloïse d'Argenteuil in 1115. So why do I feel I have to defend romantic love against the onslaught of male critics? Yet the more important question is: Why did Norman Jewison feel so free to eliminate Harnick and Bock's glorious musical expression of romantic love?

As the song says, Tevye and Golde have been married for 25 years. Will Hodel and Perchik still be together after 25 years? Who knows? Onstage, Act Two begins by counterpointing two potential futures for Hodel: what is to be gained and what is to be lost? Will she marry the mate her heart has chosen—which in this context is non-traditional—or will she marry "whoever Papa picks," the option that is specified as traditional in the Musical-Prologue "Tradition"?

On the stage, *Fiddler on the Roof* creates a powerful tension between these two options. But then along comes Norman Jewison, who simply removes one track and tries to run his train on the monorail of "tradition." So is Norman Jewison's adaptation "elaborately faithful"? Clearly, from the perspective of this Jewish Feminist, it is not "faithful" at all.

Finally, we are going to talk a bit about "nostalgia."

Look up *Fiddler on the Roof* plus the word "**sentimental**" in Google, as I did last week, and in 0.32 seconds you will get 3,970,000 results, with this one at the very top:

> *Fiddler on the Roof* is a **sentimental**, feel-good dollop of schmaltz that has warmed Jewish hearts for decades. Its enormous popularity has nothing to do with metaphysical content. The videocassettes are not rented by scholars in quest of ontological

truths. (www.chabad.org/library/article_cdo/aid/3036/jewish/
Tevyes-Query.htm)

Now look up *Fiddler on the Roof* plus the word "**nostalgia**" in Google, as I did last week, and in 0.27 seconds you get over 3,160,000 results with this one near the top:

> How accurate is *Fiddler's* shtetl? As Irving Howe famously put
> it, in a blistering attack written in 1964 after the show opened,
> "Anatevka in *Fiddler on the Roof* is the cutest *shtetl* we've never
> had. Irresistible bait for the **nostalgia-smitten** audience..."
> Howe was highly angered by what he saw as the damaging and
> false **nostalgia** for the shtetl world created by the show... Howe
> makes the strong argument for labeling *Fiddler's* **nostalgia** false.
> (Hillman, Page 85)

But the Robbins Papers at the New York Public Library for the Per-forming Arts, clearly indicate that this was not Jerome Robbins's intention. In fact, Robbins was concerned about sentimentality and nostalgia from the beginning, warning the members of his team against these very emotions at every opportunity.

> Do not romanticize the characters... We are not to see them
> thru the misty nostalgia of a time past... The effect of the work
> on their clothes and bodies must be apparent... The honey
> mists of time do not make life beautiful for them.

I found a reference to a fascinating book in the endnotes in the back of *The Invention of Tradition* called *The Future of Nostalgia*. The woman who wrote it—Svetlana Boym—was born in a city called Leningrad that is now known, once again, as Saint Petersburg. She came to the United States as a child in the wave of Jewish immigrants allowed to leave the former Soviet Union and emigrate to the United States or Israel or wherever—in that wave in the late 1980s—right before the breakup of the Soviet Union. Svet-lana Boym is now a Professor of Slavic Literature at Harvard University.

The Future of Nostalgia is primarily about the work of Joseph Brodsky, Vladimir Nabokov, and other well-known literary exiles (both Jewish and non-Jewish) from the former Soviet Union, but what is most important to me is the critical distinction Boym makes between what she calls "Restor-ative Nostalgia" versus "Reflective Nostalgia."

What does Svetlana Boym mean when she differentiates between these two uses of the term nostalgia?

Simple-minded me thinks of "Restorative Nostalgia" as "Fox News Nostalgia" → We can go back! Let's go back to those wonderful days gone by!

On the other hand, I like to think of "Reflective Nostalgia" as "PBS News Nostalgia" → We can't go back. This is how it used to be. Maybe it isn't that way anymore, but our past can still be our springboard to the future.

Those of you here tonight—those of you who know me best—know that I believe the "River of Time" only flows in one direction. I live in Brooklyn now. I miss you all. I really, really do. But Richard got a new job and now I live in Brooklyn and that is the way my "river" flowed.

I live in Brooklyn now. I am really happy to see all of you tonight, but soon I will fly back to Brooklyn because that is where I live now. I do not live in Chicago anymore. Nothing can ever change that. But even if I were to move back to Chicago tomorrow, the Chicago of tomorrow would be different from the Chicago of yesterday. And Chicago, the **real** Chicago, will grow ever more different every day that I am in Brooklyn (or wherever).

So as much as I treasure the memory of my 35 years in Chicago—and I do—I know I can never go back to Chicago as I remember it. What would the people who now live in my house on Plymouth Court think if I were to ask to move back in? Even if they said fine, some of my stuff—starting with everything I happily gave to Goodwill in the process of packing—can never be recovered… And those were just the tchotchkes. Gone. Gone.

This is the distinction Svetlana Boym is making, and I think it is really helpful in understanding why people can sometimes be so negative about the term "nostalgia," and why they associate it with "sentimentality" in the worst sense. If I believed in "Restorative Nostalgia," I might try to recreate a bit of Chicago in Brooklyn. In my case that would mean, among other things, squeezing the contents of a three-story Chicago townhouse into a two-bedroom Brooklyn apartment. But "Reflective Nostalgia" is after something else entirely.

Is *Fiddler on the Roof* nostalgic? Let us look at Robbins's memo again:

> Do not romanticize the characters... We are not to see them
> thru the misty nostalgia of a time past... The effect of the work
> on their clothes and bodies must be apparent... The honey
> mists of time do not make life beautiful for them.

This is a direct quote from the memo, exactly as Jerome Robbins dictated it to his transcriptionist. These are his thoughts, as conveyed to costume designer Patricia Zipprodt (the person who won her first Tony Award for the costumes she designed for *Fiddler on the Roof*).

And then, after he received the transcript, he wrote at the top: "These are notes for P.Z. They are good for all of us."

So let us read the words of Jerome Robbins together now, and imagine that he is speaking directly to all of us here tonight:

> Do not romanticize the characters; they are tough, working,
> resilient, tenacious; they fiercely live and hang onto their exis-
> tence; they have the word, everyone else is wrong; we are not to
> see them thru the misty nostalgia of a time past, but thru the
> everyday hard struggle to keep alive and keep their beliefs.
>
> They are not "Characters" but laborers, workmen, artisans, and
> the effect of their work on their clothes and their bodies must
> be apparent.
>
> This is a rural unsophisticated area... no newspapers, or any
> communication with the rest of the country around them. It is
> poverty stricken. Everyone just about ekes out an existence. The
> honey mists of time do not make life beautiful for them. All
> that is beautiful is their continued efforts and tenaciousness to
> hold to what they believe in.
>
> LOCATE TEVYE'S FAMILY:
> socially -- down the bottom of the ladder
> economically -- "   "   "   "
> geographically -- out of town. Farm.
>
> This is a country community... a little group of houses in the

middle of sprawling Russian countryside. The Jewish community is kept apart, separate, huddled together, isolated, and then told to keep alive. To do so they work hard and fight for existence.

FARM not CITY

RURAL not URBAN

PRACTICAL not ROMANTIC

TOUGH not PICTURESQUE

(Robbins, LPALC)

On the bottom of this slide (under the quote), I have highlighted these words: "Do not romanticize the characters… We are not to see them thru the *misty nostalgia* of a time past… The effect of the work on their clothes and their bodies must be apparent… The *honey mists of time* do not make life beautiful for them."

This is the clearest possible articulation—in his own words—of the intentions of the original creator of *Fiddler on the Roof.* Jerome Robbins had no interest in "Restorative Nostalgia." He certainly never wanted to go back and live in Anatevka. Robbins's *Fiddler on the Roof* was an exercise in "Reflective Nostalgia" → a springboard to the future.

✡ ✡ ✡ ✡ ✡

The title of this lecture is "Jerome Robbins: From Rozhanka to Broadway." So where is Rozhanka?

Today, Rozhanka is located on the border between the nation-states of Poland, Belarus, and Ukraine, but Rozhanka was once located in that part of the world known as the Russian "Pale of Settlement."

Three of my grandparents came from this part of the world too. My mother's mother—Gra'ma Hecky—always referred to it as "Russia-Poland."

> **Little Jan:** Gra'ma Hecky, where were you born?
> **Gra'ma Hecky:** Russia-Poland.
> **Little Jan** (*thought bubble*): Russia-Poland?!? Where is that???

In Gra'ma Hecky's time, the borders of the Russian "Pale of Settlement" were always shifting. The languages there were always changing. One day a town was in Lithuania. The next day it was in Poland. But most of the time, this part of the world was somehow part of Russia, and therefore under the military control of a Czar.

And this is where Harry Rabinowitz—Jerome Robbins's father—fled from at the age of 18. This is where he was living when he was conscripted into the Czar's army. The family got him out; they got him to America. This happened with many Jewish men at that time... **if** they were lucky.

When he was six years old, Lena Rabinowitz—Jerome Robbins's mother—took Jerry and his sister Sonia back to visit. They went to meet their grandparents, because Harry's parents had yet to meet their grandchildren. Harry had to stay in the USA because he was working, but Lena took the kids to Poland—Rozhanka was in Poland then—for the summer.

Robbins had wonderful memories of Rozhanka. He was treated like a prince. After all, this was in the mid-1920s, and he was the grandson from America!

Skip ahead to 1959: Jerome Robbins was in Poland doing a Ballet USA tour of Europe for the State Department... He got to Warsaw... Close enough to hire a car... So he went to Rozhanka... And it goes without saying that the entire Jewish community of Rozhanka was long gone.

What did Jerry hope to find? The unpaved streets he'd wandered as a little boy? All were gone...

> When Jerry and his companions arrived at the place where Rozhanka had been, "There was nothing there."
> (quote from Jamie Bauer: Vaill, Page 319)

Rozhanka is the place where Jerome Robbins's father Harry grew up, and Robbins obviously had a lot of emotional feelings about this particular shtetl. I believe his nostalgic stance toward Rozhanka epitomizes the term "Reflective Nostalgia."

Let me be blunt here: Do you really believe that Jerome Robbins in his heart of hearts wanted to go back to Rozhanka and have some matchmaker set him up with a woman?

At three I started Hebrew school,
At ten I learned a trade.
I hear they picked a bride for me.
I hope she's pretty.

Fiddler on the Roof was **never** intended to be an exercise in "Restorative Nostalgia." It does not **celebrate** the shtetl. It is **not** about a "simpler time" that some people wish they could go back to in order to escape from the complicated world in which we actually live now.

Fiddler on the Roof is an exercise in "Reflective Nostalgia." *Fiddler on the Roof* is a vehicle for **honoring** our past so that we can use it as a launch pad to the future.

The last words tonight belong to Hodel and Tevye in their final conversation at the train station. Obviously I cannot provide all the details that I presented last year in my lecture on Hodel again now. Suffice it to say that here—at the train station—we find the climax to Jerome Robbins's production of *Fiddler on the Roof*:

Tevye: Is he in bad trouble, that hero of yours?
Hodel: Yes, but he did nothing wrong…
Tevye: But if he did nothing wrong, he wouldn't be in trouble.
Hodel: Papa, how can you say that, a learned man like you? What wrongs did Joseph do, and Abraham, and Moses? And they had troubles.
Tevye: But why won't you tell me where Perchik is now, this Joseph of yours?
Hodel: It is far, Papa, terribly far. He is in a settlement in Siberia.
Tevye: Siberia! And he asks you to leave your father and mother and join him in that frozen wasteland, and marry him there?
Hodel: No, Papa, he did not ask me to go. I want to go.

Tevye: But, Hodel, baby…

Hodel: Papa *(Sings.)*
How can I hope to make you understand
Why I do what I do,
Why I must travel to a distant land
Far from the **home** I love?

170

Once I was happily content to be
As I was, where I was,
Close to the people who are close to me
Here in the **home** I love.

Who could see that a man would come
Who would change the shape of my dreams?
Helpless, now, I stand with him
Watching older dreams grow dim.

Oh, what a melancholy choice this is,
Wanting **home**, wanting him.
Closing my heart to every hope but his,
Leaving the **home** I love.

There where my heart has settled long ago
I must go, I must go.
Who could imagine I'd be wandering so
Far from the **home** I love?
Yet, there with my love, I'm **home**.

Tevye: Well, give him my regards, this Moses of yours. I always
thought he was a good man. Tell him I rely on his honor to treat
my daughter well. Tell him that.
Hodel: Papa, God alone knows when we shall see each other again.
Tevye: Then we will leave it in His hands.

(Stein, Harnick & Bock, Pages 123–124)

Two Scenes from the Life of Jan Lisa Huttner

My Traditions Come from Russia-Poland

SECTION 8

My *Fiddler*:
From Grodna to Brooklyn

This lecture was originally presented to the Chicago YIVO Society at Northbrook Public Library in Northbrook, Illinois, on August 13, 2014. It was also presented at the Harold Washington Library Center in Chicago on August 14, 2014, and at Wilmette Public Library in Wilmette, Illinois, on August 19, 2014.

Welcome to tonight's lecture, "My *Fiddler*: From Grodna to Brooklyn." This is my sixth lecture on *Fiddler on the Roof*, presented as part of the Chicago YIVO Society's annual Summer Festival of Yiddish Culture. But today's lecture will be significantly different from the first five.

The first five lectures were "analytical;" I looked at specific parts of *Fiddler on the Roof*—images and/or bits of text—and focused on their meaning. But today's lecture is the one my husband calls the "Me Search in the Research." How did *Fiddler on the Roof* become so important in my own life? Why have I worked so hard—for more than a decade now—to make you care? Let us go back to the beginning.

All of my work on *Fiddler on the Roof* has been building up to this year —2014—because on September 22, we will celebrate the 50th anniversary of the very first opening night performance of *Fiddler on the Roof* on Broadway. The curtain went up on September 22, 1964, and the rest is "history."

Now it is 50 years later; it is 2014, and time to celebrate a "Golden Anniversary." One of the wonderful characteristics about milestone dates is that they provide an occasion, a reason to stop and take stock. How have we reached this milestone date? Where have we come from, and where do we want to go next? I have been working for more than a decade now to try to explain to myself—and to you—why I think this particular milestone is such a special one not only for the Jewish community, but also well beyond it.

This is how I stay motivated whenever I start to doubt myself: Over four hundred years after the very first performance of *Hamlet*, people still love *Hamlet*. *Hamlet* is a perennial favorite on stages all around the world. There have also been numerous screen versions of *Hamlet*, including an animated version. Most serious actors cannot rest until *Hamlet* is somewhere on their resume. Shelves full of books have been written advancing myriad theories, so, if you want to, you can argue about *Hamlet* until you are blue in the face.

I believe that *Fiddler on the Roof* has the same kind of "legs." Fifty years after that first opening night on Broadway, audiences almost everywhere have embraced *Fiddler on the Roof*. It has not only transcended the Jewish community, it has transcended America and the English-speaking world. Applause rains down on cast members performing in faraway Japan, just as it does in… Germany.

At this point, I have dedicated more than a decade of my life to trying to understand *Fiddler on the Roof* as both an artistic accomplishment and a cultural phenomenon. I am offering my research up to you as the proxies for those who are no longer with us, most especially Jerome Robbins, but also Boris Aronson, Bea Arthur, Jerry Bock, Marc Chagall, Zero Mostel and Joseph Stein. Perhaps my observations only hit 75 percent of my targets, or perhaps only 50 percent? You are each entitled to calculate the odds for yourself.

Just as people still treasure *Hamlet*, my hope is that people will continue to appreciate *Fiddler on the Roof* long past the 75th Anniversary celebration of the first Opening Night, and even after the 100th Anniversary celebration. At some point I will be gone—and so will the rest of you—but I think *Fiddler* will keep on fiddlin' for centuries to come.

✡ ✡ ✡ ✡ ✡

So who am I anyway? I was born at the Beth Israel Hospital in Newark, New Jersey, in 1951. My first home was on Wainwright Street in the Weequahic Section of Newark. In 1961, my family moved to Livingston (right up Route 280 on the suburban side of Essex County). Even if you have never been there, you probably know this mythical place. I call it "Philip Roth Country."

As all readers of Philip Roth novels know, Neil Klugman first meets Brenda Patimkin at a Livingston, New Jersey, swim club. The first time I read

Goodbye, Columbus in college (sometime in the early '70s), I was stunned. When Brenda asks Neil (who is clearly not a member) who invited him to her exclusive club on that fateful day, Neil describes his cousin Doris:

> Doris? She's the one who's always reading *War and Peace.*
> That's how I know it's the summer, when Doris is reading
> *War and Peace.*   (Roth, Page 7)

Brenda doesn't get the joke, after all, Brenda-the-Beautiful has to rest up for her next tennis game... but I sure did.

In 1959, when Philip Roth published *Goodbye, Columbus,* I was still a kid who lived in Newark and spent summers in the Catskills. But by the time I read *Goodbye, Columbus* I had long since become "Doris." How did Philip Roth know there were intellectually-ambitious Jewish girls who found themselves obsessed with *War and Peace* way back when? Only now do I understand that *War and Peace* was as close as I—and my "Doris Sisters"—could get to where we had come from before *Fiddler on the Roof* conquered Broadway.

Remember, *Goodbye, Columbus* was written during the early years of the Cold War and well before the Eichmann Trial. In the late 1950s and early 1960s, it was far easier to imagine oneself thriving on the "dark side of the moon" than to entertain thoughts of daily life in the Russian "Pale of Settlement." Much safer, by far, to sit around the samovar with Pierre and Natasha year after year, even as we gingerly dipped a few toes into *The Diary of Anne Frank,* slowly building up to *Exodus* (with one sequence set in Auschwitz) and eventually *Mila 18* (in which the entire Warsaw Ghetto is obliterated).

I graduate from Livingston High School in 1969 and start college: St. John's College in Annapolis, Maryland. That's the "Great Books" school. Day one you are reading Homer and four years later you are immersed in Einstein, while in the interim you have climbed all the named peaks of Western Civilization. Bachelor of Arts degree in hand, I begin my master's at Harvard University... but I'm not happy there.

So I transfer to the State University of New York at Binghamton (aka SUNY-Binghamton)... but the chairman of my dissertation committee dies very tragically—and very suddenly—of cancer. Off I head to the University of Chicago and in a happy but ironic ending, I meet Mr. Right! I never finish my PhD, but I do receive my "M-r-s. Degree" in 1982. Three master's degrees. No PhD. God works in mysterious ways.

In June, 2012, after 35 years in Chicago, my husband Richard accepts a position at SUNY Downstate Medical Center (aka University Hospitals Brooklyn). Surprise! Now we live in New York. As I already said: God works in mysterious ways.

Newark. Livingston. Annapolis. Cambridge. Binghamton. Chicago. Brooklyn. Nu: Why is this lecture called "From **Grodna** to Brooklyn"?

✡ ✡ ✡ ✡ ✡

My grandmother was Sophie Slotnik Hecht. My mother was Helene Hecht Huttner. Her parents were Sophie and Harry Hecht.

Grodna—G-R-O-D-N-A—is in the northwest corner of Belarus, near the borders of Poland (to the west) and Lithuania (to the north). On most maps, it is now spelled H-R-O-D-N-O. This is where my grandmother—Sophie Slotnik Hecht—was born.

I was grandchild number two, but I was granddaughter number one (the first daughter of Sophie's first daughter). So I spent a lot of time with my Gra'ma Hecky. That is what we called her, Gra'ma Hecky (from Hecht). Gra'ma Hecky would come to our house in Livingston a couple of days before Passover and do all the cooking: she rolled hand-peeled garlic cloves into spicy meatballs, transformed hand-scaled pike into gefilte fish, and turned hand-ground liver into a chewy pâté.

Gra'ma Hecky never had any recipes; she just cooked what she knew. My job was to help out in the kitchen, so I watched her and memorized everything she did. There was a time in my life when I could make really good stuffed cabbage, but I never wrote anything down either. Now I try to remember: How much lemon juice? How much brown sugar? It was really good, but I can't remember how to make it anymore.

Imagine our Seders! Gra'ma Hecky would cook for days, and I would be in the kitchen with her chopping—and listening—while she talked about this, that, and the other thing. Gra'ma Hecky had a very heavy accent. Sometimes I would ask her: "Gra'ma Hecky, where are you from?" Her answer was always the same: "I was born in Grodna, Russia-Poland."

Russia-Poland? Where is that?!? I have an atlas and lots of history books, but I have never found a place called Russia-Poland on any map…

And yet everyone here today probably knows what she meant. Gra'ma Hecky was born in what we now call the "Pale of Settlement," on the western edge of what was once the Russian Empire before it became the Soviet Union. The borders of adjacent countries—with their plurality of languages—were always shifting. But Jews spoke Yiddish in the "Pale of Settlement," and regardless of who collected taxes on behalf of which government, that never changed.

What I know about Judaism and what I love about Judaism—**my traditions**—come from Russia-Poland. That is where my own intellectual autobiography begins. This lecture is called "From Grodna to Brooklyn" because my earliest lessons were taught in a kitchen by my Gra'ma Hecky. To the women here today: You know what I mean, right? Bob your heads. I am sure many of you also had mothers and grandmothers who provided a foundation like this for you too.

So what are my early memories of *Fiddler on the Roof*? None. A complete blank. I am standing here today at the end of a series of six lectures on *Fiddler on the Roof*, so isn't it amazing that I can provide you with details about the time I saw *Man of La Mancha* on Broadway in the mid-'60s, but I cannot tell you anything about the first time I saw *Fiddler on the Roof*? I can remember the first time I saw *Guernica* at the Museum of Modern Art. I can remember when I saw *Funny Girl* at the Claridge Theater in Montclair, New Jersey. But I have no memory of having seen *Fiddler on the Roof*—either onstage or onscreen—although, of course, I know I did. One of the mysteries of my own life—one of my "Me Search in the Research" problems—is this: How can it be that I have no early memories of *Fiddler on the Roof*, even though I remember other events from the same time period so clearly? Well, it is what it is.

So what are my first memories of *Fiddler on the Roof*? In May of 2000, Richard and I went to France with his mother to celebrate her 75th birthday. My sister-in-law Kathy wanted to have a big party in Florida, but my mother-in-law Juanita wanted an adventure. So we packed up and went to France: May 17, 2000 → May 28, 2000. I thought it was going to be a light trip.

"Oh, let's tootle around the Riviera and see stuff." I was certainly not expecting a life-changing experience.

But on the afternoon of the very first day, we went to the Marc Chagall Biblical Message Museum in Cimiez, and suddenly I was all agog. I have already described this trip to Nice many times in prior lectures, so I will not go through it all again, but suffice it to say that on May 20, 2000, my life turned inside out. I became obsessed with *Fiddler on the Roof*, and here we are…

And now I must confront my core question: What happened to me that day in Nice? Looking back on this day more than a decade later, how to explain why this experience was so mesmerizing?

The blunt answer is this: I came face-to-face with Conventional Wisdom. I went into the Marc Chagall Biblical Message Museum expecting kitsch… but I came out profoundly moved. Then I fell headlong into that paradox just as surely as Alice fell down the Rabbit Hole. And the deeper I plunged, the more I came to doubt everything I thought I knew about *Fiddler on the Roof* in the context of my own life as a Jewish Feminist.

Conventional Wisdom? Here are two specific examples.

The first piece of Conventional Wisdom comes from an article called "Fiddling with Sholem Aleichem: A History of *Fiddler on the Roof*" by Stephen J. Whitfield. It appears in a book called *Key Texts in American Jewish Culture*. Whitfield says:

> *Fiddler on the Roof,* **born in the era when fathers knew best**, had located a problem, tradition, at the heart of Sholem Aleichem's stories.

The second piece of Conventional Wisdom comes from a book called *To Broadway, To Life! The Musical Theater of Harnick and Bock*, published by Oxford University Press in 2011. (Sheldon Harnick is the person who wrote the lyrics for *Fiddler on the Roof.* Jerry Bock, who died in 2010, was the person who wrote the music.) In his foreword, series editor Geoffrey Block says this:

> Then came *Fiddler on the Roof* on September 22, 1964…
> followed by an **elaborately faithful (and musically nearly complete)** film in 1971.

So this is Conventional Wisdom about *Fiddler on the Roof*:

- Jerome Robbins's 1964 Broadway production was **"born in the era when fathers knew best."**
- Norman Jewison's 1971 film was **"elaborately faithful and musically nearly complete."**

Father Knows Best made its network debut on October 3, 1954. How many people here tonight remember the Anderson family from *Father Knows Best*? The Andersons—Jim and Margaret, plus Kitten and the rest of the kids—were a very popular television family, but their series ended in a final broadcast on May 23, 1960. The Andersons were a family of the '50s; by 1960, their time had passed.

Now think about 1964.

As I list the following historical milestones from the early '60s, keep in mind all the tropes of *Father Knows Best*. Surely recent 50th anniversary commemorative events have reminded us all that the era of *Father Knows Best* was long over by 1964!

February 19, 1963: Betty Friedan publishes *The Feminine Mystique*.

August 28, 1963: Martin Luther King, Jr. gives his "I Have a Dream" speech on the Washington Mall.

November 22, 1963: John F. Kennedy is assassinated in Dallas, Texas.

February 9, 1964: The Beatles make their first appearance on *The Ed Sullivan Show*.

March 27, 1964: The *New York Times* publishes its iconic article about the murder of Kitty Genovese.

August 4, 1964: The bodies of three Civil Rights workers—Andrew Goodman, James Chaney, and Michael Schwerner—are found in Mississippi.

August 25, 1964: Fannie Lou Hamer of the Mississippi Freedom Delegation asks to be seated at the Democratic National Convention.

October 1, 1964: Jack Weinberg is arrested at UC Berkeley, triggering the Free Speech Movement.

November 3, 1964: Lyndon Johnson defeats Barry Goldwater, winning a second presidential term in a landslide.

Now how do these dates relate to *Fiddler on the Roof*?

August 1963: Jerome Robbins agrees to direct *Fiddler on the Roof.*

- The "I Have a Dream" speech.
- The Kennedy assassination.
- The Beatles on *The Ed Sullivan Show.*
- The Kitty Genovese murder.

June 1964: *Fiddler on the Roof* opens for its out-of-town run in Detroit.

- Students head to Mississippi for "Freedom Summer."

July 1964: *Fiddler on the Roof* opens for its out-of-town run in DC.

- Three bodies are discovered in Mississippi.
- Democrats head to Atlantic City for the Democratic National Convention.

September 1964: *Fiddler on the Roof* opens on Broadway.

- The Free Speech Movement begins at Berkeley.

1965:

- Lyndon Johnson's inauguration.
- MLK leads three marches in Selma, Alabama.
- LBJ engineers passage of the Voting Rights Act.
- *Fiddler on the Roof* sweeps the Tony Awards.

Now think about this set of milestone events from the years between 1966 and 1972.

1966: Ronald Reagan elected Governor of California.

1967: Israelis win the Six-Day War.

1968: After a violent convention in Chicago, Democrats lose to Richard Nixon.

1969: The Stonewall Riots begin in Manhattan's West Village.

1970: Nixon bombs Cambodia and four students are killed at Kent State.

1971: Women celebrate the 50th anniversary of passage of the 19th Amendment.

1972: *Fiddler on the Roof* nominated for an Oscar in the Best Picture category.

If all of this—and so much more—is true, then how likely is it that this statement is also true?

> [Norman Jewison's film adaptation is] "**elaborately faithful and musically nearly complete**."

True? Of course not. The world had changed in highly significant ways.

Let us focus on this one little word "nearly." What does "*musically **nearly** complete*" mean? If it is "nearly" complete, then something must be missing...

✡ ✡ ✡ ✡ ✡

And this brings us to my favorite character: Yente-the-Matchmaker.

My 2010 lecture "Yente: From Boiberik to Broadway" (sometimes called "Yente, Yenta: How a Name Became a Noun") is the lecture I have done most often, and I simply cannot go through all the relevant details again tonight. So I will just focus on the basic question I have alluded to above: what was onstage that is missing onscreen?

Here is a picture of Bea Arthur as Yente in 1964. Do all of you remember that the first Yente-the-Matchmaker was Bea Arthur? When you are listening to the Original Broadway Cast Recording, you can hear her words:

> **Yente**: Avram, I have a perfect match for your son.
> [Who is it?]
> Rukhl, the shoemaker's daughter.
> [Rukhl, she's blind. She can barely see.]
> Tell the truth, Avram, is your son so much to look at? The way she sees and the way he looks, it's a perfect match.

This voice belongs to Bea Arthur, the same Bea Arthur we came to love on television as "Maude" in *Maude* and "Dorothy" in *The Golden Girls*. Playing Yente in *Fiddler on the Roof* was her first Broadway triumph. The next year—in 1965—she went on to win a Tony Award (Best Supporting Actress) in *Mame*, but playing Yente-the-Matchmaker in *Fiddler on the Roof* was Bea Arthur's big breakthrough.

Look closely at this image on the right. Yente-the-Matchmaker is tall, tall even compared to the men. Bea Arthur was a big powerful woman with a booming voice. In 1964, she was 42 years old. She had a lot of dialogue—although not as much as she wanted of course—and she even had her own musical number called "The Rumor."

Dueling Yentes

Now compare the image of Bea Arthur in 1964 (on the right) to the image of Molly Picon playing Yente-the-Matchmaker on the screen in 1971 (on the left). Believe me, folks, I have nothing against Molly Picon. People say: "Well, she was famous in 1971. She was very well-known." They are right. That is true. But fame alone does not explain why Jewison felt so comfortable casting her as Yente.

Look closely: Molly Picon was tiny onscreen, tiny even compared to the women. Furthermore, she has minimal dialogue, and her dialogue is always with women, never with men. Those lines above from the Musical-Prologue "Tradition" (all the dialogue about Avram and the perfect match for his son), none of those lines of dialogue are in the film. And her musical number? "The Rumor" has also been eliminated.

When I reach this point in one of my lectures on Yente-the-Matchmaker—the part where I tell people that the dialogue about Rukhl-the-Shoemaker's Daughter is gone—people in the audience invariably argue with me. They are certain I am wrong about this. So I can only tell them what I am telling you now: Watch the DVD again. I assure you, it is not there. Norman Jewison "disappeared" it.

And "The Rumor," which Jewison also removed, is often deleted in stage versions now too, so many people have never even heard it. I could talk at least an hour about why this musical number was so integral to the goings on in 1964, but tonight we must move on.

Just know that these two "Yente Moments" are missing from your DVD. Norman Jewison disappeared them, erasing them from popular consciousness.

And what about Hodel and Perchik?

The second song that Norman Jewison disappeared was "Now I Have Everything," the big love song at the beginning of the second act. Perchik-the-Revolutionary is about to leave Anatevka to join his comrades in Kiev, but first he asks Hodel—Tevye's second daughter—to marry him.

Perchik was embroiled in a movement we now call the 1905 Revolution. After some months have passed, Hodel receives a letter from Perchik. He has been arrested and sent to Siberia. As soon as she finds out, Hodel makes plans to go to Siberia and marry him there.

In "Now I Have Everything," **Perchik** sings:

I have something that I would die for,
Someone I can live for, too.

Yes, now I have everything—
Not only everything,
I have a little bit more—
Besides having everything,
I know what everything's for.

What is everything for? According to Conventional Wisdom, Sigmund Freud tells us the goal of every human life is to have a love and a work. And here, in this song, this is exactly what Perchik is saying to Hodel: Before I met you, I had a work that I was called to do, but now, in addition to my work, I have also found love. So this song is tremendously significant: "Besides having everything" (meaning my work) "I know what everything's for" (meaning my love for you).

I cannot tell you how many times I have had to defend "love" since I began writing about *Fiddler on the Roof*! There is a love song in *Fiddler on the Roof*? The horror! The horror! Some people actually think Jerome Robbins missed the whole point by injecting a romantic love song where it clearly didn't belong, namely in Sholem Aleichem's Tevye stories! "Feh!" I can hear them thinking. "Thank God Norman Jewison took that song out!"

Do these people really not know that romantic love has been part of the Western tradition since at least as far back as the troubadours of the 12th century? Have these people failed to see that romantic love has been a primary focus of some of the greatest art of Western Civilization? Am I honestly supposed to apologize for "Now I Have Everything," instead of insisting that something important is missing if we simply ignore the absence of this song in the movie version of *Fiddler on the Roof*?

Now let us return to the Marc Chagall Biblical Message Museum in Nice (France). When Norman Jewison made the onscreen tableau more "authentic," he not only eliminated most of the Chagall elements in Jerome Robbins's onstage version of *Fiddler on the Roof*, he also changed our audience experience of Anatevka.

When we look at the sets Boris Aronson designed in 1964 for the original Broadway production of *Fiddler on the Roof*, we often see a house—Tevye's house—surrounded by little up-and-down houses painted on the proscenium arch. And on the scrim curtain in back of Motel's tailor shop at night (just before the wedding scene) we also see all the little houses. The meaning here is clear: Anatevka is a community, and the people of Anatevka—including Tevye and his family—are embedded in this community.

Motel's Tailor Shop (1964)

But when we get to Norman Jewison's Anatevka, people are also running around in the forest, and walking out and about in open fields. Meanwhile, Tevye has all kinds of business to do by himself in the barn. The characters onscreen have a sense of spatial **freedom** and a degree of **privacy** that contradicts everything the story tells us about their lives. What has been lost? The community.

What has happened to the village of Anatevka? When you look at Chagall's *I and the Village* from 1911, you see all the little up-and-down houses that Aronson incorporated into his Broadway set design. Aronson's proscenium arch captures exactly what Chagall painted. *I and the Village*—now at the Museum of Modern Art in New York—is one of Chagall's most famous paintings. And even photographs from the original Broadway production of *Fiddler on the Roof* clearly demonstrate the connection.

What does it feel like to live in the village of Anatevka? Is it intimate? Yes! Is it claustrophobic? Yes again! Everyone is living on top of everyone else, and neighbors can see exactly what is happening inside each house. This is the poignant beauty of the "Sabbath Prayer" scene in Act One. When all the candles are lit, windows are aglow with the light that bounces off the faces of each family.

Think about the American equivalent: Thornton Wilder's *Our Town*. I love Grover's Corners, sure, but would I ever want to live in Grover's Corners? No. Statistically, people all around the world are gravitating from their rural hinterlands to urban magnets.

This is surely one of the reasons why *Fiddler on the Roof* has been accepted as so "universal." People from most cultures have dealt with the issue of migration from village to city. Who wants to be in a place where everybody can peer through your window, see what you are doing, then gossip about you? Remember Yente in "The Rumor" telling tales about Tevye's family? People craving privacy long for the anonymity of the city.

Conclusion? Conventional Wisdom is wrong.

I am not suggesting that you accept one version of *Fiddler on the Roof* and reject the other. I am not describing one version as "good" and one as "bad." I am simply elaborating the differences.

Fiddler on the Roof is not the same onstage and onscreen. The Robbins version (onstage) and the Jewison version (onscreen) are two separate works of art, and they are significantly different. The onscreen version is **not** "elaborately faithful" precisely because it is **not** musically complete.

✡ ✡ ✡ ✡ ✡

So what? Who cares whether or not *Fiddler on the Roof* is "the same" onscreen as it is onstage? A much-anticipated new revival—the fifth!—is set to open on Broadway sometime in 2015, so why should all this "old news" matter to anyone now?

Those of you who have traveled with me on this long, 14-year journey know that I often ask myself this very question. Why do I keep telling you that all of this should matter to you when I have trouble explaining why it matters to me? So locking myself into this presentation last spring, and telling everyone that this year's title would be "My *Fiddler*:From Grodna to

Brooklyn," was a bit like hanging the Sword of Damocles over my own head. "Now or never!" I said to myself. "If there is no answer, then it really is time to move on."

Luckily, Paul Weider inadvertently came to my rescue when he called to interview me for a post in the *JUF News*. "Here is how my mother sums up *Fiddler on the Roof*," he said. "Tevye's first daughter marries someone Jewish. Tevye's second daughter marries someone who doesn't want to be Jewish. And Tevye's third daughter marries someone who isn't Jewish at all."

My spontaneous reply was this: "On the contrary, Paul. Tzeitel marries a Bund Jew. Hodel marries a Tikkun Olam Jew. And Chava marries a mensch."

And that is the moment when the Sword of Damocles magically transformed itself into Newton's Apple. "That's it," I said to myself. "That is the core issue." Who decides who is a Jew? When one Jewish person puts the label "Jew" on another Jew, what does that label typically mean? For better or for worse, the answer is almost always... tradition.

At the beginning of the prologue to *Fiddler on the Roof*, everyone sings about tradition... But every time **we** invoke "tradition" in the context of *Fiddler on the Roof*, we must keep one obvious fact in mind: the prologue is at the beginning of the show, not the end.

Tradition. What is tradition? Let us begin with the example of Hanukkah.

What foods should we eat on Hanukkah? Are there "traditional" foods? Yes... but... for people from Ashkenazi cultures, the answer is typically potato pancakes known as "latkes." For people from Mizrahi and Sephardic cultures, the answer is typically jelly donuts known as "sufganiyot." Pancakes? Donuts? But we are all Jews, right? So what are the traditional foods of Hanukkah? The traditional foods in your home are probably the ones your grandmother made.

And what are the traditional songs of Hanukkah? Today, people in Hispanophone countries probably sing "Ocho Kandelikas" (which is in Ladino), whereas people in Anglophone countries probably sing "Oh Hanukkah, Oh Hanukkah" (which is based on a Yiddish song). "Ocho Kandelikas." "Oh Hanukkah, Oh Hanukkah." But we are all Jews, right? The traditional songs in your home are probably the ones your grandmother sang.

In fact, here in the USA, we don't even agree on how to spell this Hebrew word. Chanukah? Hanukkah? When I walk into Papyrus come November, I will surely find stacks of cards with one option right next to stacks of cards with the other.

Conclusion: Tradition is **not** an answer; tradition is an open question. And because the question of tradition can be answered in multiple ways, that means we all have choices to make. If you send your friends cards wishing them a happy C-H-A-N-U-K-A-H, you are just as Jewish as the person who sent you a card wishing you a happy H-A-N-U-K-K-A-H. Right? Of course, right. Chanukah? Hanukkah? We are all still Jews, right? Of course, right.

Like the creators of *Fiddler on the Roof*, most of the members of this audience have grown up in a syncretic American world which values a range of traditions. Many of these traditions are Jewish, but most of them are not. While working on this section of my lecture, I called an Ethiopian friend raised in Israel but now living in Manhattan. "What special foods does your family eat on Hanukkah?" I asked. "We don't celebrate Hanukkah," he said nonchalantly. "There were Jews in Ethiopia long before the Maccabees ruled Judea." And yet this wonderful African man is now married to an equally wonderful Ashkenazi woman raised on Long Island, so I hope he learns to love latkes while his son is still young!

Tradition! Tradition!! Tradition!!! What is tradition? In my life, I have had the freedom to pick from several different Jewish traditions; nevertheless, for me, **my traditions** begin with what my grandmother learned from her grandmother way back when in Russia-Poland.

✡ ✡ ✡ ✡ ✡

On one of my many research trips to the Robbins Papers at the New York Public Library for the Performing Arts at Lincoln Center, I found an original lyric sheet for the Musical-Prologue. "Who does mama teach to mend and tend and fix, preparing me to marry whoever papa picks." This lyric sheet contained a few handwritten notes in what I presume to be Sheldon Harnick's handwriting. And because of this song (and the wonderful lyrics Harnick wrote for it) most of us now believe this is an accurate description.

So why would I say this was **not** Jewish tradition in that time and in that place?

188

Example #1: Solomon Rabinowitz and Olga Loyeff. Olga Loyeff's father—Elimelech Loyeff—was a very wealthy man. Solomon Rabinowitz (the man best-known to us today as Sholem Aleichem) had bupkis. Elimelech Loyeff emphatically did not want Solomon Rabinowitz to marry his daughter Olga. Rabinowitz was a tutor who also worked directly for Loyeff, assisting him with secretarial duties related to the affairs of his large estate. So Rabinowitz was a highly placed individual, but in service nonetheless. He wasn't washing the dishes, of course, but he was still an employee.

Elimelech Loyeff undoubtedly had grand designs for his daughter, but Olga Loyeff fell in love with Solomon Rabinowitz, and she became Olga Rabinowitz on May 20, 1883. In the fullness of time, Olga Rabinowitz gave birth to four daughters and two sons, all of them fathered by Solomon Rabinowitz. Now you can read the Tevye stories of Sholem Aleichem every day of your life, but you will search in vain for a character named Yente-the-Matchmaker—or anyone like her—in the eight Tevye stories. There is a very limited role for a matchmaker named Ephraim in a couple of the Tevye stories, but Ephraim has no power or influence whatsoever.

Conclusion: No matchmakers play significant roles in either the biography of Solomon Rabinowitz or the Tevye stories of Sholem Aleichem.

Example #2: Marc and Bella Chagall. Once again, Bella Rosenberg came from a very prosperous family, whereas Marc Chagall had bupkis. He got a scholarship to go to art school in St. Petersburg, and then he went off to Paris. Back home on a visit to Vitebsk (once in Russia, but also now in Belarus), Marc met Bella. She was very well-educated, she wanted to be an actress, and of course—as we know from all his iconic paintings of her—Bella was beautiful.

Once again, this was not the match that Papa Rosenberg had imagined for his daughter, but Bella Rosenberg fell in love with Marc Chagall, and in 1915 she married him. In addition to becoming his wife and the mother of their daughter Ida, Bella Chagall was also her husband's muse. She dined with him in good times, she starved with him in bad times, and, as his fame grew, she traveled the world with him. Berlin! Paris! Jerusalem! New York!

Just like Olga Rabinowitz, Bella Chagall kept Marc Chagall going because—let's be honest—both men had a bit of the luftmensch in them. Neither of them was especially good at making money, and even when they did, they were certainly not good at holding on to it. So these two women—Olga Loyeff Rabinowitz and Bella Rosenberg Chagall—loved them, married them, and sustained them without the assistance of any matchmakers whatsoever.

Finally, there is *Life is With People: The Culture of the Shtetl* by Elizabeth Herzog and Mark Zborowski. This is the book that the *Fiddler on the Roof* team used as one of its most important sources, and even today, this Schocken publication from 1962 is a well-regarded anthropological text. It may not be totally correct in all details, of course, and there are some ongoing debates. But one topic that is not contested? The role of the matchmaker.

If you were a wealthy man and you had a daughter, you asked the matchmakers to look for scholars with bupkis. If you were a wealthy man and you had a son, you asked the matchmakers to look for daughters of poor rabbis. The commodities that matchmakers exchanged were money and yichus (the word for lineage/pedigree in both Hebrew and Yiddish).

We can see this scenario played out in Barbra Streisand's 1983 movie *Yentl*. Hadass (the Amy Irving character) is the daughter of a rich man named Reb Alter Vishkower (the Steven Hill character). Reb Alter is rich, so he wants Hadass to marry a scholar.

Note, however, that even in *Yentl*, matchmakers play a minimal role. And this is not just true in Streisand's onscreen adaptation, it is also true in Isaac Bashevis Singer's original story (first published in English in 1961).

In Singer's version, after Yentl's father—a well-respected rabbi—dies, "marriage brokers" want to marry her off, but she announces a totally fictitious plan to live with an aunt. Dressed like a man, Yentl goes to a new town, where she is accepted into a yeshiva. Yentl—now known by the male name Anshel—falls in love with her study partner Avigdor (the Mandy Patinkin character).

Avigdor is supposed to marry Hadass, but after Reb Alter cancels their wedding, Yentl proposes. Just go with it... here is the relevant part:

> **Yentl**: I want to marry you.
> **Hadass**: On such matters, you must speak to my father.
> **Yentl**: I know.
> **Hadass**: The custom is to send a matchmaker. (Singer, Page 156)

But Yentl does no such thing. Finding herself face-to-face with Reb Alter, she decides to speak with him directly. Startled, Reb Alter repeats his daughter's words, "The custom is to send a matchmaker." And yet, soon after this "man-to-man" conversation, Reb Alter announces the betrothal himself. No matchmaker required.

In *Life is With People*, Herzog and Zborowski explicitly state: "Poor people had the **privilege** of marrying for love." Why? Because they had nothing to trade. If he is a butcher and she is the daughter of a dairyman, they do not need Yente-the-Matchmaker to take a fee to arrange things. In Sholem Aleichem's story "Modern Children," Lazar Wolf simply says to Tzeitel: "I have something to talk to your father about. Send him around." Yente is not in the story (that is, the story as originally told by Sholem Aleichem) at all.

Rich. Poor. Sholem Aleichem and Isaac Bashevis Singer—two great Yiddish authors—agree that matchmakers might have been convenient sometimes, but they were never necessary.

✡ ✡ ✡ ✡ ✡

So back to *Fiddler on the Roof*. What is tradition? When we see Tzeitel with Motel getting married under a chuppah at the end of Act One, is this tradition?

Now here is an illustration of Perchik pulling down the mechitzah which separates the men and the women at Tzeitel's wedding.

Perchik pulls down the mechitzah and people are aghast:

> **Perchik** (*to* Hodel): Who will dance with me?
> **Mendel**: That's a sin!
> **Perchik**: It's no sin to dance at a wedding.
> **Avram**: But with a girl?
> **Lazar**: That's what comes from bringing a wild man into your house.
> **Tevye**: He's not a wild man. His ideas are a little different, but—
> **Mendel**: It's a sin.
> **Perchik**: It's no sin. Ask the rabbi. Ask him.
> **Tevye**: Well, Rabbi?
> **Rabbi**: Dancing… Well, it's not exactly forbidden, but…
> **Tevye**: There, you see? It's not forbidden.
> **Perchik** (*to* Hodel): And it's no sin. Now will someone dance with me?

Golde: Hodel!
Hodel: It's only a dance, Mama.
Perchik: Play! (*Perchik and Hodel dance.*)
(Stein, Pages 98–99)

And the next thing you know, everybody is dancing… including the rabbi!

Perchik Tears down the Mechitzah

So at what point did Jewish people in Eastern Europe decide to put up a barrier between men and women? At what point did they decide that men and women could not dance together? When, where, why, and how did all of **this** become "tradition"?

And who should make the matches when the services of a matchmaker are required? A ruthless businesswoman who has her own agenda? This is certainly how Rebecca Finnegan played Yente in a brilliant production at Marriott Lincolnshire in 2010. She clearly has disposable income—she is deliberately dressed up as the richest woman in town—precisely because she

© Marriot Lincolshire Theatre (2010)

worked for it. When Tzeitel marries Motel instead of Lazar Wolf, Tzeitel not only humiliates Yente, she also threatens her revenue stream.

On the screen, on the other hand, Molly Picon is always dressed in widow's weeds, reinforcing the perception that she is just a harmless old busybody, a gossip, and a meddler.

On the stage, Yente and Lazar Wolf "storm off" as soon as the dancing begins. ("Storm off." Those are Joseph Stein's exact instructions.) But onscreen, Molly Picon cries at the wedding, visibly lost in a romantic reverie. Clearly, this is yet another one of Norman Jewison's tiny but highly significant changes.

Should we have a choice? When I put this presentation together, I found a huge number of LGBT marriage photos online. Some photos show two men getting married. Some photos show two women getting married. Some photos show transgender partners getting married. This is the point at which I must say something: Every time someone on Fox News starts talking about "traditional marriage," I can feel Jerome Robbins doing another flip in his grave. 1964 was four years before the Stonewall Riots, a very precarious time to be "out" as a famous bisexual man. Best to keep his sexuality hidden… certainly in public.

Everyone else on the *Fiddler* team—Boris Aronson, Sheldon Harnick, Jerry Bock, Joseph Stein—could marry for love. Everyone except Jerome Robbins. Jerome Robbins was the one person who, in 1964, could **not** marry for love. So this whole question of "tradition," recently co-opted and enshrined as "traditional marriage," I am sure this was a deeply personal issue for Jerome Robbins. Should we have a choice about whom to marry? I am sure Jerome Robbins believed the answer should be yes.

And most important of all: Who decides who is a Jew?

In the last scene of *Fiddler on the Roof*, Chava and Fyedka announce that they are moving to Cracow.

> **Chava**: Papa, we came to say goodbye. We are also leaving this place. We are going to Cracow.
> **Fyedka**: We cannot stay among people who can do such things to others.
> **Chava**: We wanted you to know that. Goodbye, Papa, Mama.
> **Fyedka**: Yes, we are also moving. Some are driven away by edicts, and others by silence. Come, Chava.
> **Tzeitel**: Goodbye, Chava, Fyedka.
> **Tevye** (*under his breath*): God be with you!
> **Tzeitel** (*aloud*): God be with you!
> **Chava**: We will write to you in America. If you like.
> **Golde**: We will be staying with Uncle Abram.
> **Chava**: Yes, Mama.   (Stein, Pages 150–151)

And so, in the end, the family connection is secure. Is this a good thing or a bad thing? Many people think this moment of reconciliation shows weakness on Tevye's part. Tevye blinks; he caves in. But for me, this is one of the moments that shows us just how resilient Tevye really is.

And in the interim, this moment has become one of Jewish culture's great ironies. Something happened that no one could ever have predicted. Who could have guessed way back in 1964, that 31 years later, *Schindler's List* would sweep the Oscars?

As far as I know, no one ever thought to ask Joseph Stein why he sent Chava and Fyedka to Cracow. That certainly does not happen in any of the Tevye stories of Sholem Aleichem. My guess is that Stein sent them to Cracow because Fyedka knew he would find a great university there, therefore Chava knew it was a place where Jews would likely be thriving. Chava and Fyedka leave Anatevka because they do not want to live among the persecutors, and they specifically select a destination where they know they will find a community of educated Jews.

Decades later, Oskar Schindler and Isaak Stern are in Cracow making a list—Schindler's list—and Chava and Fyedka and their children... If any of them were still there in Cracow at that time, what would they be? No Nazi would wait for an answer from the priest in Anatevka. Chava and her children would be labeled Jews.

So who decides who is a Jew? Will we as Jews expel other Jews from our tent? Will we hand that decision over to other people? "Your mother is Jewish, so you are Jewish, so get on the train!" Who decides who is a Jew? The implications are enormous.

In 2014, as we celebrate the 50th anniversary of the first Broadway performance of *Fiddler on the Roof*, we have a choice to make. We can choose the Jerome Robbins version from 1964 (which is progressive and egalitarian), or we can choose Norman Jewison's version from 1971 (which is regressive and patriarchal).

Choices... And I have made mine!

We Suffer in Silence
Fiddler on the Roof *Act Two, Scene 8*

Yente's dialogue by Joseph Stein. Golde's thought bubble by Jan Lisa Huttner.
Based on the final page of Sholem Aleichem's story "Tevye Leaves for the Holy Land."

"God Almighty, how cleverly You run this world of Yours: Here You create a horse
and here you create a Tevye, and one fate is enough for both of them!
The only difference is that a man has a mouth and can grumble
till he's hoarse, while a horse can't grumble till he is a man.
That's why he is only a horse." (Halkin, Page 116)

Questions Asked / Questions Answered

Early in 2014, when I decided to self-publish "something" in honor of the Golden Anniversary of the first Broadway performance of *Fiddler on the Roof*, I threw myself into preparations for a little book which I fondly described (with a wink and a nod) as my "appetizer course."

By the end of 2014, I had learned the hard way that self-publishing is a grueling process. As a lifelong book lover, I took the job very seriously. I invested an enormous amount of my own time and energy in the project, and I also paid for the services of a small army of people—for project management, cover design, photo clearance, copy editing, upload assistance, and so forth—in an effort to achieve the most professional-looking outcome. When I held my first print-on-demand copy of *Tevye's Daughters: No Laughing Matter* in my hands, I felt genuine pride. It was print-on-demand, so I could make copies whenever I wanted to, and so could everyone else. It was all worth it.

When I made the decision to self-publish "the meal," however, I was considerably older and wiser. Although I had written various book proposals for several potential agents (in the formats they had dictated), no commitment from a publisher ever materialized. Therefore, I decided to create my own format and push forward.

So I built my "meal" with the ingredients that were already available, namely the six lectures I had given for the Chicago YIVO Society's Summer Festival of Yiddish Culture from 2009 to 2014. I always knew my title was going to begin with "Diamond Fiddler," so I called this new book *Diamond Fiddler: Lectures on* Fiddler on the Roof.

Initially, each lecture ended with a transition section called "what I have learned since," in which I included provocative questions from relevant Q&A sessions. Then I realized something that should have been obvious: there was a great deal of circling. Since specific issues returned again and again, I could not merely append "answers" to the ends of individual lectures.

That is when I decided to write a separate section called Questions Asked/Questions Answered.

Once again, still winking and nodding, I thought of this section initially as the FAQ section (meaning "Frequently Asked Questions"). But over time, I came to think of it with a bit more exasperation: Here are answers to frequently asked questions so that you never have to ask them again!

The first one was obvious: No one should ask the question "Which Fiddler is *the* Fiddler?" ever again because we know the answer. It is not a mystery. The answer is the Chagall painting called *Green Violinist* that is owned by the Guggenheim Museum in Manhattan. Got it? Okay. Stop asking.

But once I had that out of my system, I gave myself permission to really think about questions that truly were open and much more complex than the Chagall question. Suddenly, after 16 years, I was learning completely new facts (e.g. about Frances Butwin and her role in the *Fiddler on the Roof* story) and formulating new opinions (e.g. about Chava and Fyedka).

Frankly, the idea that even after 16 years of research there were still buried treasures hiding in plain sight thrilled me. It confirmed my sense that the basic "stuff" of *Fiddler on the Roof* is so rich and so deep that even with all of the research I have done, new people will find new jewels after I am gone. Yes, there are still many "open questions" and I am sure that someday people will walk through some of the doors that I have opened… and ask them.

QUESTION 1: WHICH FIDDLER IS *THE* FIDDLER?

On September 5, 2003, the *Forward* published my article "Everybody's Fiddler," in which I asserted—for the first time—that a real 19th century klezmer musician named Stempenyu was the missing link connecting Sholem Aleichem, Marc Chagall, and *Fiddler on the Roof*. This article appeared in print with a very large color reproduction of Marc Chagall's beloved painting *Green Violinist* (you know, the painting at the Guggenheim).

> With a century of scholarship to ground us, *Fiddler's* upcoming 40th anniversary (in September 2004) encourages us to look at the musical's two major sources—Sholem Aleichem and Marc Chagall—with fresh eyes. Having studied the subject myself for several years, I think there was a clear point of convergence, a person who became an archetype. His name was Stempenyu.

Skip to 2016, and this article continues to be available to all online:

www.forward.com/articles/8071/everybody-s-fiddler/

On August 17, 2009, after more than five years of additional research, I gave a lecture at Evanston Public Library as part of the Chicago YIVO Society's Summer Festival of Yiddish Culture. The audio from this lecture, called "Stempenyu: From Berdichev to Broadway," was posted by the *JUF News* (for whom I have written regular monthly columns on Jewish culture since October 2005) on December 11, 2009, and it is still available as a podcast from iTunes:

itunes.apple.com/us/podcast/juf-podcasts/id258160589

I also gave an updated version of "Stempenyu: From Berdichev to Broadway" at Oakton Community College as part of Chicago's first Limmud program on February 14, 2010.

Forward? Limmud? YIVO? Even if you have never lived in Chicago and have never read a single issue of the *JUF News*, the *Forward*, Limmud, and YIVO are all well-respected names on the Jewish cultural scene.

Furthermore, in May 2008, Melville House Publishing reissued Hannah Berman's translation of *Stempenyu: A Jewish Romance* in their series The Art of the Novella. Of course, Amazon—which clearly knows way too much about me—sent me an announcement, and I placed my order immediately. When I received my copy, I found this note on the inside of the front cover flap:

> Held recently by **scholars** to be the story that inspired Marc Chagall's "Fiddler on the Roof" painting [which in turn inspired the play that was subsequently based on Aleichem's Tevye stories, not this novella], *Stempenyu* is the hysterical story of a young village girl who falls for a wildly popular klezmer fiddler—a character based upon an actual Yiddish musician whose fame set off a kind of pop hysteria in the shtetl...

Wanting to remain anonymous, I asked a friend to contact Melville House Publishing to ask them who these "scholars" were, and they responded to her with a link to my article in the *Forward*.

So one would think that anyone really interested in any of these topics—Sholem Aleichem, Marc Chagall, *Fiddler on the Roof*—would have had plenty of ways to find my answer to this question (Which Fiddler is *the* Fiddler?)... but no. Everyone just carried on as if none of this had ever appeared in print and/or online.

When the Arena Theatre in Washington, D.C., began promoting its 50th anniversary revival of *Fiddler on the Roof* in 2014, two related articles appeared in the *Washington Post*.

The first article—by Melinda Henneberger—was published on June 14, 2014, and says this:

> Based on the stories of Sholem Aleichem, with a title inspired by Marc Chagall's painting "The Fiddler," the story follows a poor dairyman's attempts to hold on to what matters as his daughters are rebelling and his whole way of life is disappearing.

The link in this Henneberger article directs readers to a Chagall painting from 1947 called *The Blue Violinist*:

www.wikiart.org/en/marc-chagall/the-blue-fiddler-1947

The second article—by Menachem Wecker—was published on October 24, 2014, with a link that directs readers to a Chagall painting from 1912-1913 called "The Fiddler":

www.stedelijk.nl/en/artwork/753-le-violoniste

In Wecker's article, "Marc Chagall: The French painter who inspired the title 'Fiddler on the Roof,'" he says this:

> Despite consensus that *Fiddler* creators Jerry Bock, Sheldon Harnick and Joseph Stein had Chagall on the brain, there is some dispute about which Chagall works helped coin the title.

Wecker's article then became the source for the study guide that accompanied the new Broadway revival (which opened in New York on December 20, 2015):

> DID YOU KNOW? The title *Fiddler on the Roof* is derived from Marc Chagall's 1913 painting "The Fiddler." Chagall's work also influenced Boris Aronson's scenery for the original production. Chagall's artwork tended to romanticize the bleak Shtetl life.

And the study guide says this, even though the costume for the new Broadway *Fiddler*—with its vibrant purple coat worn over a white tallis—clearly invokes the *Green Violinist*.

ff2media.com/secondcitytzivi/2015/12/20/the-fifth-bw-fiddler/

So here is my final answer to the question: Which Chagall "fiddler" is *the* fiddler on the roof? Answer: *Green Violinist*.

My case rests on three sets of evidentiary references:

• Internal References
• External References
• Textual References

Internal Evidence

First look at the painting *Green Violinist* on page 57. Notice the placement of the arms, the head, and the leg on the roof. Look at the violin *this* fiddler is holding. See how it is all one color?

Now look at the cover of the *Fiddler on the Roof* 1964 Playbill.

Fiddler on the Roof

© PLAYBILL INC.

Now look again at *The Fiddler/Le Violioniste* (1912–1913).

www.stedelijk.nl/en/artwork/753-le-violoniste

This fiddler is looking left rather than right. His hands are in a different position, and his violin is two-toned. Not such a good match after all…

Now look again at *The Blue Violinist* (1947).

www.wikiart.org/en/marc-chagall/the-blue-fiddler-1947

He is much younger. He doesn't have a beard. His chair may be sitting on a roof, but he clearly is not. No match at all.

As Yente would assert about *Green Violinist*: "**It's a perfect match.**"

External Evidence

First of all, please note that *Green Violinist* is owned by the Guggenheim Museum located in Manhattan, which is where it was—as part of the permanent collection—in 1964. So if any of the members of the *Fiddler* team wanted to go look at paintings by Marc Chagall in the early '60s, this is one of the paintings to be found, quite literally, in their own backyard.

Here is one of the facts we know for sure from the documentation at the archives at New York Public Library for the Performing Arts. One of the first actions Jerome Robbins took after agreeing to direct the musical—then referred to as *Tevye*—was to contact Marc Chagall. Robbins wanted Chagall to do all the sets for what was to become *Fiddler on the Roof.*

Chagall declined, saying he was too busy. Then Boris Aronson offered to design the sets. After learning of Aronson's work with Chagall in Moscow and Berlin in the 1920s, Robbins said yes. He said yes over the objections of producer Hal Prince, who later admitted he had been wrong about Aronson. Prince and Aronson began a collaboration on *Fiddler on the Roof* that eventually resulted in four Tony Awards for Aronson… and many more for Prince.

The bottom line here is that we know for sure that Jerome Robbins had Chagall in **his** mind from the very beginning, and the artistic vision of Marc Chagall was central to Robbins's conception of *Fiddler on the Roof* from start to finish.

Once he took on the directing role, Robbins had his team members do an enormous amount of research. They went to Hasidic weddings to watch men dance. They read anthropological texts and did additional background research in the YIVO archives. So is it hard to picture them making a trip to the Guggenheim? No. Of course not.

The first piece of external evidence, therefore, is the sheer physical proximity of this specific painting: *Green Violinist.*

The second piece of external evidence comes from the huge source book *Marc Chagall,* Franz Meyer's monumental text on Chagall's work. It was published in France in 1963, then it was published (in English) by Harry N. Abrams, New York, in 1964. In addition to all its other virtues, Meyer's book provides a complete record of where everything was in 1964.

That is how we know that in 1964, *The Blue Violinist* from 1947 was in a private collection. And that is how we know that in 1964, *The Fiddler* from 1912–13 was in the Stedelijk Museum in Amsterdam (where it can still be found today).

A massive number of Chagall canvases are identified by name in this book. Some of them are shown in black and white, while others are in color, but quite tiny. However, the plate with *Green Violinist* is a large, full color reproduction clearly labeled "Guggenheim Museum."

So what was accessible to people living in Manhattan in 1964, people who—unlike us—did not have the benefit of Google? Answer: *Green Violinist*… right down the street… at the Guggenheim!

The final piece of external evidence is in Boris Aronson's monograph *Marc Chagall*, published in German, Russian, and Yiddish in 1922. Here again there is a large reproduction of the *Music* panel from the Moscow State Yiddish Theatre, the very same image that was to become *Green Violinist* after Chagall left Moscow and painted it again a few years later.

Textual Evidence

In my lecture on Stempenyu, I point to the bottom right hand corner of *Green Violinist*.

© Dover (2000)

Part of my evidence for saying that Sholem Aleichem's novella *Stempenyu* is the inspiration for Marc Chagall's painting *Green Violinist* is the presence of the **bird** (representing Rochelle), the **ladder** (representing the Jewish people), and the barren **tree** (representing the Russian Pale of Settlement), all of which appear in the exact location on the canvas where Chagall also placed his own signature.

Yes, by 1964, Sholem Aleichem's novella *Stempenyu* was long forgotten by almost everyone. But who definitely did know about *Stempenyu*? Boris Aronson, the same Boris Aronson who designed the sets for Maurice Schwartz's production of *Stempenyu the Fiddler* at the Yiddish Art Theatre in 1929.

So until someone comes up with good reasons why we should look anywhere else, I rest my case.

Green Violinist. It's a perfect match!

QUESTION 2: WHAT DID JOE STEIN BUY AT O'MALLEY'S BOOK STORE?

Sometime in March 2003, I learned that Sheldon Harnick and Joseph Stein were scheduled to speak at a conference on musical theater at Hofstra University on Long Island. At that time, of course, I was still living in Chicago. I remember giving serious consideration to flying in for the day, but for some reason I decided against it. I think I had a scheduling conflict, but I don't quite remember. So I tried to get a Brooklyn-based friend to go in my place, but he was not available either. What to do?

Somehow (and I honestly think I have willfully suppressed the details), I convinced someone at Hofstra to tape the session for me and send me an audio file. I think it was a "him." I think I paid him for his efforts. And I think I felt very guilty about the whole thing... Nevertheless, I was determined to "listen in," even if I was unable to be there in person to participate in the Q&A. So I received a tape from someone, and then I sent it to my transcriptionist.

This conference was actually a very big, three-day event, with lots of famous people in attendance, and yet I can find no record of it beyond a pdf of the program booklet on the Hofstra website. As far as I can tell, no book, article, or anything else intended for the general public, was released after the event.

So I ask you to take the following quotes on faith, because as far as I know, this is the only time Joseph Stein ever described his trip to O'Malley's. Regardless, I am absolutely sure this was the first time that I ever heard about O'Malley's, and my subsequent actions will make no sense if I do not start with Stein's Hofstra session. This O'Malley's anecdote is based on the actual transcript, although all punctuation, spelling, et cetera is my own.

Date: Thursday, March 27, 2003
Time: 12:00–1:15 PM
Place: Sondra and David S. Mack Student Center
   Hofstra University: Hempstead, New York
Session: The Making of a Musical: *Fiddler on the Roof*
Participants: Sheldon Harnick & Joseph Stein
   with moderator Herman A. Berliner (Provost & Sr. VP of Academic Affairs)

Sheldon Harnick: Through the years, and it has now been almost 40 years since *Fiddler on the Roof* opened, the memories that we have have diverged, Joe Stein and I. So I just want to say at the beginning: Whatever I say is true; whatever Joe says is highly questionable. (Hearty audience laughter.)

What **is** true is that we met on *The Body Beautiful*, which was not successful, but it was a joyous meeting and we loved working together. Then, some years later, a friend—and I cannot remember who it was—somebody sent me the Sholem Aleichem novel called *Wandering Stars*. I read it and I thought it was wonderful. I gave it to Jerry Bock to read, and he loved it, and we thought, maybe there is a musical in this. "Let's call Joe Stein." So we did.

Joe read it and he said: "It **is** wonderful, but it is too big. It covers something like eighty years in time. It has an enormous cast. It's just too sprawling. But, since we love the work of this author, Sholem Aleichem, let's look around and see other things that he wrote, and maybe there will be something there that would suggest a musical." And I don't remember at this point who discovered the *Tevye's Daughters* stories...

Joseph Stein: Well, I did I think. I remembered the Tevye stories from... My father used to read me stories from Sholem Aleichem. It came back to me, and I thought about the possibility of using some of those stories as a basis for a musical.

And it was very difficult getting copies of that. It was out of print. There was no way of getting it. I finally found one in—of all places—an old bookstore. A bookstore that had old books. And it was called O'Malley's. (Huge audience laughter.)

And O'Malley's Books had *The Old Country* by Sholem Aleichem, and from that we used three stories—three very short monologues about Tevye—as the basis for the story that we created which became *Fiddler on the Roof*...

And there were some Yiddishists who did object that we weren't exactly true to Sholem Aleichem, which we were not. I mean, the fact is that *Fiddler on the Roof* was based on three monologues, short stories that were written for a different audience. It was not written for the theater. It was not written as a musical. So obviously it had to be—could totally be—adapted for our purposes, but to be true to the feeling, the rhythm, and the emotion of the original. And that is what I tried to do...

Sheldon Harnick: Bear in mind, as Joe said, when we were looking for copies of this book, it was out of print.

Joseph Stein: Yes. Sholem Aleichem was no longer being read by anyone.

The *Collected Stories of Sholom Aleichem*

The very next week, my very good friends at Amazon delivered a used copy of *The Old Country* by Sholom Aleichem. Surprise! Only one of the eight stories we now call the Tevye stories was to be found within the covers of this book called *The Old Country*. Furthermore, that one story, "Tevye Wins a Fortune," was not part of the plotline of *Fiddler on the Roof.*

Say what?

I went back online. According to Amazon, the copy of *The Old Country* I had ordered as a single had been published by Crown in 1946 as part of a two-volume set called *Collected Stories of Sholom Aleichem*, translated by Julius and Frances Butwin in a "De Luxe Illustrated Edition" [sic] with illustrations by Ben Shahn. The second volume in this set was called *Tevye's Daughters.* I ordered the two-volume set.

When it arrived, I quickly realized that the contents were exactly the same as the contents of a book I already had, another book **also** called *Tevye's Daughters*, which had been published by Sholom Aleichem Family Publications of Shelter Island, New York, in 1999. A quick check of the copyright page confirmed the connection.

The copyright of my newly acquired *Tevye's Daughters* book (the one which was part of the two-volume set called *Collected Stories of Sholom Aleichem* reads: © COPYRIGHT, 1949, BY THE CHILDREN OF SHOLOM ALEICHEM, AND CROWN PUBLISHERS, INC.

The copyright of the second version of *Tevye's Daughters* (the one I already had on the shelf) reads: © COPYRIGHT, 1999, By the Family of Sholom Aleichem ORIGINAL COPYRIGHT 1949 By THE CHILDREN OF SHOLOM ALEICHEM, AND CROWN PUBLISHERS. Other than that, Google has very little to say about "Sholom Aleichem Family Publications of Shelter Island, NY."

Both are translated by Frances Butwin, and both open with the same dedication *"For My Parents* Gershon and Sonia Mazo." The Ben Shahn illustration that originally appeared opposite the title page in the 1949 version now appears on the cover of the 1999 version. Otherwise, they are identical.

Both copies of the first volume, *The Old Country*, were exactly the same, the newly acquired one and the one I already had. Both copyrights read "© COPYRIGHT, 1946, BY CROWN PUBLISHERS, INC." Both are translated by Julius and Frances Butwin. *The Old Country* has no dedication, but both copies open with a foreword by Frances Butwin, signed and dated "St. Paul, March 1946," which reports the death of her husband Julius in November 1945.

"Whatever Joe says is highly questionable."

For years, I thought Joe Stein had simply made a mistake. Somewhere along the line, he had also acquired the two-volume set called *Collected Stories of Sholom Aleichem*, and even though he thought the stories he used for *Fiddler on the Roof* were in the first volume (*The Old Country*), they were actually in the second volume (*Tevye's Daughters*).

For all these years from 2003 on, I used this as a case of faulty memory, and every time I told this story, the reference to O'Malley's got a big laugh. There is something inherently funny and very American about the idea that a Jewish guy who grew up in a Yiddish home had searched and searched for Sholem Aleichem stories, only to find them, at long last, in a bookstore owned by an Irish guy.

What was most important to me? What immediately caught my own eye was the fact that *Tevye's Daughters* also contains Frances Butwin's translation of "The Little Pot" ("Dos Tepl"), the monologue in which we meet Yente-the-Poultrywoman! It took me longer to appreciate that it also contains "The Man from Buenos Aires."

From the huge volume of stories left to us by Sholem Aleichem, Frances Butwin—and Frances Butwin alone—had selected 27 stories that she translated and published in a collection called *Tevye's Daughters*. And among these 27 stories, we will now find "**Modern Children**" (the story about Tzeitel and

Motel-the-Tailor), "**Hodel**" (the story about Hodel and Perchik-the-Revolutionary), "**Chava**" (the story about Chava and Fyedka-the-Russian), and "**Get Thee Out**" (the final story in which Tevye and his family are driven from their home and sent into exile), as well as "**The Little Pot**" (the story about Yente-the-Poultrywoman), and "**The Man from Buenos Aires**" (the story about human trafficking).

Tevye's Daughters also contains "The Bubble Bursts," "Shprintze," and "Tevye Goes to Palestine." In other words, the only one of the eight Tevye stories that is not in *Tevye's Daughters* is "Tevye Wins a Fortune"—"Tevye Wins a Fortune" is in *The Old Country*. In fact, it is the only one of the eight Tevye stories to be found in the first volume of the two-volume set called the *Collected Stories of Sholom Aleichem* translated by Julius and Frances Butwin in a "De Luxe Illustrated Edition" [sic] with illustrations by Ben Shahn.

The Old Country

But I just could not let it go. Had Joe Stein really made a mistake? Was this simply a case of faulty memory?

In the course of editing my lectures for this book, I went back to Amazon and discovered a used copy of *The Old Country* that appeared to have a different binding from the one on my shelf. I ordered it, it came, and bingo: this newest addition to my own bookshelf—bound in navy blue rather than in grass green—was obviously the oldest. And the 27 stories listed inside, in the table of contents, included both "Modern Children" and "Hodel."

I ran to the shelf, pulled down the green-bound version, and counted the stories in the table of contents. Twenty-seven? No! Twenty-five! In her foreword from March 1946, Frances Butwin wrote:

> There is no need to describe the quality of Sholom Aleichem's work. Here are the stories. Read them and see for yourself. There are twenty-seven stories in the book. I think you'll wish there were more.

This same foreword appears verbatim in both editions—the blue-bound version of *The Old Country* (that was published in 1946) and the green-bound version (that was published later as part of the two-volume collection)—even though the green-bound version of *The Old Country* only contains **twenty-five** stories.

I was wrong to cast aspersions on Joe Stein's memory. What he found at O'Malley's was the blue-bound version, the one with the original **twenty-seven** stories, including "Modern Children" and "Hodel," the stories that comprise the bulk of his adaptation *Fiddler on the Roof.*

However, I now see what no one ever seems to have noticed before, namely the fundamental role that Frances Butwin played in the creation of *Fiddler on the Roof.* Frances Butwin—and Frances Butwin alone—collected seven of the eight Tevye stories in a book called *Tevye's Daughters*, to which she—and she alone—added one story ("The Little Pot,") from *Monologen* and another story ("The Man from Buenos Aires") from *The Railroad Stories.*

It was all there, waiting for Joe Stein. He just had to find it.

In all the voluminous output on *Fiddler on the Roof* (including recent books by Jeremy Dauber, Barbara Isenberg, and Alisa Solomon), I know of no description of correspondence of any kind between Joe Stein and Frances Butwin, but my heart still tells me it must be "there" somewhere. My guess is that once Stein had *The Old Country* in hand, he could not rest until he found the final stories he needed to complete his libretto, and that meant finding Frances Butwin's *Tevye's Daughters*, Yente and all.

I thought I had already given names to all of the women usually excluded from the story of *Fiddler on the Roof* (most especially Rukhl Yampolsky Loyeff and Marie Waife-Goldberg), but I was wrong. Without the work of Frances Butwin, there would be no *Fiddler on the Roof* as we know it today.

QUESTION 3: ARE THE TEVYE STORIES ONE "NOVEL" WRITTEN IN REAL TIME?

My *Fiddler on the Roof* obsession began in May 2000. I had been on a trip to France called Artistic Legacies of the Riviera, and after a life-changing experience at the Marc Chagall Biblical Message Museum in Cimiez, I came home and started ordering what would soon become a mountain of materials (Books! CDs! DVDs!) from my new best friends at Amazon.com.

One of the very first items I purchased, of course, was a copy of *Tevye the Dairyman* by Sholem Aleichem. Way back in June 2000 (a full 16 years ago), Amazon had fewer choices than they have today. I selected what seemed to be the most popular one: *Tevye the Dairyman and The Railroad Stories*.

Tevye the Dairyman and The Railroad Stories, "Translated and with an introduction by Hillel Halkin," was part of the Library of Yiddish Classics. The series editor was Ruth R. Wisse of Harvard University. The publisher was Schocken Books of New York. I may not have known all that much about any of this way back in 2000, but I knew these names (Halkin. Harvard. Wisse. Schocken Books.) were all highly respectable if not downright venerable.

Halkin's translation of *Tevye the Dairyman and The Railroad Stories* was originally published by Schocken Books (which is now a part of Random House, Inc.) in 1987, with a very long and informative 41-page introduction signed and dated "Zichron Ya'akov, Israel. 1986." This same translation was reissued by Schocken Books with new covers—but with the same aforementioned 1986 introduction—in 1996 and 2004.

The first use of the term "novel" is on page 17, and I now note with interest that this first use also coincides with Halkin's first reference to *Fiddler on the Roof*.

> Readers of *Tevye the Dairyman* who are familiar with the play
> or movie *Fiddler on the Roof* will notice that, in more ways than
> one, there is scant resemblance between Sholem Aleichem's **novel**
> and the charming musical based on it.   (Halkin, xvii)

At the time, however, all this went right over my head. If Halkin thought (later on in the same paragraph) that *Fiddler on the Roof* (in contrast to *Tevye the Dairyman*) "keeps within the range of the safely sentimental," then who was I to say otherwise?

Put aside the words "safely sentimental" for the moment.

Right now my only concern is with Halkin's use of the phrase "Sholem Aleichem's **novel**." Is this correct? Are the Tevye stories a novel? Why should we think that? Was this Sholem Aleichem's intention?

Keep in mind that Solomon Rabinowitz succeeded in publishing several novels during his lifetime—including *Stempenyu* and *Wandering Stars*—under the pen name "Sholem Aleichem." But the Tevye stories, to the best of my knowledge, had never been published as one novel before this appearance—in 1987—in the Library of Yiddish Classics. I have searched everywhere for years now, and as far as I can tell, the Tevye stories had always been released—at least in English—in story **collections** like the two-volume set translated by Frances Butwin and published by Crown in 1949.

To his credit, Halkin asks this question himself in his introduction, in so many words:

> Can a work of fiction begun with no overall plan, written in installments over a twenty-year period, and ending more than once, be called (as it has been here) a **novel** at all?

And then he makes an emotionally compelling case for his affirmative answer:

> Indeed, if what perhaps most characterizes the novel as a literary form is the flow of time in it, the fact that more than in any other artistic medium we see human beings exposed to time, shaped by time, worn by time, then *Tevye* is a novel *par excellence*, perhaps the only one ever written in real time, that is, according to a scale on which time for the author and time for his characters are absolutely equivalent. Sholem Aleichem and Tevye age together: a year in the life of one is a year in the life of the other, and twenty years in the life of one is twenty years in the life of the other. Even as Sholem Aleichem sits at his desk writing down Tevye's stories, Tevye continues to grow older by the amount of time that writing takes.   (Halkin, Page xxi)

For 15 years, from 2001 forward, I simply accepted Halkin's description of this "novel *par excellence*" without question, and I continued to use the same description myself ("a novel... written in real time") in my annual YIVO lectures. Only now, looking back, can I see why it was so easy for me to accept Halkin's description.

By 2001, I had already seen *Too Far to Go* and after I saw it, I read (and in some cased re-read) most of John Updike's Maples stories. So long before I opened *Tevye the Dairyman and The Railroad Stories* for the first time, I already had a template of "a novel written in real time" in my head. As I explained in "The Me Search in the Research" (my preface): "What is observed depends on what is expected."

John Updike? Maples stories? Say what? I will spare you a long digression on John Updike. Suffice it to say, though, that if any writer ever created "a scale on which time for the author and time for his characters are absolutely equivalent," then Updike certainly qualifies.

Updike died in 2009 at the age of 76, and, like Sholem Aleichem, he left behind a massive body of work. Updike is most famous for his Pulitzer Prize-winning Rabbit series. The novels *Rabbit, Run* (1960), *Rabbit Redux* (1971), *Rabbit Is Rich* (1981), and *Rabbit at Rest* (1990) cover several decades in the life of everyman Harry "Rabbit" Angstrom. In 2000, Updike added the novella *Rabbit Remembered*.

As far as I know, no one has ever had the temerity to film any of the Rabbit books, but somewhere in the mid-'70s, a writer named William Hanley transformed one specific set of Updike stories into a screenplay. His adaptation culminated in a TV movie called *Too Far to Go* which was broadcast for the first time in March 1979. It is now available on DVD from Monterey Media, Inc.

The dramatic arc, about a couple named Richard and Joan Maple, is based on a series of stories, most of which were initially published in the *New Yorker* magazine from the mid-'50s through the mid-'70s (once again, a span of approximately 20 years). However, the Maple stories never appeared as a **collection** until 1979, when they were released together in paperback in conjunction with the NBC broadcast.

In 2009, a few months after Updike's death, a hardcover edition of *Too Far to Go* was released in Random House's prestigious Everyman's Library series. Updike used the occasion to add a wry new paragraph to his original preface. He had lung cancer. He knew he was dying. It was one of the last pieces he wrote.

> In the thirty years since the above preface was written, this collection of linked stories, quickly assembled to coincide with a made-for-television movie called *Too Far to Go*, has had a gratifying career in paperback… but this is the first hardbound edition in English. I was delighted to be told of it, and have availed myself of the opportunity to revise a few words and phrases, and to include one more Maples story, 'Grandparenting.' The couple surprised me, in the mid-Eighties, by reappearing in a wintry Hartford, married to others but brought together by the birth of their first grandchild. I have not encountered them since, though mutual friends assure me that they are both still alive and look well, considering.

Had John Updike ever read the Tevye stories? I parse this paragraph and feel certain the answer is yes. Regardless, by the time I read any stories by Sholem Aleichem, I had already read a great many stories by John Updike, and *Too Far to Go* (both on the screen and on the page) had clearly made an indelible impression on me.

Returning to my preface: "What is anomalous depends on what is accepted."

✡ ✡ ✡ ✡ ✡

Now back to Sholem Aleichem. The answer to the question "What did Joe Stein buy at O'Malley's Book Store?" led to a new question: When were the Tevye stories first published together as one "novel" in a single collection?

Right now, I can only answer the question "When were the Tevye stories first published together as one 'novel' in a single collection?" for English. I cannot answer this question for Yiddish, Hebrew, or any other language. But the answer for English (the language that provided the source text for *Fiddler on the Roof*) has become the occasion for yet another paradigm shift.

The question "What did Joe Stein buy at O'Malley's Book Store?" led me to Frances Butwin, who published a book called *Tevye's Daughters* in 1949.

But that book had 27 stories in it, of which only seven are part of the Tevye series. Furthermore, to this day, the story "Tevye Wins a Fortune" is still to be found only in *The Old Country*, even though "Modern Children" and "Hodel" were both moved from *The Old Country* and republished in *Tevye's Daughters*—with no explanation and as if for the first time—in 1949.

So when were the Tevye stories first published in English as a complete set? And would Frances Butwin have published them as a complete set herself if someone had given her the opportunity to do so? The answer to the first question is 1987, an answer that is both specific and quite revealing. The answer to the second question is "probably not."

Here is what Frances Butwin actually says in her introduction to *Tevye's Daughters*, which is signed and dated "St. Paul, August, 1948":

> In spite of the fact that these stories [presumably referring to all 27 stories in this book] are separated by intervals of time and that each one presents a complete incident with its own climax and denouement, taken together they have the unity of a novel. On the surface, this novel is a family chronicle whose theme is the timeless and never-resolved conflict between the younger and older generations. Examined more closely, *Tevye's Daughters* is something more than a family saga. It is a story of social conflict laid at a precise turn of history—the last days of Tsarist Russia… The political events of those years are reflected both directly and indirectly in the tragedies of *Tevye's Daughters*. (Butwin, Page x).

From Frances Butwin's point of view, then, the seven Tevye stories that she published in *Tevye's Daughters* did not stand alone as a novel. They required the 20 additional stories also collected in this book, augmented by the 25 stories she had already published—with her late husband Julius—in *The Old Country* in 1946.

And after 1949? We already know in Joseph Stein's own words how hard he had to search before he finally found a copy of *The Old Country* at O'Malley's. Frances Butwin had achieved the peak of her fame in 1949. In the 1950s, once her books were out of print, she went back to school and became a librarian.

As far as I can tell, if we exclude the two scripts Arnold Perl wrote for *The World of Sholom Aleichem* (1956) and *Tevya's Daughters* (1959), then very little either by or about Sholem Aleichem was published in the 1950s.

And then, much to everyone's surprise, *Fiddler on the Roof* became a huge Broadway hit in 1964! And suddenly Frances Butwin's translations were in demand once again!

© Jan Lisa Huttner (2018)

In January 1965, Pocket Books, Inc. published a mini-collection called *The Tevye Stories and Others by Sholom Aleichem* with these words on the cover:

Warmhearted, rollicking tales of life in "the old country"—on which the Broadway hit musical FIDDLER ON THE ROOF is based.

This book contains both Crown introductions—from 1946 and 1948—along with Francis Butwin's dedication "*For My Parents* Gershon and Sonia Mazo."

There are 16 stories in the table of contents. Seven of them are Tevye stories (although in an odd order). For reasons known only to the publisher, the final story "Lekh-Lekho" (Get Thee Out)—which is so critical to the final moments of *Fiddler on the Roof*—is **not** included in this little 254-page book. Neither is "The Little Pot."

At some point, both books in the Butwin collection were reissued. The publication dates on the two copyright pages are exactly the same (1946 and 1949), however the covers—also exactly the same in every other respect—now carry the words:

> The stories on which the great musical
> FIDDLER ON THE ROOF is based.

In 1982, Simon & Schuster published *The Best of Sholom Aleichem*, a collection edited by Irving Howe and Ruth R. Wisse. The copyright information, which is quite cumbersome, specifies that this slightly larger paperback is "A Washington Square Press Publication of POCKET BOOKS, a Simon & Schuster division of GULF & WESTERN CORPORATION" [*sic*]. The original copyright holder, however, was New Republic Books © 1979 ("Published by arrangement with New Republic Books").

The New Republic Books edition begins with a 26-page introduction in the form of a dialogue:

> How do two editors write an essay together when one [Irving Howe] lives in New York City and the other [Ruth Wisse] in Montreal? They follow the epistolary tradition of Yiddish literature and send one another letters. This is what we did, sent real letters that we soon began to look forward to receiving. It could have gone on almost forever, but we stopped because Sholom Aleichem said, "Enough, children, enough."   (Howe & Wisse, Page ix)

The stories in *The Best of Sholom Aleichem* are grouped into four parts.

Part One has 12 stories, five of which are from *The Old Country* (with translation credited to Julius and Frances Butwin), and one of which comes from *Tevye's Daughters* (with translation credited to Frances Butwin alone).

Part Two has four stories, all of which are Tevye stories and three of which come from *Tevye's Daughters* (with translation credited to Frances Butwin). The only one of these four not translated by Frances Butwin is the first Tevye story, "Tevye Strikes It Rich." This is also the one Tevye story which remained in *The Old Country* and never appeared in *Tevye's Daughters*. The person who translated this story for Howe and Wisse was… Hillel Halkin.

Part Three and Part Four both have three stories each (supplied by a mix of translators). Eliminating Halkin and the Butwins, the rest of the people who contributed translations to Parts One, Three, and Four, include: Saul Bellow, Reuben Bercovitch, Sacvan Bercovitch, Etta Blum, Gershon Freidlin, Nathan Halper, Seymour Levitan, Isaac Rosenfeld, Miriam Waddington, Leonard Wolf, and Seth Wolitz. Each of them translated one story apiece except for Sacvan Bercovitch and Etta Blum (who both provided two).

That means approximately one-third of these stories had been made available by the Butwins more than 30 years before, but two-thirds of them were newly available (including the Sacvan Bercovitch translation of "The Little Pot," which he simply calls "The Pot").

Sixteen people contributed to *The Best of Sholom Aleichem*, four of whom (including one of the two editors) were women. However, Frances Butwin's outsized presence gives this volume from 1979 an almost equal male/female balance.

There is no reference to *Fiddler on the Roof* on either the cover of the New Republic Books hardcover from 1979 or the Washington Square Press paperback from 1982, but there are two references in the introduction. The first is an oblique and dismissive snippet from Irving Howe:

> To see Sholom Aleichem in this way [Howe's way] seems a necessary corrective to the view, now prevalent in Jewish life, that softens him into a toothless entertainer, a jolly gleeman of the shtetl, a fiddler **cozy** on his roof.   (Howe & Wisse, Page xiv)

But five pages later comes this more positive—and highly specific—comment from Wisse:

> Tevye has been endowed [by Sholom Aleichem] with such substantiality, so much adaptive vigor of speech and vision, that the dire events he recounts almost cease to matter. He gives proof of his creative survival even as he describes the destruction of its source. (I thought it was very fine when the Broadway production of *Fiddler on the Roof* placed Tevye, in the finale, on a revolving stage, as though he were taking his world along with him wherever he went.)   (Howe & Wisse, Page xix)

Later still, Wisse addresses the "one novel hypothesis" and debunks it as follows:

> Even in the main, archetypal figures of Sholom Aleichem are not full-blown heroes of novels, but characters or speakers in short

story sequences, written over a period of years and later assembled in book form. The stature and personalities of Tevye, Menachem-Mendel, Mottel the Cantor's Son, as well as the town of Kasrilevke (Sholom Aleichem's fourth, collective "hero"), emerge from a run of episodes, each one only slightly different from the one before it, that cumulatively establish their dimensions. As distinct from the normal novel, which develops a single architectonic structure, growing from introduction to a central point of resolution, Sholem Aleichem's major works beat like waves against a shore, one chapter resembling and reinforcing the last in variations on a theme.   (Howe & Wisse, Page xxxiii)

Not to be outdone, in 1983 Crown distributed a huge new hardcover book by Avenel Books called *Favorite Tales of Sholom Aleichem*, which turns out to be nothing more than the two Butwin books, now consolidated into one big, heavy tome. After the exact same dedication ("For My Parents Gershon and Sonia Mazo") plus the table of contents, come these words:

Publisher's Note: *Favorite Tales of Sholom Aleichem* brings together in one volume the stories that first appeared in *The Old Country*, translated by Julius and Frances Butwin, and in *Tevye's Daughters*, translated by Frances Butwin. The introduction to these collected tales is comprised of Frances Butwin's foreword to *The Old Country* and her introduction to *Tevye's Daughters*, altered slightly, with her permission, to bring them into accord with the omnibus volume of the stories.   (Avenel Books, Page xi)

However, the only "slight alteration" I could find was the date at the end:

AVENEL VERSION	CROWN VERSION
Frances Butwin	F.B.
Minneapolis	St. Paul
1983	August, 1948

New Republic Books publishes 276 pages of *The Best of Sholom Aleichem* in 1979; Crown releases 692 pages of *Favorite Tales of Sholom Aleichem* in

1983. The "declaration of war" is in the cover design. Whereas *The Best of Sholom Aleichem* makes no reference to *Fiddler on the Roof*, *Favorite Tales of Sholom Aleichem* puts a huge dancing man on the cover with these words:

> 55 short stories and sketches from the Old Country—including the wonderful tales of Tevye and his daughters that became *Fiddler on the Roof.*

Then it was Ruth Wisse's turn again. As the series editor for Schocken Books' Library of Yiddish Classics, she chose Halkin to translate *Tevye the Dairyman and The Railroad Stories*. And ironically it was Halkin who wrote the introduction—in 1986—in which *Tevye the Dairyman* is described for the first time as "a novel *par excellence*, perhaps the only one ever written in real time."

The clue to the importance of all of this is to be found in the dates. Halkin wrote his introduction in 1986, and Schocken Books published this book in 1987. Was anything else happening in 1987?

Although it took a bit more time before details were released to the general public, plans for the Silver Anniversary of the first Broadway opening night were already underway. Here is an announcement from UPI's archives which is dated August 4, 1989 (a few weeks before the actual September 22, 1989 Silver Anniversary date):

> Topol has signed to do the musical through December on an itinerary that will take him to Kansas City, Columbus, Detroit, Boston, Cleveland, Pittsburgh, New Orleans, Miami, Chicago, and New Haven.

Topol arrived at the Gershwin Theatre on Broadway on November 18, 1990. This revival—the fourth of the six listed on the Internet Broadway Database (IBDB)—ran through June 16, 1991.

Can I prove to you that Schocken Books knew all this was on the horizon when they published *Tevye the Dairyman and The Railroad Stories* in 1987? No, I cannot. But my gut tells me that someone somewhere was already aware—if only subliminally—of the parallels with the *Too Far to Go* case.

Tevye the Dairyman and The Railroad Stories was published by Schocken Books; *Too Far to Go* was published by Fawcett Books; both of them were divisions of Random House.

Publish a new English translation of the Tevye stories which, for the very first time, contains all eight of Sholem Aleichem's original stories in the order in which he himself released them? Make sure the names *Tevye the Dairyman* and Sholem Aleichem are prominent on the cover, but omit any reference to *Fiddler on the Roof* so as not to alienate anyone who still clings to the Yiddish? The marketing potential of doing all of this right before the Silver Anniversary of *Fiddler on the Roof*'s first Broadway opening night was obvious.

In 1996, Random House reissued *Tevye the Dairyman and The Railroad Stories* as a paperback. This was the version I purchased in 2000. The title *Tevye the Dairyman* dominates this cover, and the name Sholem Aleichem is still prominent on the cover too. But the words *The Railroad Stories* now appear in much smaller letters so that no one will be distracted by them. My guess is that by this point, the production team assumed that most people would be coming to *Tevye the Dairyman* by way of *Fiddler on the Roof*. If so, then they would likely consider *The Railroad Stories* mere filler. Even I did not take *The Railroad Stories* too seriously until I had reason to re-read "The Man from Buenos Aires."

Then Random House released the very same translation with the very same introduction (still signed Zichron Ya'akov, Israel 1986) 18 years later in 2004, just in time for the fifth of the six revivals listed on the Internet Broadway Database. This one—timed to the 40th Anniversary of *Fiddler on the Roof*'s first Broadway opening night—played at the Minskoff Theatre from February 26, 2004 through January 8, 2006. This time, the words FIDDLER ON THE ROOF (in capital letters at the top) were even bigger than the name Sholem Aleichem, and the visual design makes the connection explicit.

✡ ✡ ✡ ✡ ✡

To me, this long strange road suggests that no one ever thought to publish Sholem Aleichem's eight Tevye stories as one "novel" until it was clear to everyone that a 25th anniversary celebration represented a significant marketing opportunity.

Perhaps Wisse, who seemed to appreciate that *Fiddler on the Roof* had—with some justification—become an international sensation, would have been more than fine with a reference to *Fiddler on the Roof* on the cover. Perhaps it was Halkin who put his foot down, refusing to allow it. Halkin is, after all, the person who wrote these preposterous words in his introduction: "there is **scant resemblance** between Sholem Aleichem's novel and the **charming** musical based on it."

Credit goes to Joseph Stein, who, like William Hanley—the man who created *Too Far to Go* from Updike's Maples stories—crafted a brilliant narrative from a set of disparate stories (in Stein's case, stories translated into English for all posterity by Frances Butwin). My heart tells me Sholem Aleichem would have been just as appreciative and just as gracious as John Updike was. Meanwhile I am here, as their mutual friend, to assure them all that Tevye is looking quite well, considering.

QUESTION 4: IS YENTE A YENTA?

On March 14, 2015, I did a Women's History Month presentation for the Temple Beth Emeth Brooklyn Sisterhood called "Yente/Yenta: How a Name became a Noun." This was a variation on the numerous Yente/Yenta lectures I had already done in Chicago, of course, but I also added a few tidbits I had learned in the interim.

Particularly helpful was a 2008 book by Rella Israely Cohn—which I had only just discovered—called *Yiddish Given Names*. Cohn devotes a full page to the name Yente, which concludes as follows:

> …negative connotations ('vulgar, coarse, gossipy') are modern. The original etymological meaning has been reversed. Harkavy does not have Yente; he does have a verb yentshen, 'to groan, complain, grumble'. Did the verb change the connotation of the name, or is the verb recent, deriving from the name?
>
> (Cohn, Page 339)

Once again, several members of my audience flew into a rage. Once again, they swore they had **personal** memories of the word "yenta" used as a pejorative ('vulgar, coarse, gossipy') well before 1971.

One woman was particularly irate. Since we were close in age, I asked blunt questions:

"How can you be so sure that you 'remember' this one little detail from childhood with such certainty? Isn't it possible that your current 'memories' are affected by what has long since become common usage?"

She stormed out of the room in a huff. Judging from the look on her face, I think she wanted to strangle me… and I mean that quite literally.

Why does my attempt to differentiate between Yente (the name) and yenta (the noun) cause such consistent outrage?

I began this particular Yente/Yenta presentation at Temple Beth Emeth Brooklyn the way I usually do:

> Would it surprise you to learn there is no character named Yente in any of Sholem Aleichem's eight Tevye stories?

Then I followed up with the same three questions I always ask:

- Why did the creators of *Fiddler on the Roof* feel the need to add this character?
- Where did the creators of *Fiddler on the Roof* get Yente from anyway… thin air??
- What happens when we change the actress playing Yente from Bea Arthur to Molly Picon???

Back to O'Malley's Book Store

By this point in *Diamond Fiddler*, my answers to each of the three questions above should be almost as familiar to you as they are to me. But my recent trip with you to O'Malley's Book Store makes me even more confident that I have been on the right track—persistently—from 2010 (when I gave my first Yente/Yenta presentation at Chicago's Harold Washington Library Center) through 2015 (when I gave my most recent Yente/Yenta presentation at Brooklyn's Temple Beth Emeth).

The person who plucked "The Little Pot" from Sholem Aleichem's vast treasure trove and made it one of the 27 stories included in a collection called *Tevye's Daughters* was Frances Butwin. So what was Frances Butwin thinking way back in the late 1940s? Did Frances Butwin (who was, after all, a native Yiddish speaker who was actually born in "the old country") think that Sholem Aleichem had named his poultrywoman "Yente" to indicate that she was a "vulgar, coarse, gossipy" character? I'll tell you. I don't know.

The nine-page introduction to *Tevye's Daughters* signed "F.B. St. Paul, August, 1948" only talks about Tevye, and as far as I know the text of this introduction has never been changed in any of the numerous editions published after 1949. Even the one you can now purchase in paperback (published by Sholom Aleichem Family Publications) has the very same introduction, word for word, from the header "Introduction" to the sign off "F.B. St. Paul, August, 1948."

Frances Butwin's Monograph

But wait!

In 1977, G.K. Hall & Co. of Boston issued a monograph called *Sholom Aleichem* in its Twayne's World Authors Series: A Survey of The World's Literature. Who wrote this monograph? Right there, on the "About the Authors" page, are two paragraphs of biographical information about Frances Butwin, plus a brief paragraph about her new collaborator (not her husband Julius, but her son Joseph).

By this point, Frances Butwin's days as a best-selling author were long gone. Remember, even though the Butwin books were popular in the 1940s, Joseph Stein had to look long and hard before finding his copy in O'Malley's Book Store in 1963.

Joseph Butwin, on the other hand, had received a PhD from Harvard University, and by 1977, he was teaching English Literature at the University of Washington in Seattle. On the "About the Authors" page, it says "his work is primarily a study of comedy embodied in the figure of the clown."

The "general editor" of the Twayne's World Authors Series was Sylvia E. Bowman of Indiana University. But the editors for Yiddish Literature were Edward Alexander and Fred Lukoff, both of whom are identified as faculty members at... University of Washington.

So it is very likely that this monograph would never have been published had Joseph Butwin not been a faculty member at the University of Washington at that time. Nevertheless, I hope he will forgive me if I attribute most of the actual thinking that went into the five page section on "The Little Pot" to his mother Frances Butwin.

> Yente's speech is a thesis without a thesis sentence; it is an argument that hinges on hidden principles... Ultimately a sense of order may be shared by the author and the reader but it is not known to the speaker and may be lost on the listener. The listener may know better, but the speaker is lost in a maze, and we are above it. The difference between the speaker's knowledge and ours is a condition of the irony that controls Sholom Aleichem's monologues. (Butwins, Pages 110–111)

If Yente-the-Poultrywoman gave voice to a paradigmatic story that revealed nothing less that the "condition of the **irony** that controls Sholom Aleichem's monologues" in 1948 (when Frances Butwin originally singled "The Little Pot" out for inclusion in *Tevye's Daughters*), then why diminish her now as "vulgar, coarse, gossipy" in 2016?

226

So I am baffled by the fact that this book—published in 1977—contains only one oblique reference to *Fiddler on the Roof*:

> …the world that knows Tevye has been multiplied since the 1940s by translations that bring him to an audience that does not read or speak Yiddish and is not necessarily Jewish. More recently, of course, a **musical comedy performed on stage and on film** has given the name of Tevye to the world of people who never read the Yiddish original or the translations.   (Butwins, Page 9)

Nevermind that by this point—in 1977—the theatrical version of *Fiddler on the Roof* (which opened in 1964) still held the record for the most performed production in the history of Broadway, while the film adaptation (released in 1971) had received three Oscar nominations.

The Butwins—in this case Frances and her son Joseph—have dismissed *Fiddler on the Roof* in this one sentence at the end of the first paragraph of their preface without even giving it a name. Therefore, reference to it is so fleeting that the title—*Fiddler on the Roof*—does not even make it into the index, let alone the list called "WORKS—DRAMA" which does include both "*Stempenyu* (dramatization)" and "*Tevye* (dramatization)."

It is almost as if their designation "musical comedy" is intended as a curse. Note that Wikipedia describes *Fiddler on the Roof* variously as a "musical," a "musical dramatic adaptation," and an "American musical comedy-drama," while IBDB (Internet Broadway Database) includes it in the categories "Musical, Comedy, Drama," and IMDb (Internet Movie Database) uses the categories "Drama, Family, Musical." One is left wondering if Frances Butwin and her son Joseph even saw *Fiddler on the Roof*? If yes, then perhaps they were in that small group of people who were **not** crying at the end.

I frankly find all this almost as disconcerting as the fact that Marie Waife-Goldberg makes no mention of *Fiddler on the Roof* whatsoever in *My Father, Sholom Aleichem*, even though it was originally published in 1968 (three years after the Robbins version swept the Tony Awards). Since she includes details about her trip to Kiev in 1966, we can only assume that at some point Marie Waife-Goldberg made a deliberate decision to exclude all mention of *Fiddler on the Roof* in *My Father, Sholom Aleichem*.

What explains these mysterious black holes? To quote Tevye again: "I'll tell you. I don't know." But I do think I am now able to put a name on yet another Invisible Woman.

Yente Abramovitsh

In my lecture on Stempenyu, I introduced an author named Sholem Yankev Abramovitsh, best-known by his Yiddish pen-name Mendele Mocher Sforim (Mendele-the-Bookseller). Abramovitsh was born in 1835—so he was 24 years older than Rabinowitz—and he died in 1917—so he outlived Rabinowitz by one year. Beyond his own tight-knit family, Abramovitsh was very likely Rabinowitz's best personal friend and certainly his closest collaborator. In *My Father, Sholom Aleichem*, Marie Waife-Goldberg introduces him as follows:

> Mendele had become a literary celebrity in both Hebrew and
> Yiddish before Sholom Aleichem was born. My father called him
> Zayde (grandfather), a nickname that stuck to him from then on.
> (Waife-Goldberg, Page 88)

Mendele appears frequently in her subsequent descriptions of literary events and conferences, but he is also present in this deeply intimate moment:

> My father was away at the Hague for the [1907] Zionist Congress
> when Babushka [Marie's pet name for her grandmother Rukhl
> Yampolsky Loyeff] went to the hospital for her operation… He
> hurried straight home upon hearing Babushka's condition had
> worsened, and he was as distressed at her passing as was my moth-
> er… His dear friend and literary "Grandfather," Mendele, read the
> prayer at her internment, and my father recited the Kaddish, as a
> son would, and as she had expressed a wish before her death that
> he do.   (Waife-Goldberg, Pages 230–231)

So Mendele was with the Rabinowitz family in their period of deep mourning, but was he there alone?

As one would expect, *The YIVO Encyclopedia of Jews in Eastern Europe* has a great deal to say about Mendele, including personal details like these:

> After the dissolution of his first marriage, Abramovitsh married
> the daughter of a respected notary from Berdichev and moved
> to that bustling commercial center in Volhynia, where he spent a
> restful decade (1858-1868). At the home of his in-laws, Abramo-
> vitsh devoted his time to secular studies, a series of literary proj-
> ects, and communal and charitable activities. (Volume 1, Page 2)

Yet never once does the author of this section of *The YIVO Encyclopedia of Jews in Eastern Europe* feel called upon to mention the name of either wife (although we do learn some details about his son Mikhail).

But buried deep within Dan Miron's massive tome *From Continuity to Contiguity: Toward a New Jewish Literary Thinking*, we find this:

> Preparing enlarged versions of *Dos kleyne mentshele* and *Fishke der krumer*, Abramovitsh launched in 1879 the publication of *Mendele's Collected Works*, opening the first volume with a brilliant general introduction entitled "Mendele the Book Peddler's Introduction as He Appeared Before the Public with his Works." Here Mendele offered "his readers" a detailed physical portrait of himself... and even coyly revealed the name of his spouse (**Yente**), "since as everyone knows, our Jewish writers have a habit of inserting their pious wives into their books, calling them by their proper names." (Miron, Page 443)

And here she is:

Yente Abramovitsh with Her Granddaughter
(circa 1915)

Abramovitsh Family Photo
(circa 1915)

I submit to you that Yente-the-Poultrywoman is named "Yente" in honor of Yente Abramovitsh, just as Tevye's favorite daughter is named "Hodel" in honor of his own wife Olga [Hodel] Rabinowitz. Keeping names "in the family" is one of Judaism's most honored traditions. Perhaps Rabinowitz wanted his literary children to be known by a few special names after he was gone?

My heart tells me that Solomon and Olga Rabinowitz were likely very well-acquainted with both Sholem Yankev Abramovitsh and Yente Abramovitsh. And since her name was not a pejorative in her own day, why should we scorn it today?

The character of Yente-the-Matchmaker as created by Joseph Stein— and originally embodied by Bea Arthur—was fully worthy of her venerable name. The person who turned Yente into a yenta was Norman Jewison, that non-Jewish guy from Canada, in an adaptation of *Fiddler on the Roof* that is anything but "elaborately faithful."

As I demonstrated in my lecture on Yente, this chart helps prove my point.

YENTE (DARK) ----> YENTA (LIGHT)

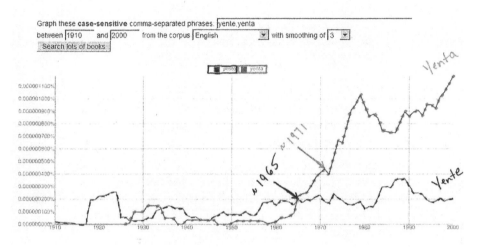

From Wikipedia (2011)

One More Mystery

And yet, even now, one mystery remains. Where did the arc for the Yente-the-Matchmaker character come from? After all, when we compare the arc of the Yente-the-Poultrywoman character and the arc of the Ephraim-the-Matchmaker character, there are barely any overlaps. So did Joseph Stein invent the arc for his Yente-the-Matchmaker character from whole cloth?

Allow me to introduce "Auntie Toive from Berdichev" as she appears in Sholem Aleichem's autobiography *From the Fair*, and you can decide for yourself.

One day [in Sofievka] passed and then another, one week and then another. Then an unexpected catastrophe struck, brought on by an outsider who opened up the old man's eyes to the ongoing romance [between Solomon and Olga/Hodel]. This person happened to be a wise, farseeing woman, a relative of old Loyev from Berditchev named Toive. We call her "Auntie Toive from Berditchev." When you get to know her, you will see how appropriate her name is. To her we'll devote a separate chapter.

Chapter 73. Auntie Toive from Berditchev

Auntie Toive watches the youngsters—
the catastrophe—out into the world—
intercepted letter—wandering in the night

Actually, Toive wasn't an aunt to anyone. She was no more than a cousin to old Loyev [Elimelech]... Her clever eye glance, however, seemed to penetrate you... She managed the business affairs and was quite wealthy.

Now, after an absence of many years, Auntie Toive came to visit the Loyevs... she saw everything through her Berditchev eyes and marveled at everything. She talked familiarly to old Loyev and told him explicitly what she thought, what pleased her, and what did not...

Aunt Toive liked the teacher. Sholem was a fine lad—she had nothing against him, and he knew his stuff too. And what's more, he came from a good family—that made it even better. But where was it written that a tutor had to be so close to his pupil? In her opinion, this teacher was too chummy with his charge. How did she know this? Aunt Toive had an all seeing eye. Aunt Toive appointed herself to watch the young couple's every step... Aunt Toive from Berditchev noticed from the very first day that the girl was dying for the lad and that he was head over heels in love with the girl.

"It's plain as day to anyone," she declared, "except for someone who's either blind in both eyes, or simply doesn't want to see what's happening under his nose... If it's a match—why well and good, but the mother and the father have to know. And if it's a love affair? A romance? Then the parents should *certainly* know—for it's much healthier and better and nicer to give your daughter to a poor teacher who has no more than a couple of shirts to his name than to wait until this self-same teacher runs off with the daughter on some dark night...

These were Aunt Toive's complaints... She revealed them to her cousin [Elimelech Loyev] in absolute secrecy half an hour before her departure. Her words reverberated in old Loyev's heart... he was furious and didn't say a word to anyone for the rest of the day. He secluded himself in his room and did not show his face...

Something was going on. Something was brewing... The pupil, ready to go for a walk with her tutor, was stopped at the last minute... Something extraordinary was happening in the house. A strange silence that precedes a storm...

Who would have thought that a couple of ambiguous words from Aunt Toive from Berditchev would cook up such a storm and prompt such a revolution in the house? Had Aunt Toive known sooner what repercussions her words would cause, perhaps she wouldn't have butted in where she wasn't needed... Was it the boy's fault that he was poor? "Being poor is no shame" and "Happiness is in the hands of God" were among the proverbs she fed [her cousin] Elimelech.

Words, however, no longer availed. The old man maintained that actually he had nothing against Sholem, but how dare they conduct a romance in his house without his knowledge? His daughter's possible engagement to a poor lad didn't bother him. Now it did? It was he, her father, who was supposed to introduce such a young man to her. And she must not choose him herself, without having consulted her father! This is what vexed him more than anything else.

The young couple became aware of all these complaints and remarks only much later. But at this time, like a pair of innocent lambs, they did not know who had betrayed them. They only felt that something was brewing.   (Leviant, Pages 249-252)

Marie Waife-Goldberg tells much the same story in *My Father, Sholem Aleichem*, however, she does add these reflections all her own:

My father did not speak to old Loyev of his love for his daughter, and this was a grievous mistake. Whether the old man would have embraced Sholom it is hard to say–but he might have done so, for he was not the man to seek a rich husband for his daughter. He did, after all, like Sholom very much, and he appreciated his knowledge and abilities. Certainly a direct approach would not have evoked the violent reaction that ensued when he heard of his daughter's 'romance' from Aunt Toive. (Waife-Goldberg, Page 74)

Now compare all of the above to the following snippet of dialogue between Golde and Yente when Motel comes looking for Tzeitel in Act One, Scene 1.

> **Yente**: What does that poor little tailor, Motel, want with Tzeitel?
> **Golde**: They have been friends since they were babies together. They talk. They play...
> **Yente** (*suspiciously*): They play? What do they play?
> **Golde**: Who knows? They're just children.
> **Yente**: From such children, come other children.
> **Golde**: Motel, he's a nothing...   (Stein, Pages 13-14)

There is a clear parallel between Auntie Toive and Yente-the-Matchmaker. They have the same dramatic function in these two romance narratives—one fact, one fiction. So here is the mystery: How did Joseph Stein know about Auntie Toive?

Marie Waife-Goldberg did not publish *My Father, Sholom Aleichem* until 1968, and Viking Penguin did not publish Curt Leviant's translation of *From the Fair* until 1985. True, Tissa's eldest daughter Tamara Berkowitz (Sholem Aleichem's first grandchild) had published an English translation called *Great Fair: Scenes from My Childhood* in 1955 (under her married name Tamara Kahana). But even if Stein had thought to look for it, and even if he had found a copy of it somewhere, he would have learned nothing about Auntie Toive from it. *Great Fair* ends with chapter 60, well before anyone connected with the Loyev Family first appeared in the life of Solomon Rabinowitz.

So once again, all I can do is quote Tevye (shrug and all): "I'll tell you, I don't know." But when a match is this perfect, should we really just chalk it up to mere coincidence? Oh, and, do remember that—according to Dan Miron—Berdichev just happens to be where Yente Abramovitsh was living when she married Mendele.

And a Surprising "Final Answer"

I gave my first lecture about Yente-the-Matchmaker on August 20, 2010. At that time, of course, one of my primary resources was Hillel Halkin's translation of the Tevye stories as they appear in his collection *Tevye the Dairyman and The Railroad Stories*. This is the English translation originally published in the Schocken Books Library of Yiddish Classics in 1987 (right before the Silver Anniversary of the first Broadway performance of *Fiddler on the Roof* on September 22, 1989).

A short time later, Amazon sent me a message about a new set of Tevye stories. This version was called *Tevye the Dairyman and Motel the Cantor's Son*. The translator was Aliza Shevrin. The publisher was Penguin Classics. The copyright date was 2009. Was I interested? Of course!

As soon as Shevrin's *Tevye the Dairyman and Motel the Cantor's Son* arrived, I immediately read Dan Miron's introduction, and then I settled in to begin "re-reading" Sholem Aleichem. But I was stopped dead in my tracks on **the second page of the very first story** "The Great Windfall" when I saw this:

> It was exactly nine or ten years ago and maybe a bit more. At that time, I wasn't at all the man you see today. Of course, I was the same Tevye but not really the same. How do they say: the same **yente** but sporting a different hat. (Shevrin, Page 6)

Say what? Did Sholem Aleichem actually use the name Yente as a noun way back in 1895?!? And if so, why had I never noticed this before?

This answer is simple. Hillel Halkin either missed it, or he saw it but he did not care. Here is his translation of the same passage from "Tevye Strikes It Rich":

> What I'm trying to tell you is that it took place exactly a dog's age ago, nine or ten years to the day, if not a bit more or less. I was the same man then that I am now, only not at all like me; that is, I was Tevye then too, but not the same Tevye you're looking at. How does the saying go? **It's still the same lady, she's just not so shady.** Halkin, Page 4)

Now in 2016—six years later—I have acquired even more translations. Here is what Miriam Katz says in *Sholem-Aleykhem's Tevye the Dairyman*, the version published by Pangloss Press (publishers of Judaica in History & Culture) in 1994. From "The Grand Prize":

> In those days I was not the same person I am now. That is, I was the same Tevye, but different. **As they say, the same old woman but under a different veil.** (Katz, Page 10)

Of course, I know what you want to know now: How did Frances But-win translate this passage? Recall that this story appears in *The Old Country* (which is the first volume of the two-volume set that became *Collected Stories of Sholom Aleichem*). Since we do not know exactly what Frances Butwin did (versus what her husband Julius Butwin did before his untimely death), we do not know what her exact contribution to this passage is. But here is how it appears in what the Butwins call "Tevye Wins a Fortune."

> In those days I was not the man I am today. That is, I *was* the
> same Tevye, and yet not exactly the same. **The same old woman,**
> **as they say, but in a different bonnet.** (Butwins, Page 22)

Julius Butwin died in 1945. *The Old Country* was published in 1946. In 1949, Frances Butwin published *Tevye's Daughters*, a second collection of stories by Sholem Aleichem that included "The Little Pot" (a monologue told from the POV of a character named Yente-the-Poultrywoman).

Since Frances Butwin published her work well before *Fiddler* arrived on Broadway in 1964, we cannot fault her for failing to notice the appearance of the name Yente used as a noun in the very first Tevye story. For Halkin and Katz, on the other hand, this must surely have been a bit of willful blindness. It is yet another instance in which someone who claimed to know Sholem Aleichem's Tevye stories backward and forward failed to see how faithful Joseph Stein had actually been to the work of the master.

As soon as I read Shevrin's translation, I ran to the shelf, and pulled down the copy I had from the National Yiddish Book Center. Did Sholem Alei-chem use the name Yente as a noun way back in 1895? Yes, he did, and here is the proof:

הײסט, טאַקי דער אײנענער מ. ב. י. ה. , נאָר פֿאָרט נישט דער,
וװי זאָגט איהר : די אײגענע יענטע, נאָר אַנדערש געשלייערט.
דהײנו וואָס ? איך בין געוועזן, נים פֿאַר אײך געדאַכט, אַ קבצן
אין זיעבען פֿאַלעם, חאָטש אַפֿילו, אַז מע וויל שמועסען דאָס אײ־
גענע וויעדער צוריק, בין איך נאָר איצט אויך נאָנץ וויים פֿון אַ
נגיד. וואָס מיר פֿעהלט צו בראָצקי'ן — מענען מיר זיך דאָם

© National Yiddish Book Center (1999)

Once again, I felt Sholem Aleichem's smile like a ray of sun on my face. Suddenly it was Easter and I had found another egg!

I made a copy of this Yiddish passage, and brought it to the next meeting of the Chicago YIVO Society Board a few weeks later. "What does all this mean?" I asked. "What do **you** think 'yente' meant when used as a noun way back in 1895?"

The Yiddishists in the group gave my question serious consideration and reached a consensus: "Dame, like '**grand dame**,' like Dame Maggie Smith and Dame Judi Dench."

I pressed them: "So still in the same linguistic family as genteel, gentry, and gentleman? Not 'gossip' or anything pejorative, right?"

Thus reassured, I used my six degrees of separation to find an email address for Aliza Shevrin, and once I had it, I sent her this question:

> What do **you** make of this use of the term "yente" by Sholem Aleichem? What would it have meant to him when he used this expression? (Since you don't capitalize it, I assume you don't think he intended it as a name.)

And here is her response:

> Dear Jan/Tzivi,
>
> How clever of you to notice such a small, but important detail… In Tevye's case, the word "yente" is really idiomatic, not a busybody, tattle-tale or snoop so much as a slightly pejorative term for a woman. The word "**dame**" comes to mind. I hope this is helpful.
>
> Zay gezunt,
>
> Aliza

So here is the surprising "final answer" to my question "Who first used the name Yente as a noun?" The answer is Sholem Aleichem, and the context makes it clear that it did not have the meaning it has today. If anything, way back in 1895, Sholem Aleichem meant it as an ironic honorific.

My gut tells me that if we knew more about Yente Abramovitsh (beyond just her photo), then we would enjoy Sholem Aleichem's wordplay all the more. However, for now, the mental image of Bea Arthur promenading through town as the "grand dame" of Anatevka will certainly do. Pearls! Pearls!!

How did Joe Stein know?

QUESTION 5: WHY NOT SHAKESPEARE'S *KING LEAR*?

On August 18, 2011, I was at Northbrook Public Library (located in one of Chicago's posh northern suburbs), speaking in front of my largest crowd to date. While it was the third in my series of presentations for the Chicago YIVO Society's Summer Festival of Yiddish Culture, it was my first time at NPL, so many people there were hearing me speak about *Fiddler on the Roof* for the first time.

I began my presentation "Hodel: From Sofievka to Siberia" with a bang:

> "Who is the main character in *Fiddler on the Roof*?" I asked. "I won't blame you if you say 'Tevye,' but today I am going to make the case that the main character in *Fiddler on the Roof* is actually Hodel. Yes, I am talking about Tevye's second daughter, Hodel, the one who marries Perchik-the-Revolutionary and goes to Siberia. And no, I am not kidding."

Suffice it to say that the Q&A after my presentation was very stimulating.

One year later, on August 7, 2012, I returned to NPL to present "Tevye's Daughters: From Chawton to Broadway" (making this the fourth in what eventually became a six-part series of annual lectures for the Chicago YIVO Society). Once again, the audience response was quite lively, and most of the comments I received on my feedback form were positive. Answers to the question "Which aspects of this presentation were most interesting to you?" elicited the following written feedback:

- The connection between the stories of Jane Austen and Sholem Aleichem.
- The musical *First Impressions*.
- I didn't expect *Pride and Prejudice* or *Downton Abbey*!
- Never heard of *First Impressions*.

Answers to the question "Which aspects of *Fiddler on the Roof* do you think I should pay more attention to in the future?" included:

- I thoroughly enjoyed the presentation.
- None. You understand all the nuances.
- You have covered it all!

Nevertheless, one gentleman in the audience looked visibly distressed, so I called on him first when I began the Q&A. "Why aren't you talking about *King Lear*," he sputtered. "King Lear had daughters too!"

I was frankly blindsided. King Lear definitely did have daughters, so why had I never considered **them** before?

The truth is that I had begun thinking of Hodel as the main female character in *Fiddler on the Roof* quite early in my research, and the arc of the Elizabeth Bennet character in *Pride and Prejudice* had always been a critical part of my rationale.

When I took my first writing course in 2002, I used my weekly deadlines to produce the first of several book proposals. The result was a 42-page outline called "*Fiddler on the Roof*: Sources & Synergies (A 40th Anniversary Celebration)."

Once my instructor considered my outline "done," I mailed it out to several contacts for feedback. This was the point at which I was told that even with the best book proposal in the history of Planet Earth, an unknown author had zero chance of being published unless she had a strong "platform."

Since it was already May 2003, I moved my target date for publication from **2004** (the year of the 40th anniversary of the first Broadway performance) to **2014** (the year of the 50th anniversary of the first Broadway performance). Knowing that this 50th anniversary would be the Golden Anniversary, I told myself the timing would be that much more auspicious.

Then I set about building a platform based on a Venn diagram which depicted my target market as the "sweet spot" where Women, Jews, and Broadway Aficionados overlapped—a target market already known to be especially sweet for people who sell books.

This diligently built platform now includes:

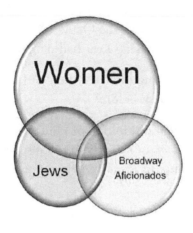

© Jan Lisa Huttner (2003)

- Regular columns for the *JUF News*, *World Jewish Digest*, WomenArts, etc.
- Features in the *Forward*, *Jewish Film World*, etc.
- Guest posts on *Huffington Post*, *Women's eNews*, etc.
- Dozens of presentations (including all of the lectures on *Fiddler on the Roof* in this current compilation).

I also built an active presence on Facebook, started several blogs, and joined relevant professional organizations (including the National Federation of Press Women and the International Women's Writing Guild) and numerous online groups (including the American Jewish Press Association and the Association for Jewish Theatre). Now that I live in Brooklyn, I am a member of multiple organizations (including the Center for Jewish History and JCC Manhattan) where I go several times each month to attend lectures.

Eventually I sent newly revised proposals to various agents (and others), but as the years passed, the publishing business continued to deteriorate. Many neighborhood bookstores have since closed, no shopping malls are anchored by a Borders Books anymore, media companies are in freefall, and here we are.

Now back to Hodel and Elizabeth Bennet.

What Did I Know and When Did I Know It?

Here is what I said in my **2003** outline:

Who is Hodel?

In the Rabinowitz version, Hodel is Tevye's second daughter out of seven. She makes minor appearances in the first three chapters, plays the central role in the fourth chapter, and then disappears. There is no Hodel character in the Schwartz version. In the Perl version, however, she has a through-line, that is, she is an important character in both acts. During Act One, Scene 2, Hodel is the one who tells Tevya that Tzeitel does not want to marry Lazar, and she is the one who argues that Tzeitel should have the right to veto the match. In Act Two, she meets, falls in love with, and marries Perchik, and then she follows him to Siberia.

In the Robbins version, Tevye has five and only five daughters: Tzeitel, Hodel, Chava, Shprintze, and Bielke. Hodel is the second of the five daughters, and she is clearly her father's favorite. She is the focal female character in *Fiddler on the Roof*, and the climax of Joseph Stein's libretto comes when she has to explain to her beloved father, Tevye, why she is leaving home to follow Perchik to Siberia.

THE MAIN CHARACTERS				
Version One = Rabinowitz Version	Version Two = Schwartz Version	Version Three = Perl Version	**Version Four** = **Robbins Version**	Version Five = Jewison Version
TEVYE THE DAIRYMAN	*TEVYA*	*TEVYA & HIS DAUGHTERS*	*FIDDLER ON THE ROOF*	*FIDDLER ON THE ROOF*
Tevye	Tevya	Tevya	**Tevye**	Tevye
Golde	Goldie	Golde	**Golde**	Golde
Tsaytl	Zeitel	Tzeitl	**Tzeitel**	Tzeitel
Hodl	N/A	Hodel	**Hodel**	Hodel
Chava	Khave	Chava	**Chava**	Chava
Motl	N/A	Mottel	**Motel**	Motel
Pertchik	N/A	Feferal	**Perchik**	Perchik
Chvedka	Fedya	Fedka	**Fyedka**	Fyedka

NOTE: Since Yiddish uses Hebrew characters, there are no proscribed English transliterations. For example, Tevye's eldest daughter appears as "Tsaytl" in Hillel Halkin's translation of *Tevye the Dairyman*, but as "Tzeitel" in Joseph Stein's libretto for *Fiddler on the Roof*. For the sake of consistency, I will always use the Stein spellings as they appear in the Robbins Version.

© Jan Lisa Huttner (2003)

In fact, the way Stein develops the Hodel character bears striking parallels to one of literature's favorite heroines: Miss Elizabeth Bennet of *Pride and Prejudice*. Was this a deliberate choice on Stein's part? I haven't found anything in the literature to support this claim yet, however, we can be sure he was familiar with *Pride and Prejudice*. It was made into a very popular film by George Cukor in 1940, and the musical version—*First Impressions*—opened on Broadway in 1959.

Regardless of Stein's conscious intentions, I believe that the similarities between Stein's Hodel character and Austen's Elizabeth Bennet character help to explain why so many **women** were immediately drawn to *Fiddler on the Roof* despite the negative reviews of the early critics (every one of whom was male)…

Hodel and Perchik obtain Tevye's blessing on their union, then Perchik leaves for Kiev where he is arrested in a demonstration. Learning that he will be sent to Siberia, Hodel packs and Teyve takes her to the train station. The emotional climax of the Robbins version comes here at the train station, when Hodel tries to explain to Tevye **why** she is going so "Far From the Home I Love."

Hodel makes two critical points in her "big solo number." **Point One**: Hodel is making a conscious decision to leave the familiar little world of Anatevka. No one is forcing her to do this. She is not Perchik's wife yet. She could send him a "Dear John" letter, blame her parents, or find some way out of her engagement if she really wanted to do so. But she goes because she wants to go. Why? **Point Two**: The very meaning of the word "home" has changed for her.

So Hodel is the first Anatevkan to leave Anatevka. She does so voluntarily; there is no edict from the Czar forcing Hodel out. She goes to build a new life and a new family with her mate of choice. Why? Because "there with my love I'm **home**."

Elizabeth Bennet does the same thing. When *Pride and Prejudice* ends, it is easy to imagine Jane Bennet and Charles Bingley as a married couple with children, happily socializing with Mr. and Mrs. Bennet on a routine basis. But you can be sure that visits from Elizabeth and Fitzwilliam Darcy will be few and far between. Elizabeth is moving to a new world; she is moving into Mr. Darcy's world. The rest of the Bennets (save the new Mrs. Bingley, of course) will be hard pressed to follow her there.

This pattern, women leaving their birth homes to marry their mates of choice and establish new families of their own, is also a core feature of the American identity. We are a nation of migrants. We move from other countries when we first come to America, and then we move on to "greener pastures" within the USA whenever the spirit moves us.

This pattern was particularly prevalent in the 1950s, when returning soldiers used the GI Bill to obtain a professional education and then move their families to newly-built suburbs. I doubt there is a woman in any *Fiddler on the Roof* audience who is not moved to tears when Hodel tells her beloved father: "There where my heart has settled long ago I must go, I must go. Who could imagine I'd be wand'ring so far from the home I love? Yet, there with my love, I'm home."

In her 1995 introduction to The Modern Library edition of *Pride and Prejudice*, Anna Quindlen writes: "She [Jane Austen] wrote not of war and peace, but of men, money, and marriage, the battlefield for women of her day and, surely, of our own... but *Pride and Prejudice* is also about that thing that all great novels consider, **the search for self**. And it is the first great novel to teach us that that search is as surely undertaken in the drawing room making small talk as in the pursuit of a great white whale."

In *Fiddler on the Roof*, the person making this journey from "member of the chorus" (during the Musical-Prologue "Tradition") to "psychological individual" (at the train station) is Hodel. Psychological individuality—with freedom of choice and conscience—this is one of our highest American values, and yet, it often comes at the cost of community bonds. Our Founders were profoundly wise men. They promised us "life, liberty, and the **pursuit** of happiness;" they never promised us happiness itself.

Now Back to 2016

Even all these years later—from 2003 to 2016—I would not change any of this. Quite the contrary, my convictions when describing Hodel as a "psychological individual" have grown ever stronger based on additional textual analysis and evidence in books that were not even available when I first began my research way back when.

Yes, Mr. Bennet has five daughters and Tevye also has five daughters, but it is more than that. Each one of these daughters has a specific **arc**, and I am fascinated by the parallels between the various internal components of my two chosen texts.

In both cases, the first daughter makes the most conventional marriage. In *Pride and Prejudice*, Jane Bennet marries Charles Bingley, and in *Fiddler on the Roof*, Tzeitel marries Motel-the-Tailor. Regardless of the obstacles which confront these two pairs of lovers along the way, in neither case is their eventual union a stretch. They are as well-matched in social status as they are in temperament.

On the other hand, Lydia Bennet's marriage to George Wickham and Chava's marriage to Fyedka-the-Russian are both covert and problematic. Both sets of parents have literally lost sight of their daughters, and they do not even know where they are. In both cases, the parents only learn about their daughters' marriages after they have already been consummated. Then, each bride is exiled by her family, and it is not clear—in context—if either of these daughters will ever see her parents again.

Note that in *Fiddler on the Roof*, Chava is the third daughter out of five, whereas in *Pride and Prejudice*, Lydia is the fifth and final daughter. But given that the two remaining daughters—Mary and Kitty in *Pride and Prejudice*, and Shprintze and Bielke in *Fiddler on the Roof*—play relatively marginal roles in each text, I think this is a minor point.

However, in both *Pride and Prejudice* and *Fiddler on the Roof*, a skeptical father is completely won over by the rationale of a daughter who may be second in birth, but is certainly first in his heart.

"Well, my dear," said Mr. Bennet when Lizzy ceased speaking, "I have no more to say. If this be the case, he deserves you. I could not have parted with you, my Lizzy, to anyone less worthy."

(Austen, Page 273)

Tevye (to Hodel at the train station): "Well, give him my regards, this Moses of yours. I always thought he was a good man. Tell him I rely on his honor to treat my daughter well. Tell him that."

(Stein, Page 124)

Suffice it to say that none of these internal dynamics have any parallels whatsoever in *King Lear*, so I am not the least bit concerned about the invocation of *King Lear* as a challenge to my analysis. And yet, the fact that a man in my audience became so visibly agitated about this does lead me to wonder anew about why no one else has ever recognized any of these plot points, which were—and still are—so obvious to me.

Thinking back on that day at Northbrook Public Library, I realize now that the women in my audience were simply much more familiar with specific *Pride and Prejudice* characters than the men were. While Jane Austen novels are still considered "classics" in polite society, my guess is that (with the advent of "Chick Lit," "Chick Flicks," and similar diminutives) fewer men embrace her work now than they did in the past. In my experience, women flock to updates likes *Bridget Jones's Diary* and *Bride and Prejudice*, whereas men seek reasons to steer clear. Even my own husband, married to **me** for over 30 years now, was happy to send me off to *Bridget Jones's Baby* in the company of a gal pal.

Looking through the indexes of the books on my shelf about Sholem Aleichem, I see that almost all of them mention Charles Dickens and Mark Twain, but not one of them mentions Jane Austen.

This includes books by the following male authors:

- Jeremy Dauber
- Gennady Estraikh
- David Roskies

And also includes books by the following female authors:

- Barbara Isenberg

- Anita Norich

- Alisa Solomon

And, sadly, it even includes the book simply called *Sholom Aleichem* by Frances and Joseph Butwin, as well as *My Father, Sholom Aleichem* by Marie Waife-Goldberg.

However, at this point, I am not only convinced that Joseph Stein had *Pride and Prejudice* at the back of his mind when he wrote his libretto for *Fiddler on the Roof*, I am also convinced that Sholem Aleichem incorporated elements of *Pride and Prejudice* into his Tevye stories too.

Consider the implications of this quote from *Jane's Fame: How Jane Austen Conquered the World* by Claire Harman (published in the United States in 2009):

> Even farther away, in Russia, Austen's novels were becoming known without any translation. The author would have been amazed to hear that as early as June 1816, an article in a Russian journal praising contemporary English women novelists singled out the anonymous author of *Emma* for her successful "pictures of quiet family life." And though there is no direct evidence that Alexander Pushkin ever read *Pride and Prejudice,* the similarities between the novel and his masterpiece *Eugene Onegin* (published in serial form between 1825 and 1832), have convinced several critics that he knew the book very well, perhaps in one of its early French versions. (Harman, Page 74)

Now remember that Sholem Aleichem (the author) was actually a man named Solomon Rabinowitz who had four daughters and one female ward, as well as a wife who loved literature. In this house filled with women who were all educated and well-read, can it possibly be that he had never heard the name Elizabeth Bennet? I doubt it!

And here is another tantalizing snippet from an Israeli novel called *Valley of Strength*. The main character is a young Jewish woman named Fania who flees to Palestine (which, in the late 19th century, was a province in the Ottoman Empire) after a pogrom in Russia destroys her home.

"Are you new to Safed?" asked the doctor.

"I'm from Rosh Pinnah. I see you have a fine library. May I take a look?"

"By all means! But the books are in English."

"Jane Austen is my favorite!" cried Fania in an emotional voice, clasping her hands over her heart, to the utter amazement of the doctor.

"Dickens, I love too," she added hastily, her eyes flashing. "I've read *David Copperfield* three times. But Jane Austen is the best of them all." (Lapid, Page 213)

And We End Where It All Begins

Finally, I return once again to the five daughters of Zelophehad. When I published *Tevye's Daughters: No Laughing Matter* in 2014 (fondly referred to as "the appetizer course"), I asserted with conviction that both Jane Austen and Solomon Rabinowitz had read their Bible cover to cover, so they surely knew the passages about the daughters of Zelophehad in the Book of Numbers. I asserted this—on page 29—but I did not have any proof.

Now I do.

In the course of preparing *Diamond Fiddler* for publication, I went back to all my source texts to validate my quotes. And so I dutifully went back to Leviant's *From the Fair: The Autobiography of Sholom Aleichem*, and when I did—lo and behold—I found this:

"Listen here, young fellow, let me ask you something," old Loyev sang out. "My son tells me that you're just as knowledgeable in our holy Jewish books as in their secular ones. Do you remember what Rashi says about the daughters of Zelophehad?"

Then commenced a long-winded discussion on Rashi. And Rashi led to the Talmud. At which followed a learned disquisition about scholarship and Haskala, as is usual among Jews who are at home in all the commentaries. This caused a sensation, a furor so great that old man Loyev placed his hand on Sholom's shoulders...

(Leviant, Pages 231-232)

Sure enough, Rashi does have many interesting points to make about the Daughters of Zelophehad in his extensive commentary on the Book of

Numbers. Not coincidentally, Rashi was the father of three daughters—Miriam, Rachel, and Yocheved—but no sons. These three women are all said to have been educated by their famous father, and Ashkenazi lore tells us they all married scholars, and gave birth to even more scholars. "Rashi's Daughters" even have their own Wikipedia entry: "These women married three of their father's finest students and were the mothers of the leaders of the next generation of French Talmudic scholars."

I wonder now if Solomon Rabinowitz and Elimelech Loyev really talked about the Daughters of Zelophehad on the momentous day when they first met one another. After all, by the time he wrote *From the Fair*, Rabinowitz was an old man writing about something that had happened decades before.

By that time, of course, Rabinowitz had long since become the father of four daughters (and had also been responsible for the dowry of his ward). In those same years, Rabinowitz had also created a character named Tevye who started out with seven daughters, but in the end, he only ended up writing stories for five of them.

Maybe Soloman Rabinowitz and Elimelech Loyev—his future father-in-law—did discuss Rashi's commentary on the Daughters of Zelophehad that day, maybe not. Regardless, the man who wrote the Tevye stories certainly refers to the Daughters of Zelophehad—by name—when recounting a pivotal moment in his own life, and that is all I need to know.

One last question: Why are the Daughters of Zelophehad so obscure now, especially given the ever-growing set of books and articles about Jane Austen? I give a feminist explanation in *Tevye's Daughters: No Laughing Matter*, but I also think there is a simple answer too.

Who was the person who built the ark? Ninety-nine percent of English speakers will say "Noah." Even if they know nothing else about the Hebrew Bible, they know—for sure—that Noah built the ark. Even so, they are wrong.

Look at the Hebrew text and you will see that the person who built the ark was actually "No'akh."

Put two people named "Noah" in the King James Bible? This must have caused considerable heartburn for the 15th century [male] scholars who slaved over the first translation. Best to get rid of one of them. Let Noah be the guy

עֵץ חַיִּים

ETZ HAYIM

TORAH AND COMMENTARY

NOAH

נח

9This is the line of Noah.—Noah was a righteous man; he was blameless in his age; Noah walked with God.—10Noah begot three sons: Shem, Ham, and Japheth. 11The earth became corrupt before God; the earth was filled with lawlessness. 12When God

⁹ אֵלֶּה תּוֹלְדֹת נֹחַ נֹחַ אִישׁ צַדִּיק תָּמִים הָיָה בְּדֹרֹתָיו אֶת־הָאֱלֹהִים הִתְהַלֶּךְ־נֹחַ: ¹⁰ וַיּוֹלֶד נֹחַ שְׁלֹשָׁה בָנִים אֶת־שֵׁם אֶת־חָם וְאֶת־יָפֶת: ¹¹ וַתִּשָּׁחֵת הָאָרֶץ לִפְנֵי הָאֱלֹהִים וַתִּמָּלֵא

NOAH AND THE FLOOD (6:9–9:17)

NUMBERS 27:2 PINHAS

במדבר כז פינחס 926

nassite family—son of Hepher son of Gilead son of Machir son of Manasseh son of Joseph—came forward. The names of the daughters were Mahlah, Noah, Hoglah, Milcah, and Tirzah. 2They stood before Moses, Eleazar the priest, the chieftains, and the whole assembly, at the entrance of the Tent of Meeting, and they said, 3"Our father died in the wilderness. He was not one of the faction, Korah's faction, which banded together against the LORD, but died for his own sin; and he has left no sons. 4Let not our father's name be lost to his clan just because

בֶּן־גִּלְעָד בֶּן־מָכִיר בֶּן־מְנַשֶּׁה לְמִשְׁפְּחֹת מְנַשֶּׁה בֶן־יוֹסֵף וְאֵלֶּה שְׁמוֹת בְּנֹתָיו מַחְלָה נֹעָה וְחָגְלָה וּמִלְכָּה וְתִרְצָה: ² וַתַּעֲמֹדְנָה לִפְנֵי מֹשֶׁה וְלִפְנֵי אֶלְעָזָר הַכֹּהֵן וְלִפְנֵי הַנְּשִׂיאִם וְכָל־הָעֵדָה פֶּתַח אֹהֶל־מוֹעֵד לֵאמֹר: ³ אָבִינוּ מֵת בַּמִּדְבָּר וְהוּא לֹא־הָיָה בְּתוֹךְ הָעֵדָה הַנּוֹעָדִים עַל־יְהוָה בַּעֲדַת־קֹרַח כִּי־בְחֶטְאוֹ מֵת וּבָנִים לֹא־הָיוּ לוֹ: ⁴ לָמָּה יִגָּרַע שֵׁם־אָבִינוּ

In modern Hebrew, the letter Hey can appear in three forms:

ה ה ה
Book Print | Manual Print | Cursive

In modern Hebrew, the letter Chet can appear in three forms:

ח ח ח
Book Print | Manual Print | Cursive

© The Jewish Publication Society (1999)

who built the ark. Who cares about No'ah, the second daughter of some guy named Zelophehad, anyway?

Answer? Me!

249

QUESTION 6: WHAT ABOUT THE GUYS?

When a publicist from Troika Tours contacted the *JUF News* in March, 2009, to tell us that "Topol's Farewell Tour" was on its way to Chicago in June, I asked for their full list of tour dates. Then I called my cousins in Florida and we bought tickets for a performance in April, so we could all go together. The publicist was thrilled. She sent a press kit, and promised to arrange interviews for me. The *JUF News* editors wanted everything ready well before my deadline in mid-May to accommodate their print publication date on June 1.

By that time, of course, I had been working on *Fiddler on the Roof* for close to a decade. I had already seen Theodore Bikel at the Oriental Theatre in Chicago, Alfred Molina and Harvey Fierstein at the Minskoff Theatre on Broadway, and a host of less-famous Tevyes at various local venues.

Add in the fact that I was no fan of Norman Jewison's screen adaptation (in which Chaim Topol had so memorably starred as Tevye almost four decades earlier), and I will admit to going into the Kravis Center for the Performing Arts in West Palm Beach on April 15, 2009, with a bias.

Kravis Center for Performing Arts
© Frances Gragg (2009)

But to my great surprise, Chaim Topol's stage performance won me over completely. "Topol is terrific!" I wrote in my June '09 column for the *JUF News*.

Age and experience have made Chaim Topol a true ensemble player. Although he has warm moments of genuine connection with almost every character in the huge cast, two relationships stand out. Erik Liberman is one of the best Motel-the-Tailors I've ever seen anywhere. "Every night, I get to grow from boy to man to mensch," Liberman told me when we chatted on the phone, "and every Jew in the audience will know what that means." Eric Van Tielen is also an exceptionally strong Fyed-ka-the-Russian, literally demanding that Tevye embrace him man-to-man when they dance together at the inn.

To be totally honest, I had never been much of a Motel fan before. Since one of my major complaints about the film is that Norman Jewison eliminated the song "Now I Have Every-thing," no one should be surprised by this point to hear me describe myself as a "Perchik Girl."

So I am grateful to Erik Liberman for opening my eyes, and forcing me to take a fresh look at Motel-the-Tailor. And Liber-man was just as good the second time when I saw the Troika production of *Fiddler on the Roof* at Chicago's Ford Center for the Performing Arts on June 14.

I have no doubt that early *Fiddler on the Roof* audiences understood that Perchik-the-Revolutionary was Tevye's favorite son-in-law. Joseph Stein clearly sets Perchik up as the primary agent of change in his libretto, giving him lines like in Act One, Scene 2: "Girls should learn too. Girls are people." and in Act One, Scene 6: "Congratulations, Tzeitel, for getting a rich man." (Stein's stage directions specify that this line is "sarcastic.")

In Act One, Scene 10, Perchik pulls down the mechitzah—the barrier between the men and the women—at Tzeitel's wedding so he can dance with Hodel, and in the final moments of Act One he is "hit with a club," after he "grapples" with the Russian who "throws the wedding-gift candle-sticks to the ground" during the pogrom.

Even after he knows that Perchik has defied him by refusing to ask his permission to marry Hodel (although Perchik does ask Tevye for his blessing), Tevye still tells Golde in Act Two, Scene 1: "He is a little crazy, but I like him." And when he is saying goodbye to Hodel at the train station in Act Two, Scene 3, Tevye says:

> Well, give him my regards, this **Moses** of yours. I always thought he was a good man. Tell him I rely on his honor to treat my daughter well. Tell him that.

Sheldon Harnick also gives Perchik a musical boost with his lyrics. Perchik not only has a duet with Hodel in Act Two, Scene 1 ("Now I Have Everything"), which expresses the Freudian ideal of a love and a work, but Harnick also has Hodel wish for him in Act One, Scene 1. She sings the words "For Papa, make him a scholar" in "Matchmaker," and, like magic, Perchik—a scholar!—appears at the dinner table in Act One, Scene 3. Tevye—her Papa—has invited Perchik into their home to spend the Sabbath, and the moment they are introduced, Hodel and Perchik lock eyes.

There is also no doubt that Jerome Robbins intended all of this. In his personal notes (which I have read with my own eyes at the Library for the Performing Arts at Lincoln Center), Robbins specifically invokes Mississippi Freedom Summer. And as Alisa Solomon writes in *Wonder of Wonders: A Cultural History of* Fiddler on the Roof:

> Frustrated and searching for a way to make [Bert] Convy understand Perchik's revolutionary zeal, Robbins told him—only a month after the murders of James Chaney, Andrew Goodman, and Michael Schwerner—to imagine that he was a student on his way to Mississippi to assist with voter registration. "You are not going to Coney Island for a ride on the Ferris wheel," Robbins prodded. "You are going on a dangerous mission [Robbins said in reference to Act Two, Scene 1]. That's the urgency I want to feel in this scene." (Solomon, Page 194)

Then along comes Norman Jewison, and not only is the song "Now I Have Everything" eliminated, but so is the Moses reference. Tevye no longer tells Hodel that he "always thought Perchik was a good man." Tevye no longer instructs Hodel to "Tell Perchik I rely on his **honor** to treat my daughter well."

Who benefits from all these changes, which surely must be considered minor by those who believe that the screen version is "elaborately faithful" to the stage version? Motel-the-Tailor!

When the 1965 Tony Award nominations were announced, acting nominations went to Zero Mostel for his performance as Tevye and Maria Karnilova for her performance as Golde. The night of the Tony Awards, Mostel was named Best Actor in a Musical, and Karnilova was named Best Featured Actress in a Musical.

On the other hand, when the 1972 Oscar nominations were announced, acting nominations went to Chaim Topol for his performance as Tevye (Best Actor in a Leading Role) and Leonard Frey for his performance as Motel (Best Actor in a Supporting Role). In the event, Gene Hackman won the Best Actor Oscar for his role in *The French Connection* and Ben Johnson won the Best Supporting Actor Oscar for his role in *The Last Picture Show*. But as the cliché goes "it's an honor just to be nominated," and in 1972, the Oscar honors went to the actors—both men—who played Tevye and Motel.

None of the actresses, not even beloved Molly Picon—who was the best-known member of the entire cast at that time—rated a mention, even though the film itself received eight nominations (including Best Picture) and won three (albeit all in technical categories). In fact, no women at all were nominated for Oscars for their work on the film adaptation of *Fiddler on the Roof*, not even the costume designers—Joan Bridge and Elizabeth Haffenden—even though costume designer Patricia Zipprodt was one of the Tony winners in 1965.

Since 1972, Motel-the-Tailor has typically been Tevye's most privileged son-in-law on stage as well. While the 2004 Broadway revival received six nominations, the only nominations in any of the four acting categories went to Alfred Molina (Best Actor in a Musical) and John Cariani (Best Actor in a Supporting Role). Me? I thought Robert Petkoff was superb as Perchik, whereas Cariani's Motel was only so-so. I invite you to listen to the 2004 cast album and judge for yourself.

When the media blitz for the 2015 Broadway revival began, Adam Kantor's name was everywhere, and his performance as Motel-the-Tailor was mentioned in almost every subsequent review. On the other hand, when Ben Rappaport was cast as Perchik, it barely registered. Perchik was one of the last major parts to be announced, almost as an afterthought. I invite you to buy the 2015 cast album and hear for yourself how "Now I Have Everything" was truncated in that production.

"Now I Have Everything"			
PERCHIK	**HODEL**	**WHERE**	**WHEN**
2:03	Convy	Migenes	Broadway	1964
2:57	**Petkoff**	**Kelly**	**Broadway**	**2004**
2:05	Humbley	Silber	London	2007
1:55	Rappaport	Massell	Broadway	2015
2:08	Petkoff	Kelly	Broadway	2004A
0:49	Petkoff	Kelly	Broadway	2004B

NOTES: In 1964, the only song under two minutes was "The Rumor" (1:51). In 2004, a lovely reprise was added to "Now I Have Everything" which brought it up to 2:57, and also closed the character arc by adding a few notes from "Matchmaker" at the end, thus reminding us that Hodel had said "for Papa, make him a scholar" just before Perchik appeared onstage. But in 2015, it became the shortest song on the CD. Of course, it is not on the movie soundtrack at all because Jewison deleted it.

© Jan Lisa Huttner (2016)

All that said, however, when I watched Erik Liberman's performance for the second time at Chicago's Ford Center for the Performing Arts (two months after our phone interview in West Palm Beach), I realized that he had hit the nail right on the head. In the course of every performance, Motel-the-Tailor does indeed grow from boy to man to **mensch** (which, as Wikipedia tells us, is used in Yiddish to signify that the person is a "**person of integrity and honor, someone to admire and emulate**"), and every Jew in the audience **does** know what that means.

Motel-the-Tailor is a loveable character, and we should cherish the pleasure of his acquaintance regardless of the fact that Norman Jewison dissed Perchik onscreen in order to elevate him. Certainly, I have watched all the subsequent Motels I have seen on stage with more appreciation, even though I am still (and will always be) a "Perchik Girl."

"We gave each other our pledge."

Why is Motel always hanging around Tevye's place anyway? When he shows up for dinner on Shabbat, why does Golde simply set a place for him as if she had been half expecting him all along? Put another way, why isn't Motel—an unmarried, unattached bachelor—spending the Sabbath with his own family? The only one who questions his status in Tevye's household is Yente. ("What does that poor little tailor, Motel, want with Tzeitel?")

In the Rabinowitz version, we learn that Motel has a legitimate place within Tevye's family. When Tevye is telling Golde about his dream, he reports the following conversation with the ghost of Golde's Grandma Tzeitel:

> "Mazel tov!" she says to me. "I'm so pleased to hear that you've chosen a fine young man for your Tzeitel, your eldest daughter who's named for me. He's called Motel Kamzoil, after my **cousin** Mordechai, and he's an excellent fellow, even if he is a tailor…"
> (Halkin, Page 51)

Arnold Perl repeats this reference to "Mordechai" (elevating him in the process from "cousin" with a small "c" to "Uncle" with a capital "U") in his stage play *Tevya's Daughters* :

> Tevye: Listen, your grandmother says, Motel Kamzoil is named for **Uncle** Mordechai. It's a sign he'll make Tzeitel a good husband…
> Golde: After all, since he's named for my **Uncle** Mordechai…
> (Perl, Page 26)

The Robbins version has great fun with this relationship in the wonderful lyrics Sheldon Harnick wrote for Grandma Tzeitel in "Tevye's Dream":

> A worthy boy is he,
> Of pious family.
> They named him after my
> Dear **Uncle** Mordechai,
> The tailor Motel Kamzoil.
> (Harnick & Bock, Page 74)

In *Fiddler on the Roof*, the character of Motel's mother Shandel gets exactly one line of dialogue in each of three widely-dispersed crowd scenes. In the wedding scene, Stein also writes stage directions for her ("Motel enters, followed by his **parents** and relations."), but he does not give these characters any dialogue. Also, there are no other references, either explicit or implicit, to Motel's father. And when Mordcha-the-Innkeeper is describing the gifts at the reception, there do not appear to be any gifts from anyone in Motel's family.

In the context of the Robbins version, I think Motel is meant to be thought of as someone who has lost his father. Since he is a cousin, Tevye and Golde have semi-adopted him. He has the run of their house. When he shows up, they feed him. Before they learn otherwise, they think of him simply as one of "the kids."

So when Motel asserts himself by asking for Tzeitel's hand in marriage, Tevye initially responds by treating him like a kid. That is why Tevye's comment to the audience ("He's beginning to talk like a man.") signals the turning point in his decision process. Maybe Tevye never thought of Motel as a husband for Tzeitel, but, just as Erik Liberman says, Motel becomes a man right before our eyes precisely because Tevye is seeing Motel as "a man" for the very first time.

As Tevye tells Golde later (speaking to her through the voice of Grandma Tzeitel):

> For such a match I prayed.
> In heaven it was made.
> A fine upstanding boy,
> A comfort and a joy,
> The tailor Motel Kamzoil.
> (Harnick & Bock, Page 75)

By the end of the Robbins version, Motel has validated Tevye's faith in him. He tells Golde with confidence: "We'll all be together soon. Motel, Tzeitel and the baby, they'll come too, you'll see. That Motel is a **person**."

Now, think how different this final scene would have played out if, in fact, Tzeitel had married Lazar Wolf-the-Butcher.

Golde let Yente talk her into this match—even though they both knew that Tevye did not like Lazar Wolf—because Lazar Wolf was one of the richest men in Anatevka. And Tevye agreed to go along with the match—even though he had no respect for Lazar Wolf—because: "with a butcher, my daughter surely will never know hunger."

And yet, by the end of *Fiddler on the Roof*, when Lazar Wolf says goodbye to Tevye on his way out of town, his wealth has been reduced to the contents of one suitcase. Furthermore, Lazar Wolf's destination is even flimsier than Tevye's. With no relatives of his own, his only plan is to go to America and throw himself on the mercy of one of Fruma Sarah's brothers. (Remember Fruma Sarah? Lazar Wolf's ferocious wife of Blessed Memory?) So assuming Tzeitel and Lazar Wolf even made it all the way to Chicago, what good would a butcher shop in Anatevka have been to Tzeitel once she was actually there?

> (Lazar enters, carrying a large suitcase.)
>
> **Lazar**: Well, Tevye, I'm on my way.
> **Tevye**: Where are you going?
> **Lazar**: Chicago. In America. My wife, Fruma Sarah,
> may she rest in peace, has a brother there.
> **Tevye**: That's nice.
> **Lazar**: I hate him, but a relative is a relative! (*They embrace.*)
> **Lazar**: Goodbye, Tevye.   (Stein, Pages 148-149)

These are the fates that Joseph Stein decreed. This is how he—and Jerome Robbins—chose to end the Tzeitel/Motel/Lazar Wolf character arcs in *Fiddler on the Roof* (even though these are very different from the futures Sholem Aleichem had envisioned for them). Had she become Lazar Wolf's wife, Tzeitel would likely have grown old hungry for both love as well as food. But married to Motel-the-Tailor, she at least she has a companion in life and they both know "what everything's for."

Before we leave Motel-the-Tailor and move on to Fyedka-the-Russian, I would like to point out another "little tweak" I really liked in the much-maligned 2004 Broadway revival of *Fiddler on the Roof*. The group leaving under Motel's wing at the very end had three members rather than two: Tzeitel, their baby, and Motel's mother Shandel.

I wish more directors would emulate this subtle but significant addition. First, it helps the audience understand why Tzeitel and Motel cannot go to America right away with Tevye and the rest of the family. Motel needs enough money for three passages (for his mother, his wife, and himself), and that is a lot of money for a young tailor. Second, wrapping up this one loose end makes Motel even more menschlikh, and no one in the audience needs to worry about the fate of his widowed mother Shandel.

> **Tevye:** Work hard, Motel. Come to us soon.
> **Motel:** I will, Reb Tevye. I'll work hard.
>
> (Stein, Page 152)

"A bird may love a fish, but where will they live?"

Time has been very kind to Motel-the-Tailor. And time has also been kind to Fyedka-the-Russian, but for very different reasons.

As I have explained it above, Motel is a suitable husband for Tzeitel in *Fiddler on the Roof* in part because he has always been a member of the family anyway. At the start of Act One, Tevye and Golde basically consider him just another one of "the kids," often underfoot and always at the table whenever dinner is about to be served on Shabbat.

> **Tevye** (to Perchik): I have five pleasant daughters. This is mine… this is mine… this is mine… this is mine… this is mine… (*Motel enters. Tevye almost kisses him in sequence.*) This is **not** mine. Perchik, this is Motel Kamzoil and he is…
> **Golde:** Motel, you're also eating with us? (*Motel gestures, "Yes, if I may."*) Of course, another blessing. (Stein, Pages 32–33)

But by the end of Act Two, Motel has come into his own, and Tevye accords him recognition not just as a man but as a mensch.

> **Tevye** (to Golde): We'll all be together soon. Motel, Tzeitel and the baby, they'll come too, you'll see. That Motel is a **person**.
>
> (Stein, Page 147)

As Erik Liberman points out, when Tevye says this to Golde, every Jew in the audience knows what he means because the word "person" is used here with the meaning "person of integrity and honor" (the words used on Wikipedia to define "mensch").

In the case of Perchik, Tevye always knows that Perchik is a suitable husband for Hodel because when he enters the action, he is the answer to a prayer. Hodel asks for a scholar in Act One, Scene 1 at the start of "Matchmaker," because she knows that is what Tevye wants for her. ("For Papa, make him a scholar.")

When Perchik arrives in Anatevka in the very next scene—already on the run from his nefarious activities in Kiev—Tevye is eager to embrace him. Even though his neighbors are wary of Perchik, the minute he hears that this talkative stranger is a "student," Tevye invites Perchik into his home to spend the Sabbath (a home in which there are five unmarried daughters).

In the next scene (Act One, Scene 3), when Perchik—with whom Hodel immediately begins to banter—says of her: "Your daughter has a quick and witty tongue," Tevye takes this as flattery: "The wit she gets from me." Then, after Golde snaps at him, Tevye adds: "The tongue she gets from her mother."

Perhaps Golde interjects herself at this point simply because she is in a rush to get everyone to the dinner table so she can light the Shabbat candles? But maybe she is on the alert—mentally chewing on Yente's warning about Motel—so she senses the danger in adding another penniless young man to her family circle? Regardless, the die is already cast. Even after Hodel and Perchik defy him by planning to marry without his permission, Tevye still says to Golde:

> He's a good man, Golde, I like him.
> He's a little crazy, but I like him.
> (Stein, Page 115)

In the case of Fyedka-the-Russian, however, no matter how much Chava pleads with him, Tevye refuses to believe that Fyedka is a suitable husband for Chava. So what is wrong with Fyedka?

The usual answer is that Fyedka-the-Russia is not Jewish, but I think there is more to it than that. I think it is also the case that Tevye does not know him. Chava may well be in love with Fyedka, but Tevye never gets a chance to interact with Fyedka the way he connects **man-to-man** with both Motel and Perchik. Since Stein never gives Fyedka a chance to speak for himself, Tevye has no opportunity to form an independent opinion of him. Therefore, since Tevye does not know this potential new son-in-law as a **person**, all he can do is fall back on the one thing he does know: Fyed-ka-the-Russian is a gentile.

When Stein created the Fyedka character, he clearly took his lead from Sholem Aleichem, who also robbed Fyedka of any chance to speak for himself. However, Sholem Aleichem does allow the village priest to speak on his behalf, and the priest—someone with a voice of authority who commands as much respect as Tevye is likely to give to any of his gentile neighbors—actually speaks quite well of him:

> No harm will come to your daughter… She's about to be married—and to a young man any girl would envy her for… He's a fine, upstanding fellow, and educated too, entirely **self-taught**. He's in love with your daughter and wants to marry her. The only problem is, he is not a Jew.   (Halkin, Page 75)

Yes, Sholem Aleichem gave him the name "Fyedka Galagan," but the disreputable Galagan family which plays such a big role in the Maurice Schwartz film *Tevye* (released in 1939, just after Kristallnacht), has no place at all in either Sholem Aleichem's Tevye stories or Joseph Stein's *Fiddler on the Roof*.

And yes, the word "galagan" may have negative connotations ("galagan" comes into Yiddish from the Russian word for "hooligan," and has become "balagan" in Modern Hebrew, meaning chaos or fiasco), but Sholem Aleichem himself might have used it to credit Fyedka—also referred to in the "Chava" story as Fyedka-the-Town Scribe—with having raised himself up from bad circumstances.

In the screenplay that Maurice Schwartz wrote for his film *Tevye*, Chava uses the edict of expulsion as an excuse to escape **from** the Galagan family. On the other hand, in "Lekh-Lekho"—the final story in *Tevye the Dairyman*—Sholem Aleichem gives her people to run **to**:

> …she is your daughter as much as ever, says Tzeitel, because the minute she heard we had to leave, she made up her mind to come with us. Whatever happens to us, she said to me, will happen to her too—if we're homeless, so will she be—and the proof of it, Papa, is, that's her bundle right there on the floor…
>   (Halkin, Page 129)

Regardless, the surname Galagan is never referenced in *Fiddler on the Roof*, nor do we ever meet any of the members of Fyedka's family. In fact, even the priest is gone. The only thing Tevye knows about the priest's role in Chava's life is what he learns from Golde:

> **Golde** (to Tevye): I looked all over for Chava. I even went
> to the priest. He told me—they were married.
>
> (Stein, Page 135)

Tevye's dilemma in *Fiddler on the Roof* is somewhat similar to Michael Corleone's dilemma at the beginning of *The Godfather: Part II*. Michael's widowed sister Connie comes to him—as the head of the Corleone family—and asks to marry someone named Merle. But even though he knows in his heart that Connie will defy him, Michael refuses her request: "I don't know this Merle. I don't know what he does."

By casting actor Troy Donahue in the role of Merle, director Francis Ford Coppola made it abundantly clear that Michael was making the right decision. Michael may not know Merle, but way back in 1972, *The Godfather* audience knew Troy Donahue. So the original *The Godfather: Part II* audience saw Merle—in context—as an aging "pretty boy" who would use Connie for her money (which the audience also knows is really Michael's money). Therefore, no one in the audience is surprised when the Connie/Merle marriage turns into a dismal failure, and Connie returns home to beg Michael to forgive her after their mother dies.

On the other hand, every *Fiddler on the Roof* audience gets to know Fyedka in a positive light, even if Tevye does not. In Act One, Scene 8, Motel asks Chava to manage his tailor shop for a few minutes while he goes off to buy a wedding hat. Soon, a couple of Russian boys come into the shop and begin to harass her, but Fyedka follows them in and chases them away, and then apologizes to Chava for their bad behavior.

> I've often noticed you at the bookseller's. Not many girls in this
> village like to read. Would you like to borrow this book? It's very
> good. It's by Heinrich Heine. Happens to be Jewish, I believe.
> After you return it, I'll ask you how you like it, and we'll talk
> about it for a while. Then we'll talk about life, how we feel about
> things…
> (Stein, Page 87)

Fyedka appears next in Act Two, Scene 5 of Stein's libretto, although we know from Yente's comment to Tzeitel—in Act Two, Scene 2—that they have long since become a topic of local gossip. Fyedka wants to talk to Tevye man-to-man, but Chava will not let him.

> **Fyedka:** Chava, let me talk to your father.
> **Chava:** No, that would be the worst thing, I'm sure of it.
> **Fyedka:** Let me try.
> **Chava:** No, I'll talk to him. I promise.   (Stein, Page 130)

In the list of mistakes Chava makes in *Fiddler on the Roof*, this is her biggest mistake.

Note that the audience is in a similar position while watching *My Big Fat Greek Wedding* (the modest romantic comedy that became the highest-grossing independent film in American history in 2002). By the time "Toula" (Nia Vardalos) finally brings "Ian" (John Corbett) home to meet her father "Gus Portokalos" (Michael Constantine), we—the members of the audience—have long since come to love him. We know Ian is a good man, and we know he is a good match for Toula. Despite his initial intransigence, Toula's patriarchal father eventually comes to accept Ian too. ("After all, this is America. Some of us are apples and some of us are oranges, but in the end, we're all fruit.")

In Act Two, Scene 8, the last scene in *Fiddler on the Roof*, Chava and Fyedka come to the house to tell Tevye and Golde that they are moving to Cracow. And this is point at which Fyedka finally speaks directly to Tevye, from his heart, for the very first time. Remarkably, even in the midst of his own pain and trauma, Tevye is able to hear the truth from this good man:

> **Fydeka:** Yes, we are also moving. Some are driven away by edicts, others by silence. Come, Chava.

Tzeitel immediately knows the ice is broken:

> **Tzeitel:** Goodbye, Chava, Fyedka.
> **Tevye** (to *Tzeitel, prompting her under his breath*): God be with you!
> **Tzeitel** (*looks at him, then speaks to Chava, gently*): God be with you!

To ensure that the audience understands that now Chava and Fyedka—just like Tzeitel and Motel—leave Anatevka with hopes of one day joining the rest of the family in America, Stein ends this exchange as follows:

Chava: We will write to you in America. If you like.
Golde: We will be staying with Uncle Abram.
Chava: Yes, Mama.   (Stein, Pages 150–151)

So when we first meet him in both Sholem Aleichem's "Chava" story and in *Fiddler on the Roof,* Fyedka-the-Russian is an idealistic, bookish poet. But by the end of *Fiddler on the Roof,* Fyedka has also convinced Tevye that he has the makings of a mensch. As the years passed from 1964 to today, Fyedka has gradually shed all of the negative attributes left over from the Maurice Schwarz days—doubts that probably still weighed his character down in the Stein days—and became the man I think Jerome Robbins always wanted him to be.

When you have seen as many performances of *Fiddler on the Roof* as I have over the years, little details become signifiers. For example, I now play a little game with myself: During the opening number—the Musical-Prologue "Tradition"—I try to guess which character is which, based on their costumes. In most productions, when the chorus of Mamas first appears, both Golde and Yente are usually somewhere in the chorus of Mamas. And in most productions, when the chorus of daughters first appears, all five of Tevye's daughters are usually somewhere in the chorus of The Daughters.

Similarly, when the Russian men come into the Inn in Act One, Scene 4, Fyedka is always a member of the group. Me? I have seen so many performances of *Fiddler on the Roof* over time that I can look at undifferentiated crowd scenes, place mental bets on who is who, and almost always win the bet. The best costume designers plant subtle clues (for example, Motel often has a tape measure around his collar, Perchik has a backpack, and Fyedka carries a book), that have subliminal effects on audience members. Even if these signifiers do not leap out to others, they certainly speak volumes to me.

I cannot tell you exactly when, but at some point I began to notice that Fyedka's role at the Inn had grown larger. In Stein's libretto (as well as on the Jewison DVD), the Jewish men at the Inn and the Russian men at the Inn begin the scene in separate spheres. Then Lazar Wolf-the-Butcher announces "I'm taking myself a bride… Tevye's eldest, Tzeitel," and all the Jewish men begin drinking, singing and dancing: "To Life! To Life! L'Chaim!"

Meanwhile, the Russian men watch from the sidelines, cheering them on, but not participating. Suddenly, one of the Russian men begins to sing:

> Za va sha, Zdarovia, Heaven bless you both, Nazdrovia,
> To your health, and may we live together in peace.
>
> (Stein, Page 50)

And soon all of the men—Jewish **and** Russian—are singing and dancing together, culminating in "*a wild finale pile-up on the bar.*" Anyone who has ever seen *Fiddler on the Roof* anywhere at any time knows this scene. It is one of the most memorable moments in the musical.

In Stein's libretto for Robbins, as well as in the screenplay Stein wrote for Norman Jewison, this guy is just "a Russian"—he is nobody, just a gypsy in the chorus. But at some point in time, this anonymous Russian became... Fyedka! In most productions, it is now Fyedka who jumps up on a table, sings "Za va sha, Zdarovia... may we live together in peace," then thrusts out his hand, jumps down from the table, and starts dancing—hand-in-hand—with Tevye!

From the audience perspective, this subtle change has enormous implications. In Act Two, Scene 5, when Fyedka says to Chava "let me talk to your father," we know that Fyedka knows exactly who Tevye is, and Tevye probably knows who Fyedka is too. After all, Anatevka is a pretty small place, and they are likely to have locked eyes a few times in the interim. So Fyedka asks once more, this time practically begging: "Let me try." But unlike her sisters, Chava—who was not at the Inn—chooses to go it alone... and the consequences are disastrous.

As I said above, I cannot point to a specific moment when I first noticed all of this, but I do remember exactly when I first discussed it with someone. On April 21, 2009—approximately a week after my chat with Erik Liberman—I did a telephone interview with Sammy Dallas Bayes, the director of the Troika production (fondly known as "Topol's Farewell Tour") that I had just seen in West Palm Beach. I was back in Chicago and I called him, and here is the exact record of our conversation:

> **Jan:** The decision to make Fyedka so prominent in the scene at the Inn so that he's the one who stands up on the table and starts singing... Can you talk about that decision and why you made it? In my little yellow book [Stein's libretto], it just says "Russian." It does not say "Fyedka."

264

Sammy: Well, first of all, I thought it was important that Fyedka be pulled out a little bit from the other Russians. His scenes are not that big, and to bring him forth I've always looked for "a Russian" that could do that. If Fyedka could do that solo, I thought it gave him more of a presence in the show. Originally [in 1964] that character was played by an actor, and acting ability was his most important quality. But when we did out-of-town tryouts, the show kept changing, and that part became smaller because of scenes in which Fyedka was eliminated or written down. Consequently, I figured, because it's such an important role—I mean Chava and Fyedka really cause a complete break with tradition— that it was important to give his character more **presence** within the play itself. And the Inn, to me, was a good place to do it.

Jan: I love it. It is one of the things that I look for now, because I think conceptually—in the development of these characters—it makes a critical difference. If I tell people about this ("Fyedka is singing at the Inn!"), they look at me like I am crazy. They never understand why I am so excited. So, as far as you know, who was the first person who ever thought to do this?

Sammy: It was me.

Jan: It was you?

Sammy: Yeah. I did it before it became sort of a thing. Fyedka has to sing the solo.

Jan: I am so happy to know who to credit for this, because I think it is brilliant. It changes the dynamic on stage in a really important way. When Chava says in Act Two "He has a name," and Tevye replies "I know he has a name," your decision "to bring Fyedka forth" at the Inn gives the audience permission to believe that Tevye really does know who Fyedka is.

Sammy: Right. I didn't start directing the show until the '90s, but when I did start doing it, I felt that that character was slighted. And I knew he was slighted because I knew the reasons why, because I was there during out-of-town tryouts in Detroit and Washington, D.C. In 1964, I was one of the dancers. A lot of Fyedka's dialogue was cut away, so this helped to bring him forward in Tevye's eyes and in the eyes of the audience. He became more of a prominent figure.

Jan: Yes, and Eric Van Tielen—the young man you cast as Fyedka in the current production—he is fabulous. When he gets up and sings at the Inn, I think everybody in the audience immediately falls in love with him. When we root for him, the whole story grows more powerful. Tevye's predicament is made more poignant when the Fyedka onstage is such an obviously good guy.

Sammy: Fyedka was always supposed to be a good guy. But like I said, you never got a chance to see enough of him before to know that he was a really good guy.

Jan: Congratulations, Sammy. Mazel Tov!

Sammy: Thank you.

When I did this interview, I knew that Sammy Dallas Bayes had been one of the dancers in the original 1964 Broadway production. Then he worked directly with Jerome Robbins as a choreographic assistant, and then he became one of the "keepers of the flame" after Robbins died in 1998. Years later, I was on the phone with him, talking about the challenge of directing Topol's Farewell Tour. If anyone can be trusted to speak for Jerome Robbins today, I think Sammy Dallas Bayes qualifies. Fyedka? "Fyedka was always supposed to be a good guy."

Husbands Become Sons-in-Law

"I have five daughters!" Tevye tells us: "I have five daughters!" At the Inn, however, he admits the obvious to Lazar Wolf-the-Butcher: "I always wanted a son."

In the best productions of *Fiddler on the Roof*, Tevye gets his wish. While each of these characters must convince everyone in the audience that they are marrying for love, they should also convince us that they all love Tevye too. Yes, Motel-the-Tailor genuinely loves Tzeitel, Perchik-the-Revolutionary genuinely loves Hodel, and Fyedka-the-Russian genuinely loves Chava. They all want to be good husbands, but they also want to be Tevye's sons-in-law. The men who will win Tevye's acceptance become part of a very special family. They have menschlikh. They are **people**.

QUESTION 7: WAS KITTY GENOVESE JEWISH?

Many audience members were likely surprised to hear such prominent mention of the Kitty Genovese case in my "timeline lectures" from 2014 (presented in this book as "From Gold to Diamond: Moving Beyond Our Father's *Fiddler*"). To tell you the truth, the relevance of the Kitty Genovese case came as something of a surprise to me as well.

If I had published the book I had hoped to publish way back in 2004, I never would have known to include Kitty Genovese.

But by 2003, I had committed myself to a search for "sources and synergies," and the more I looked, the more I found. Paying close attention to the minute details of *Fiddler on the Roof* (as a "text" in book form, as well as on CDs and DVDs, and in live performances) had opened my ears as well as my eyes, and I was able to hear more and see more with each passing year.

Fiddler on the Roof:
Sources & Synergies
✡ A Fortieth Anniversary Celebration ✡

6/14/03 Draft by:

Jan Lisa Huttner
Creative Director
FILMS FOR TWO: The Online Guide for Busy Couples
www.films42.com

© Jan Lisa Huttner (2003)

And so, by the time 2014 finally rolled around, my antennae were fully functional. Delving into the Kitty Genovese case has thus become just one more benefit of my years of immersion in all the individual elements that make *Fiddler on the Roof* such a timeless masterpiece.

Of course, the answer to the question "Was Kitty Genovese Jewish?" is an emphatic NO.

Catherine Susan Genovese was a Catholic woman who was born in Brooklyn (NY) on July 7, 1935, and murdered in Queens (NY) on March 13, 1964. However, the day of her death was a private tragedy. Even as her family and friends began their grieving process on March 13, relatively few people outside her immediate circle of acquaintances knew that anything had happened to her, let alone the full weight of the monstrous details.

The name "Kitty Genovese" did not become more widely known until two weeks later when the *New York Times* published a story with the sensational headline "37 Who Saw Murder Didn't Call the Police" and the subheader "Apathy at Stabbing of Queens Woman Shocks Inspector."

That was the day—March 27, 1964—that the story of Kitty Genovese made the leap from private sorrow to public symbol. And the reporters primarily responsible for this transformation from private to public were all Jewish. A.M. Rosenthal and Martin Gansberg wrote for the *New York Times*. Mike Wallace (best-known now for his role on CBS's *60 Minutes*) was already at CBS News. Gabe Pressman worked for WNBC (the NBC flagship station in New York).

And so, when stories about the 50th anniversary of Kitty Genovese's death began appearing in the media in the middle of March 2014, my antennae started sending my brain "FidDar" messages. I went back and reread various stories in *Tevye the Dairyman*, and then looked for matching plot elements in *Fiddler on the Roof*. The echoes of the Kitty Genovese case in Joseph Stein's libretto were unmistakable.

Most significant is the way Stein reworks "Get Thee Out," which is the last of the eight Tevye stories. Sholem Aleichem's story "Get Thee Out" is diffuse and verbose. There is no one specific moment to which we can apply the word "climax."

Like all of the Tevye stories, "Lekh-Lekho" ("Get Thee Out") is a monologue. In this instance, Tevye starts by telling Sholem Aleichem about the day his neighbors showed up at his door to threaten him with a "kind of pogrom."

> "We've come to you, Tevel," says Ivan Paparilo… "because we want to have a pogrom."
>
> "Congratulations!" I said to them in my cheeriest voice. "What's

taken you so long… Everywhere else the pogroms are already over."

But Ivan Paparilo was in no mood to joke… "We just aren't certain what kind of pogrom to have."

I looked at all those good people whispering to each other… and I thought, Tevye, this is serious!   (Halkin, Page 121)

Rambling on, Tevye is clearly making light of his palpable fear of physical violence. After all, he is talking about something that never happened. Tevye took the hint, and left well before there could be a pogrom of **any** kind. And so, by the time he meets up with Sholem Aleichem (the character, not the author), and tells the tale, Tevye has long since composed himself and moved on (both literally and figuratively).

On stage, however, this incident must happen in "real time." Therefore, Stein took Sholem Aleichem's story and made it shorter, tighter, and considerably more tense and terrifying.

Here is the dialogue from Act Two, Scene 7, along with some of Stein's stage directions:

> **Avram**: Golde, is Reb Tevye home?
> **Golde**: Yes, but he's in the house. Why, is there some trouble?
> **Avram** (to Bielke *and* Shprintze): Call your father… Reb Tevye, have you seen the constable today?
> **Tevye**: No. Why?
> **Lazar**: There are some rumors in town. We thought because you knew him so well, maybe he told you what is true and what is not.
> **Tevye**: What rumors?
> **Avram**: Someone from Zolodin told me there was an edict issued in St. Petersburg that… (*He stops as the* Constable *enters with* two men.)
> **Tevye**: Welcome, your Honor. What's the good news in the world?
> **Constable**: I see you have company.
> **Tevye**: They are my friends.
> **Constable**: It's just as well. What I have to say is for their ears also… I came here to tell you that you are going to have to leave Anatevka… Not just you, of course, but all of you… It affects all of you. You have to leave.
> **Tevye**: But this corner of the world has always been our home. Why should we leave?

Constable (*irritated*): I don't know why. There's trouble in the world. Troublemakers.

Tevye (*ironically*): Like us!

Constable: You aren't the only ones. Your people must leave all the villages... The whole district must be emptied. I have an order here, and it says you must sell your homes and be out of here in three days...

Tevye: And you who have known us all your life, you'd carry out this order?

Constable: I have nothing to do with it, don't you understand?

Tevye (*bitterly*): We understand.   (Stein, Pages 137–140)

When the Constable and his men—the same men singing "L'Chaim/ To Life" and dancing at the inn in Act One—divorce themselves from their Jewish neighbors ("you who have known us all your life") in Act Two, and stand aside while something horrible is happening right in front of them, this is Stein's Kitty Genovese moment.

Why? Because Stein could have used the words so often attributed to Adolf Eichmann (the infamous words "just following orders"), but he chose not to. After all, the "just following orders" excuse would have been very familiar to everyone who saw *Fiddler on the Roof* in 1964. I have no doubt that A.M. Rosenthal and Martin Gansberg of the *New York Times* knew all about Hannah Arendt's Eichmann articles. Ditto Mike Wallace of CBS and Gabe Pressman of NBC.

Viking Press published Hannah Arendt's *Eichmann in Jerusalem: A Report on the Banality of Evil* in 1963, based on a series of articles she began publishing in the *New Yorker* magazine in February 1963 (in other words, less than one year before the murder of Kitty Genovese).

So Stein could have written "just following orders" dialogue for the Constable. He didn't. He used the words of Kitty's neighbors instead. "I have nothing to do with it," says the Constable, distancing himself from Tevye and the Jews of Anatevka (people he has known all of his life).

Note that Stein later wrote a new scene for the film (presumably at the request of director Norman Jewison) in which he conjures up an additional layer of bureaucrats—not found in Sholem Aleichem—to determine the fate of Anatevka's Jews. So maybe this invocation of the murder of Kitty Genovese on the stage was not deliberate on Stein's part? Maybe it was just "in the air," as so often happens with great art? That proves nothing other than what I have said a dozen times already in this book: what is on the screen in the Jewison version is not **the same** as what was on the stage in the Robbins version.

These People Are Our Neighbors

Think back to Frances Butwin who, with her husband Julius, produced a best-selling book called *The Old Country* in 1946, and then added a second volume called *Tevye's Daughters* in 1949 (after Julius's death). Taken together, these two books—which were soon packaged as a two-volume set called *Collected Stories of Sholom Aleichem* with artwork by Ben Shahn—succeeded in capturing the intimate grief of Jews who were just then learning the truth about the Holocaust. That trauma is expressed in a collection of stories that now speaks for itself: I, Frances Butwin, have given you the key to a world that is no more.

But in the 1950s, a great silence descended on the subject of the Holocaust. The blackout (no doubt related to the Blacklist) was so complete that Frances Butwin's books were soon out of print. By the mid '50s, she was no longer a best-selling author doing book-signing events; she was a widow scrambling to make a living as a librarian in order to support her daughter and two young sons.

One of the objects that brought Holocaust consciousness back to America in the late '50s was a little European import first published in Amsterdam in 1947 called *Het Achterhuis Dagboekbrieven van 14 Juni 1942 –1 Augustus 1944* (*The Annex Diary Notes from 14 June 1942 –1 August 1944*). It was soon translated into English, appearing in 1952 as *Anne Frank: The Diary of a Young Girl*. In 1955, it became a play called *The Diary of Anne Frank*, and in 1959, *The Diary of Anne Frank* became an Oscar-winning film.

This is not the place to rehash any Anne Frank controversies as to why and how such a tragic story became so "optimistic," "humanist," "universalist," etc. I simply want to illustrate two points about *The Diary of Anne Frank*.

First of all, Anne's diary ends when Anne is captured by the Nazis. So we will never know what thoughts Anne might have had about the "brotherhood of man" after she had been transported from Westerbork to Auschwitz to Bergen-Belsen. In calendar time, it was only a few months, but in her life, this was literally the end. Anne Frank died in Bergen-Belsen sometime in the spring of 1945.

More important, with respect to a discussion of Kitty Genovese, is the fact that all of the neighbors in *The Diary of Anne Frank* act heroically. It is Miep Gies who not only provides food for the people in the "secret annex" (always at the risk of her own life), but also Miep who saves Anne's diary. She gave it to Anne's father Otto when he returned to Amsterdam (the only resident of the Secret Annex to survive the Holocaust), and he arranged for its publication.

So if you are an American and you are living in the 1950s and you are reading *Anne Frank: The Diary of a Young Girl* and/or you are watching *The Diary of Anne Frank* (on stage and/or on screen), you are likely to have positive feelings about Anne's neighbors—especially in contrast to those evil German Nazis. You may even have said to yourself: "If I had been there, I would have been Miep. I would have been one of the people who helped. After all, these people were our neighbors."

Of course, now we know that, in fact, most Dutch citizens either did nothing or were collaborators. We know all the details now. Now we know that the Frank family was betrayed by another neighbor.

And all of this happened in Amsterdam. Tell the same story and the further East you go, from Berlin, to Warsaw, to Kiev, the less benign and more murderous the neighbors become. But still, in cultural history—as opposed to real history—the neighbors in *The Diary of Anne Frank* are always a benevolent force. They are saviors who fought in the Resistance against the Nazis, risking everything, including their very lives.

Skip ahead less than ten years in calendar time to *Fiddler on the Roof,* and suddenly (after reading about the Eichmann Trial) many Americans— especially Jewish Americans—might well wonder just how "good" their own neighbors really are. What changed in American culture? Kitty Genovese was murdered on March 13. On March 27, the *New York Times* wrote "Apathy at Stabbing of Queens Woman Shocks Inspector."

It is one thing for all those German soldiers—presumably acting under Nazi command—to keep parroting: "I was just following orders." It is quite another thing when neighbors in an ordinary residential enclave in America are apathetic. "I have nothing to do with it."

> **Constable:** I have nothing to do with it, don't you understand?
> **Tevye** (*bitterly*): We understand.

In the Air

In the blink of an eye, it is March, 2014, and I am still working on my book about *Fiddler on the Roof*—this book I have been actively working on now for the better part of a decade—and one after another, the media covers all the major milestones of one incredible year: 1964.

So many milestones of cataclysmic importance to remember, beginning with the Kennedy assassination in November '63 and culminating in the inauguration of Lyndon Johnson (after a huge landslide victory) in January '65. All of these events are happening in 1964, everything that would have been "in the air" as the *Fiddler* team made its way from a Manhattan rehearsal space to theaters in Detroit and D.C., and then, finally, to Broadway on September 22, 1964.

The *New Yorker* magazine arrives in my mailbox in early March of 2014 with a very long and very interesting article by Nicholas Lemann. Its title is "A Call For Help: What the Kitty Genovese Story Really Means."

This article is in the review section of the *New Yorker* because Lemann is covering two new books which have just been published to commemorate the 50th anniversary of the murder of Kitty Genovese:

- *Kitty Genovese: A True Account of a Public Murder and its Private Consequences* (Catherine Pelonero)
- *Kitty Genovese: The Murder, The Bystanders, The Crime that Changed America* (Kevin Cook)

I read Lemann. I read both books. I add Kitty Genovese's name to my next presentation timeline.

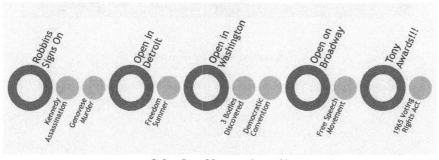

© Jan Lisa Huttner (2016)

It has taken decades, Joe, but now, finally, "We understand."

Miriam and the Women

"Then Miriam took a timbrel in her hand, and all the women went out after her to dance with timbrels." (Exodus 15:20 Etz Hayim 412)

Women dancing with Bea Arthur as Miriam (from left): Jane Austen, Frances Butwin, Marie Waife-Goldberg, and Svetlana Boym. Jan Lisa Huttner illuminates them.

SECTION 10

Epilogue:
The "Me Found" through the Research

July 2016. The day came when I said to my husband: "You know I won't be able to finish this book until after the election, right?" And Richard—usually so reserved and taciturn—turned as green and engorged as the Incredible Hulk. "No," he roared, "I don't know that!"

Who could blame him? Richard had now been living with my *Fiddler* obsession since May 2000. In context, that meant The Fiddler had been fiddling away in the background of our lives all through Bush versus Gore (2000), Bush versus Kerry (2004), McCain versus Obama (2008), Obama versus Romney (2012), and now Clinton versus Sanders (2016), the primary contest at the threshold of Clinton versus Trump. . . 16 years and five American presidential election cycles.

And yet, I knew it was true. "Richard," I said, agitated yet adamant. "I won't be able to write the epilogue until I know the ending."

The decision to call this book *Diamond Fiddler* had been a statement of faith on my part. Way back in 2003, when people I trusted told me to "build a platform" to make my research on *Fiddler on the Roof* more valuable to potential publishers, I jumped in with both feet. I worked diligently on my platform, digging ever deeper as a scholar (as evident in my growing list of articles and presentations) while reaping the rewards of public validation (as evident in my growing list of awards and connections).

When life threw me curves, most significantly my mother's sudden death in 2007 and my husband's decision to look for a new job in 2012, I just kept fiddling. I sold our condo in Chicago and moved us to Brooklyn, always prideful in my ability to "turn lemons into lemonade." I kept reaching out to new agents and modifying my book proposal to suit their specifications, but once it became clear to me that no publisher would commit, I decided to self-publish *Tevye's Daughters: No Laughing Matter*.

True, *Tevye's Daughters* was only one strand of my research, but publishing it met my commitment to do something significant in honor of the 50th anniversary of the first Broadway performance. And so I moved my target from publishing a celebration of *Fiddler on the Roof*'s 50th anniversary on **September 22, 2014**, to publishing a book honoring the observance of Sholem Aleichem's 100th Yahrzeit on **May 13, 2016**.

✡ ✡ ✡ ✡ ✡

The title *Diamond Fiddler*—chosen sometime in 2013—reflects my belief that once the Golden Anniversary events of 2014 are part of history, next up will be Diamond Anniversary events in 2039 (in honor of the 75th anniversary of the first Broadway performance) and then Centennial events in 2064 (in honor of the 100th anniversary of the first Broadway performance). I am writing to the future, a future I know I will never see, but one in which I have complete faith.

I believe in Jerome Robbins's expansive vision. Despite setbacks along the way, I truly believe that "the arc of the moral universe is long but it bends toward justice." These words, always associated now with Martin Luther King, Jr., were a part of the American abolitionist movement from the beginning. The first online citation is in a sermon called "Of Justice and the Conscience" published by a Unitarian minister named Theodore Parker in 1853.

In 1932—in the middle of the Great Depression—Ted Robinson used these words in a column he wrote for the *Cleveland Plain Dealer*. And in 1940—one year after Hitler's troops invaded Poland—Rabbi Jacob Kohn of Temple Sinai in Los Angeles used these words in his Rosh Hashanah sermon:

> Our faith is kept alive by the knowledge, founded on long experience, that the arc of history is long and bends toward justice. We have seen so many ancient tyrannies pass from earth since Egypt and Rome held dominion that our eyes are directed not to the tragic present, but to the beyond, wherein the arc of history will be found bending toward justice, victory and freedom.
> (Reported in the *Los Angeles Times* on October 3, 1940)

My heart tells me Jerome Robbins wanted his audience to experience the truth in these words (which **he** surely associated with Dr. King) in every performance of *Fiddler on the Roof*. This is the intrinsic optimism of Robbins's vision, the reason why Tevye says "God be with you!" as Chava and Fyedka "exit" with their suitcases on their way to Cracow; the reason why Tevye says "Work hard, Motel. Come to us soon." as Tzeitel and Motel "exit with their cart" on their way to Warsaw; the reason why Tevye "beckons" to the fiddler at the very last moment before the final curtain falls.

> *Tevye begins to pull his wagon upstage, revealing the fiddler, playing his theme. Tevye stops, turns, beckons to* **him**. *The Fiddler tucks his violin under his arm and follows the family upstage as the curtain falls.*   (Stein, Page 153)

✡ ✡ ✡ ✡ ✡

But my faith in the future was deeply confounded by the column David Brooks posted on the *New York Times* website on July 29, 2016. "The Sanders people have 90 percent of the Democratic Party's passion," Brooks wrote, "and 95 percent of the ideas." My rage against Brooks knew no bounds. I fumed about this line as I went about my day, and then, after Brooks said more of the same that night on the *PBS NewsHour,* I delivered the words that made Richard apoplectic.

"You know I won't be able to finish this book until after the election, right?"

"No, I don't know that!" my Incredible Hulk roared back.

"Richard," I continued, desperate to explain myself, "last night, after Hillary accepted the DNC nomination, I danced around the room in tears. You saw me! You took a picture of me—dancing in front of the television— which I immediately uploaded to Facebook!" I could not compose myself. I spoke loudly and aggressively, bordering on hysteria:

"This morning my Facebook feed was filled with women. Women dancing alone. Women dancing with their friends. Women hugging daughters who had been allowed to stay up late to watch this historic event. Women embracing their mothers, both of them in tears. Hillary watching Chelsea introduce her. Hillary and Chelsea swimming in a sea of balloons. **But David Brooks thinks** 'the Sanders people have 90 percent of the Democratic Party's passion and 95 percent of the ideas.' David Brooks has not only **obliterated** Hillary, he is **negating** me! He is **negating** all of these women!! He is even

negating their mothers and their daughters!!! We have no passion? We have no ideas ?!?"

I knew Richard would vote for Hillary Rodham Clinton on **November 8, 2016.** I even knew that David Brooks, a "moderate Republican," might well vote for Hillary Rodham Clinton too. But his **July 29, 2016** column ended with a chilling prediction:

> The Democrats had by far the better of the conventions. But the final and shocking possibility is this: In immediate political terms it may not make a difference.

What could Richard say in the face of my onslaught? Nothing. He said nothing. By the time I had finished explaining the substance of Brooks's column and the depth of my dismay, I knew he had already disengaged. I knew no more words would be forthcoming, so I read his face. Richard's face said: "Do what you want."

Now we know the ending. David Brooks was right. In fact, the Democrats not only had a far better convention, the Democrats had a far better candidate and ran a far better campaign. But it made no difference. Hillary Rodham Clinton lost, and even as I write this epilogue, Hillary Rodham Clinton is in the process of being disappeared.

On Thursday, **November 10, 2016,** one day after Hillary's concession speech, Donald and Melania Trump went to the White House. The evening news was filled with photos. President Obama and President-Elect Trump shook hands in the Oval Office, man-to-man, while Michelle Obama gave Melania Trump the grand tour. At some point, a neighbor in Chappaqua, New York, also posted a casual photo of Hillary Rodham Clinton walking her dog. Photos of all three dyads went viral on Facebook: BHO and DJT, Michelle and Melania, Hillary and her dog.

I stopped watching the news. I turned all of my radios from WNYC (New York Public Radio) to WQXR ("the most listened to classical music station in the United States"). I cut my time on Facebook down to an absolute minimum. I vowed to do my best to keep Richard's life from turning into a nightmare. Then I started thinking about what to say in this epilogue.

By this point, I expect my readers to appreciate the importance of historical context. Way back in 1964, the backers of *Fiddler on the Roof* expected a flop. The first critic to publish a review of *Fiddler on the Roof* said: "There are no memorable songs in this musical." (That was TEW, writing for *Variety* in June, after the first out-of-town performance at the Fisher Theatre in Detroit.) Things were a bit better by September. The six critics quoted in *Opening Night on Broadway* had some positive comments (mostly about Zero Mostel's performance as Tevye), but also used harsh words like "arid areas," "overabundance of self-pity," and "unfortunate weaknesses" as well. On his Broadway Scorecard, Suskin shows two "rave" reviews and four "favorable" reviews, but no "mixed," "unfavorable," or "pan" reviews.

> Here was a classic made brilliant by an imaginative production, rather than the material itself... Fortunately, the several flaws were more than compensated for by the Messrs. Robbins, Aronson, et al... Mostel surely carried the show past the less-than-overwhelmed critics.   (Suskin, Pages 207-210)

Suffice it to say here that much of this book attempts to show how historical context helps to explain why *Fiddler on the Roof* evaded the fate anticipated by all of the "experts" way back in 1964. Of course, I believe it was **the material itself**, material which has proved more than resilient in every kind of production no matter the budget and regardless of the strength of each cast. Nevertheless, if *Fiddler on the Roof* had made its Broadway debut in 1962, or in 1966, or in any other year than 1964, I doubt there would have been quite so many celebratory events in 2014.

By all objective measures, *Fiddler on the Roof* captured its historical moment in 1964, and yet, lightning failed to strike twice in 2014. It now falls to me to connect the 50th anniversary of *Fiddler on the Roof* in 2014 with the election of Donald Trump in 2016.

Barack Obama had barely begun his second term in January 2013 when pundits started yammering on about the imminent "coronation" of Hillary Rodham Clinton in 2017. My immediate stance was cautious optimism.

I wanted to believe that Hillary Rodham Clinton would one day become America's 45th President, but I always knew use of the term "coronation" was ludicrous. However events were destined to unfold, I never expected anything to be easy for her… or for me.

I became a member of Team Hillary in 1991. Really, it's true. A good friend of mine was married to someone who had worked on Harold Washington's campaign for Mayor of Chicago in 1982. Ten years later, my friend told me that David Wilhelm (someone high-up in the Washington campaign) had just been hired to manage Bill Clinton's 1992 presidential campaign. She knew this because her husband had been offered a job down in Arkansas as part of Wilhelm's support staff.

Bill who? I had never heard of Bill Clinton, but I was a loyal friend, so I started reading up on him, and, of course, the more I learned about Bill Clinton, the more I learned about Hillary Rodham Clinton as well. I remember saying to Richard: "I don't know about this Bill Clinton guy, but I love this lady Hillary." Just like that. Right from the beginning. The more I read about Hillary Rodham Clinton, the more I loved her. So I worked on Bill Clinton's 1992 campaign and I worked on Bill Clinton's 1996 campaign, and through it all, the more I came to know about Hillary Rodham Clinton, the more I loved her.

Richard and I had endless arguments about MonicaGate in 1998. I wanted Bill Clinton to resign. I thought that having an affair with an intern—consensual or not—was an abuse of power, and he needed to own it. Richard said the impeachment trial was a farce and I agreed. I did not want Bill Clinton to be impeached, I just wanted President William Jefferson Clinton to step down, so that Vice President Albert Arnold Gore, Jr. could step up. I thought if Al Gore had two years in office, there would be no stopping him when he ran for his first full term as President in 2000. Of course, neither of us had any say in the matter. Bill Clinton did not resign. Al Gore was not elected President in 2000.

But on that sad morning—Wednesday, **November 8**, **2000**—when the Bush/Gore presidential race was still too close to call, there was a ray of light. Wonder of wonders. Miracle of miracles. Hillary Rodham Clinton had won her bid to replace Daniel Patrick Moynihan in the U.S. Senate. On **January 3, 2001**, Hillary Rodham Clinton would become the new Junior Senator from the state of New York. I read the headlines in the *New York Times* on the morning of **November 8, 2000**, and my heart truly was "laden with happiness and tears."

So on **January 20, 2007**, when Hillary announced her intention to run in the Democratic Primary, I was all in. And I stayed all in after Barack Obama announced his candidacy on **February 10, 2007**, even though Obama was the clear choice of most of my Chicago neighbors. Hillary conceded on **June 7, 2008**. She immediately pledged her full support to Obama and vowed to do everything in her power to help him win the White House… and so did I. I bought one T-shirt that said "Hillary has my heart. Barack has my vote." to encourage any woman still harboring doubts to join me. I bought more T-shirts—some for me and some for Richard—that simply said "ProBama Nation."

The night Barack Obama was elected, I sobbed. Our first African American President! What a triumph! The day of the inauguration, I joined a diverse group of women at the Hyde Park Arts Center (a few blocks from the Obama family residence) and we danced in front of the television all afternoon like giddy fools.

Meanwhile, Hillary Rodham Clinton became America's third female Secretary of State (after Madeleine Albright and Condoleezza Rice). She traveled the world with tireless dedication. She was in the Situation Room the day Osama Bin Laden was captured and killed by executive order. But then, a worm in the apple: Photos of the Situation Room that included U.S. Secretary of State Hillary Rodham Clinton were considered "immodest" by some of my fellow Jews, so Ultra-Orthodox newspapers airbrushed her out. On a critical day in world history, Jewish men disappeared Hillary Rodham Clinton from the Situation Room.

I was not surprised, but I was certainly shocked, and I knew then and there what was to come. Coronation? There would never be a "coronation." Hillary Rodham Clinton would run for President in 2016. She would fight hard on every single day for every single vote, and I would fight with her. And maybe this time…

And for all this time—from the day Hillary Rodham Clinton was elected to the Senate on Tuesday, **November 7, 2000** until she conceded the presidency to Donald Trump on Wednesday, **November 9, 2016**—for all this time, I had been working on *Fiddler on the Roof*. And at every step of the way, I had also faced rejection after rejection. No matter how many articles I posted, no matter how many lectures I gave, no one showed any interest in publishing my book.

Way back in 2003, I had been told to "build a platform," so I did. I told everyone I was going to publish a book about *Fiddler on the Roof* in September 2014 in conjunction with the 50th anniversary of the first Broadway opening night, so I did. I self-published *Tevye's Daughters: No Laughing Matter*, and sent copies to all the scholars in my bibliography. These copies went to people who were supposed to care about Jewish culture in general—and Sholem Aleichem in particular—but not a one of them (mostly men, but some women too) ever got back to me.

In one way or the other, I had interviewed dozens of people connected with Jewish culture in general—and *Fiddler on the Roof* in particular—over the years, so they all knew who I was. All of them had thanked me when I promoted their work, but not a one of them offered any support (either formal or informal) when I started to promote *Tevye's Daughters* on Amazon and Facebook. I called *Tevye's Daughters* "my appetizer course," and asked for feedback so I could continue "cooking the meal." Silence. I knew better than to take rejection from agents and publishers personally; after all, since the time I had started fiddling, the publishing industry had come close to collapse. But silence from people whom I had met face to face and or actively corresponded with was emotionally wrenching.

✡✡✡✡✡

While on her way to this much-hyped "coronation," Hillary Rodham Clinton faced an unexpected challenge for the Democratic Party nomination from Vermon's Senator Bernie Sanders (someone who was never a registered Democrat and is not a registered Democrat now). She kept going. She campaigned from coast to coast and everywhere in between, losing most of the caucus states but winning most of the primary states. Was there a systematic difference between caucus states and primary states? No one in the media seemed interested in the disparity. Millions of people all around the country voted for her, yet most pundits still insisted that people did not "like her and her candidacy "lacked enthusiasm."

And just like Hillary Rodham Clinton, I kept going too. Going to the Broadway Theatre on Broadway and 53ʳᵈ Street on Friday, **November 20, 2015**, to see the very first performance of the fifth Broadway revival of *Fiddler on the Roof*. Going to the Brotherhood Synagogue at Gramercy Park on Sunday, **May 22, 2016**, to observe Sholem Aleichem's 100ᵗʰ Yahrzeit. Going to the Center for Jewish History on Thursday, **September 8, 2016**, to hear an elegant lecture called "Thirteen Ways of Looking at Sholem Aleichem: Notes from a Yiddish Writer's Biographer." Going and going and going, only to witness—time and again—how women were not only being disappeared from both the life and work of Sholem Aleichem, but also from the latest production of *Fiddler on the Roof* too.

On **September 15, 2015**, I had created a Facebook group called Hillary's Auxiliary. By Election Day, Hillary's Auxiliary had attracted more than 90,000 followers, but all of my work—the time, energy and cash that went into Hillary's Auxiliary—was invisible to those who controlled the conversation about the 2016 Presidential campaign. On **June 20, 2016**, BBC Radio ran a segment on a Facebook group called Babes for Bernie, so I looked them up. Babes for Bernie had 6,492 "likes" on Facebook that day (and now it has 6,762 "likes").

By that point, on the other hand, Hillary's Auxiliary already had more than 30,000 "likes" on Facebook. Nevertheless, no one in the media ever showed any interest in doing a segment on Hillary's Auxiliary. Numerous journalists were my "Facebook Friends" and "friends of friends," so hundreds of people had access to my daily posts. But since Hillary's Auxiliary did not fit either the "people do not **like** her" or "her candidacy lacks **enthusiasm**" narratives, no one cared about us.

Similarly, I had lectured and published for more than a decade by the time of Sholem Aleichem's 100ᵗʰ Yahrzeit, but that did not seem to matter either. For me, knowing that Jewish men were playing outsized roles in both sets of conversations, the parallel was obvious. I could feel the effort of swimming against wave after wave of Jewish male disapproval, sometimes just feeling ignored, but other times feeling their outright contempt for me, my efforts, and women in general.

All through 2015 and 2016, I read stacks of print and online publications (including the *Economist*, the *Forward*, the *New Republic*, the *New York Review of Books*, the *New York Times*, and the *Washington Post*). I surfed a host of television stations including news and commentary programs on CNN, MSNBC, PBS, and sometimes even FOX, as well as "comedy commentary/fake news" on Comedy Central, HBO and TBS. And I listened to public radio broadcasts for hours every day (including the late night broadcasts from the BBC). So although I never did a scientific poll, I do consider myself very well informed.

From my own experience, based not only on everything I listened to, watched, and read, but also on all the people I traded messages with face-to-face and/or on Facebook, here is my guestimate:

At least 75 percent of female Jewish voters (and probably more) voted for Hillary Rodham Clinton on **November 8, 2016**. Most of us voted with joy, pride, and yes, enthusiasm. And although there was some anxiety after FBI Director James Comey dropped a bombshell on Friday, **October 28, 2016**, less than two weeks before Election Day, most of us thought everything would be okay in the end. We expected her to squeak through and win the day.

But at most 50 percent of male Jewish voters (and probably less) voted for Hillary Rodham Clinton on **November 8, 2016**. And very few of them—statistically speaking—voted for her with joy, pride, or anything remotely resembling "enthusiasm."

Here is a summary of relevant results as posted by the *Forward* on **November 9, 2016**:

> 71% of Jews supported the democratic nominee in this year's election—slightly more than the 69% who voted for Obama in 2012, but significantly less than the 78% who turned out for Obama in 2008, the 74% who voted for Kerry in 2004, or the 79% who voted for Gore in 2000.
>
> Pew's data is for the American electorate in general, but Orthodox Jews are unlikely to have been an exception to this rule: A

September 2016 poll conducted by the American Jewish Committee found that approximately 50% of Orthodox voters favored Trump while 21% supported Clinton (a full 15% said they would not vote).

After I read this statistical information from the *Forward*, I parsed the number 71 ("71% of Jews supported the Democratic nominee in this year's election…"). I thought about what I knew, based on anecdotal evidence as well as feedback on Hillary's Auxiliary (where "anti-$hillary" posts from supporters of Bernie Sanders were as frequent and as noxious as "anti-Killary" posts from supporters of Donald Trump). I considered the full spectrum of Jewish male voters.

- The Jewish men on the Far Left clearly supported Bernie Sanders. Some of them undoubtedly "held their noses" and voted for Hillary Rodham Clinton (those are actually the exact words of one male Facebook friend on the day of the election), but many probably did not. I do not know if they voted third party or decided not to vote at all, but I do know that they did not, in general, vote for Hillary Rodham Clinton.

- The Jewish men on the Far Right (most of whom are also Orthodox) voted proudly and volubly for Donald Trump. Men who had no qualms about disappearing Hillary Rodham Clinton from the Situation Room after the assassination of Osama Bin Laden were never likely to vote for her regardless of rationale.

- Jewish men in the Center Right, dismayed by Donald Trump, may well have voted for Hillary Rodham Clinton, but only after disparaging her character and credentials.

So most of the male Jewish vote undoubtedly came from the Center Left. I am sure many gay men in this category supported Hillary Rodham Clinton enthusiastically, and for good reason.

In the end, how many Jewish men actually voted for Hillary Rodham Clinton because they believed in her in any way comparable to the way I—and almost every Jewish woman I know—voted for her? Statistically speaking, my guess is very few. I never felt Jewish men of any political persuasion were either proud of the fact that the DNC had nominated a woman (even though in my memory most of them had been **very** proud that the DNC had nominated a black man in 2008), nor did they ever feel the need to express any happiness **for me** as I had expressed happiness for my African American friends and acquaintances in 2008.

Quite the contrary, right up until the day of the election, my male friends insisted on telling me how flawed she was, so much so that on the morning of **November 8, 2016**—when I was still anxious but hopeful—I began replying to their Facebook posts with a link to a YouTube clip of Barbra Streisand singing "Don't Rain on My Parade." And once the results were known, they were quick to blame Hillary Rodham Clinton (as well as me and all of her female supporters), even though everyone knew that the Electoral College vote had been an exceedingly close, and Hillary Rodham Clinton was already trouncing Donald Trump in the popular vote.

I do not think anyone has focused on this topic yet, and it is certainly not my intention to try to sort it all out here. I am sure journalists and historians will continue to wrestle with the dynamics of the 2016 Presidential campaign long after America has a 46th President and beyond. What role did Senator Bernie Sanders play in crippling Hillary Rodham Clinton's attempt to become America's first female president? That is not for me to say. All I can do here is record my own reactions—the reactions of a committed Jewish Feminist—to various events as they unfolded.

On Friday, **November 20, 2015**, I went to see the very first performance of the fifth Broadway revival of *Fiddler on the Roof* at the Broadway Theatre on Broadway and 53rd Street. More on that below…

On Sunday, **May 22, 2016**, I went to the Brotherhood Synagogue at Gramercy Park to observe Sholem Aleichem's 100th Yahrzeit. The special guests included Sheldon Harnick (the only surviving member of 1964's original creative team) and world-famous violinist Itzhak Perlman. They each read one of Sholem Aleichem's best-loved stories, as did Aaron Lansky (the founder of the Yiddish Book Center in Massachusetts). Actor Shane Baker read parts of Sholem Aleichem's famous Ethical Will in Yiddish, and Sherwin Kaufman (the son of Sholem Aleichem's daughter Lyala Rabinowitz Kaufman and his only surviving grandchild) read the same parts in English.

Although there was a video clip of Lyala's daughter Bel Kaufman (who died soon after the 98th Yahrzeit in 2014 at age 103), the only woman on the program was Yelena Shmulenson, the actress who had played the character of the "Shtetl Wife" in the Coen Brothers' Oscar-nominated 2009 dramedy *A Serious Man*. She and Allen Lewis Rickman (the actor who had played "Shtetl Husband" in *A Serious Man*) did a wonderful rendition of the story "It's a Lie" in Yiddish, as a conversation between two characters (with English translation for both characters' dialogue provided by Shane Baker).

If you were counting—which I clearly was—then you would have seen six men speaking from the bemah that night, plus one lone woman who shared one piece of the packed program with two men. Sherwin Kaufman's son—Ken Kaufman—who acted as the Master of Ceremonies, read the long list of cousins present that night. Many of them were women, but none of Sholem Aleichem's numerous female descendants ever said a word or had any public role whatsoever in the festivities.

I kept hoping against hope that a famous actress like Tovah Feldshuh or a local luminary like Eleanor Reissa would magically appear to add a few of Yente-the-Poultrywoman's plaintive words from "The Little Pot" to the mix, but it never happened. No one came up to the bemah to give voice to Yente, or to Menakhem-Mendl's effusive wife Sheineh-Sheidl, or to loquacious Gitl Purishkevitch. All of Sholem Aleichem's marvelous female characters had been disappeared from the emotional observance of his 100th Yahrzeit. In fact, even the character Yelena Shmulenson voiced that night was someone with no name—a character from one of the Railroad Stories—who was very likely written as male by Sholem Aleichem, but voiced by a female at his 100th Yahrzeit so as to play on the audience's fondness for *A Serious Man*.

On Sunday, **July 24, 2016**, I watched Senator Bernie Sanders defame Congresswoman Debbie Wasserman Schultz on national television on the eve of the Democratic National Committee Convention. CNN host Jake Tapper invited the ex-candidate to attack the DNC Chair on the basis of the systematic hacking of private DNC e-mail accounts that resulted in selective disclosures by WikiLeaks. That Sunday morning, the former candidate let loose based on "information" that very few people had even read—let alone verified—at that point. As the days passed, most of this "information" was thoroughly debunked by responsible journalists like Jeffrey Toobin of the *New Yorker* and Kurt Eichenwald of *Newsweek*, and yet the damage had already been done.

Let me be blunt here:

- On Sunday, **July 24, 2016** (on the eve of the DNC Convention), two Jewish men—Sanders and Tapper—sought to destroy the reputation of a Jewish woman on national television for the sake of their own self-aggrandizement.
- On Monday, **July 25, 2016** (the first day of the DNC Convention), Congresswoman Debbie Wasserman Schultz was hounded off the podium by irate Sanders supporters—many of whom I suspect were Jewish men—and forced to resign as DNC Chair.
- On Friday, **July 29, 2016**, a Jewish man—David Brooks—used his very powerful positions at the *New York Times* and on the *PBS NewsHour* to elevate Sanders' supporters ("The Sanders people have 90 percent of the Democratic Party's passion and 95 percent of the ideas.")

Collectively, these Jewish men helped destroy the hopes and dreams of all the women on my Facebook feed—many of whom I know for a fact were also Jewish—women who had been so elated the night that Hilary Clinton became the first woman ever nominated by a major political party for the American presidency.

On Thursday, **September 8, 2016**, I went to the Center for Jewish History in Manhattan to hear an elegant lecture called "Thirteen Ways of Looking at Sholem Aleichem: Notes from a Yiddish Writer's Biographer." In the one hour plus that he spoke, Professor Jeremy Dauber failed to mention the names of any of the women in Sholem Aleichem's family. His father was identified as "Reb Nachum," and his eldest son was identified as "Mischa," but his mother was identified as "his mother" (not Chaya Esther), his wife was identified as "his wife" (not as Olga and certainly not as Hodel), and even his daughter Ernestina—who played a critical role in one of Dauber's anecdotes—was identified simply as "his daughter." All of their identities had been erased, even though Dauber surely knows, just as I know, that Solomon and Olga Rabinowitz had four daughters named Ernestina (Tissa), Lyala, Emma, and Maroussia (Musa).

These are all real events. I am merely recording the "who, what, when, where" as well as my own reactions to what I saw with my own eyes and heard with my own ears. Others no doubt saw and heard other things, but this is my story (told in the first person) as a howl of pain recorded for posterity.

On Sunday, **November 18, 2016**, once I had sufficiently recovered from Election Day, I went back to the Broadway Theatre on Broadway and 53rd Street to see one last performance of the fifth Broadway revival of *Fiddler on the Roof* before it closed forever on **December 31, 2016** (barely one year after it had opened).

I went notebook in hand and stood at the back of the dress circle checking my facts and recording my observations. Was I right to say that in 2016, Anatevka has more male residents than female residents? Yes. This is not just my imagination. This is a fact. The creative decision to focus the fifth Broadway revival on the dances of Hofesh Shechter—wonderful though they may be—had resulted in a gender imbalance in the drama.

This is abundantly clear in one critical scene at the end of Act One— namely the party scene in which all the Jews of Anatevka gather to celebrate the wedding of Tzeitel and Motel. Here is Joseph Stein's description of what we should expect to see:

> *The set opens to show the entire yard of Tevye's house. Part of it is divided down the* **center** *by a short partition* [the mechitzah]. *Several tables are set up at the rear of each section. The musicians play, and all dance and then seat themselves on benches at the tables. The women are on the left, the men are on the right. As* **the dance** [now famously known as "The Bottle Dance"] *concludes, Mordcha* [the innkeeper] *mounts a stool and signals for silence. The noise subsides.*
> (Stein, Page 91)

The Making of a Musical: Fiddler on the Roof (the book published by Richard Altman and Mervyn Kaufman in 1971) contains several different photographs of this scene, not only from New York but also from London, Paris and Berlin, as well as a still from Jewison's film. The most exemplary photograph is the one from Paris (where *Fiddler on the Roof* opened at Theatre Marigny in November 1969). Spread across the tops of pages 150 and 151, we can clearly see Perchick and Hodel getting ready to begin dancing in the middle of the stage after Perchick has pulled back the mechitzah.

Perchick is standing on the right side of the stage (meaning on the left side of the photo). Hodel is standing on the left side of the stage (meaning on the right side of the photo). The mechitzah is behind them. The photo shows tables filled with men on the left and tables filled with women on the right, and the number of men is equal to the number of women. They are all staring at Perchick and Hodel—hands clasped—in the center of the stage.

That was 1969. Since Richard Altman had been Jerome Robbins's assistant in 1964 as well as the person primarily responsible for staging the first wave of foreign productions, I have every confidence that this photo (and its companions) represents the way Jerome Robbins wanted this critical scene presented to the audience. My confidence comes directly from Altman's qualifications as the first "keeper of the flame," so well described on the book jacket.

> According to Altman, assistant to Jerome Robbins from the very start of the production, it was Robbins's innovative genius which was directly responsible for the show's "stature, universality, and longevity."   (Altman & Kaufman, front flap)

> Since he was intimately acquainted with every aspect of the play, Altman was also summoned by film director Norman Jewison to help cast the movie version.   (Altman & Kaufman, back flap)

In 2015, on the other hand, women are squeezed to the left of the mechitzah in a space that occupies approximately one-quarter of the stage. Even though, at that point, there are already more men than women on stage, when the male dancers appear, the non-dancing male characters move to the right side of the stage so the male dancers can have maximum room in the middle. This creates an even greater imbalance in the total number of male and female characters on the stage.

Most of the productions I have seen follow Stein's directions for what happens next:

> *They all dance* [where "all" generally includes everyone on stage including the rabbi], *except for* Lazar *and* Yente, *who storm off. As the dance reaches a wild climax, the* Constable *and his* men *enter, carrying clubs. The dancers see them and slowly stop.*
>
> (Stein, Page 100)

But very little of this "action" remains in 2015. By the time Perchik asks Hodel to dance with him, the male dancers—wonderful as they are—have taken up so much time that the rest of the scene is truncated. Perchik slips under the mechitzah—instead of pulling it down—leaving most of the female characters behind the mechitzah for the bulk of the scene. There is so little dancing that Lazar and Yente have no time to make an emphatic exit, and there is certainly no "wild climax." Perchik asks Hodel to dance with him, and all too soon the constable arrives, the pogrom begins, and the curtain falls on Act One.

Did anyone else notice any of these details? I doubt it, but if so, no one mentioned them in any of the many reviews posted after the fifth Broadway revival of *Fiddler on the Roof* officially opened on **December 20, 2015**. Since I live in Brooklyn now, many people I know have actually seen this new production. When I ask, they just shrug. After all, these people know *Fiddler on the Roof* very well at this point, so even if they do not see something on stage, they likely supply it from memory, just like the people who tell me that Yente's line "The way she sees and the way he looks, it's a perfect match" is on the movie soundtrack, even though it definitely is not.

Women were disappeared from the 2015 Broadway revival of *Fiddler on the Roof*, the musical "based on Sholem Aleichem's stories," in November 2015. Women were disappeared at the observance of this beloved author's 100th Yahrzeit in May 2016. Women were disappeared by his biographer in a prestigious lecture at a high-profile venue in September 2016.

Women were simultaneously disappeared from the 2016 Presidential campaign. After Debbie Wasserman Schultz was sent back to Florida in disgrace in July, Attorney General Loretta Lynch, CNN commentator Donna Brazile, and Huma Abedin—HRC's chief aide and longtime confidante—were all pushed to the sidelines too. And now Hillary Rodham Clinton, the first woman to be nominated for president by a major political party, is in the process of being disappeared from public view after a lifetime spent on the world stage.

So what? Who cares? In the defiant words of Hillary Rodham Clinton herself when she faced down Republican members of the House Oversight Committee on Benghazi on **May 8, 2013**:

> What difference at this point does it make? It is our job to figure out **what happened** and do everything we can to prevent it from ever happening again.

Way back in my preface "The Me Search in the Research," I introduced the term "paradigm."

- What is observed depends on what is expected.

- What is anomalous depends on what is accepted.

- The continuity of thought depends on the "normal" tendency to assimilate anomalies to accepted paradigms through minor accommodations.

- The novelty of paradigms depends on a need to restructure the past in order to consolidate the present.

I am circling back now to say that over the years, I had developed paradigms all my own for Hillary Rodham Clinton, *Fiddler on the Roof*, and many related things, paradigms that are considerably different from the paradigms—Conventional Wisdom—held by many others. I believe my paradigms made me acutely aware of things most of my contemporaries simply missed. I saw what I saw and knew what I knew (however blind I may have been to the significance of other events that did not meet my own expectations).

If you have come this far on this journey with me, then restoring disappeared women to their rightful place—in art and in history, and in their daily lives as well—is now your job as well as my own. For everyone who believes in Robbins's vision of *Fiddler on the Roof* as a work of art that helps the arc of history "bend towards justice," this is now "our job."

As Hillary Rodham Clinton said over 20 years ago in Beijing at the United Nations 4th World Conference on Women:

> ...human rights are women's rights, and women's rights are human rights once and for all. Let us not forget that among those rights are the right to speak freely—and the right to be heard. (September 5, 1995)

And the "me" found through the research is more committed to those principles than ever before.

Jan Lisa Huttner
Brooklyn, New York
December 10, 2016

©2016 Huttner/Rosenzweig

Jan Plans, God Laughs

Yiddish Proverb: Der mentsh trakht un got lakht (Man Plans, God Laughs).
Cherubs (clockwise from the top): Sophie, Audrey, Fanny, and Isabel.

ACKNOWLEDGMENTS

Wherever you go, there you are

"Wherever you go, there you are" was the favorite saying of Bert Thoms (my freshman math tutor at St. John's College). Although this phrase is typically attributed to Confucius, Mr. Thoms attributed it to a mythical Greek philosopher named "Bolideus," a name he created from the term "bolide." According to the American Meteor Society website: "A bolide is a special type of fireball which explodes in a bright terminal flash at its end, often with visible fragmentation." But whoever first said these words, once I heard them from the lips of Bert Thoms, I never forgot them.

By 2012, Richard and I had been married for almost thirty years, and for all of those years, we had lived in Chicago, and for most of those years, he had been an accountant at the University of Chicago Medical Center. And then, on February 17, 2012, Richard learned that a big reorganization was underway which did not include him.

I know the date because it was the date of my father's Yahrzeit, so I had asked weeks before to do the D'var Torah at Congregation KAM Isaiah Israel on that night. What would have become of us if we had not had that specific commitment on that particular night? Perhaps we would still be in bed, hiding under the covers? But we were expected at KAM that night, so we went. And I gave the D'var Torah which I had written the day before (knowing it now had whole new levels of meaning known only to me and to Richard): "These are the rules that you shall set before them…"

My father, Eddie Huttner, was not a Temple-Goin'-Kinda-Guy, and I doubt he ever wrote a D'var Torah in his whole life. But Parsha Mishpatim wrestles with complex concerns that sound very much like things my father tried to teach me in his own special way. As Rabbi Lewis John Eron of the Jewish Federation of Southern New Jersey put it in his D'var Torah for Mishpatim (which I used as a source for my own):

> Would their bitter memories [of slavery and oppression] lead to a society built on anger and resentment or to one founded on compassion and concern?

The next week, Richard called one of his old bosses to line up a reference, and after the call came this: "David said, 'If Jan will move to Brooklyn, I will hire you tomorrow.'"

I started laughing. "So, okay," I said. "We're moving to Brooklyn." What else could I say? For more than a decade, I had been telling everyone that the climax of *Fiddler on the Roof* comes at the train station when Hodel tells Tevye: "There with my love I'm home." God had decided to test me with my own hypothesis!

I have now demonstrated to my own satisfaction that "home" is not a place on a map. Home is not Chicago, or Anatevka, or even Eretz Yisrael. Home is a state of being.

So I would like to start these acknowledgements by thanking God.

Who is God? I'll tell you, I don't know. But I can tell you who God is not, at least not for me. God is not "Sistine Chapel Guy." Michelangelo's male divinity with the huge white beard—this glorious embodiment of patriarchal authority—has never been and will never be "God" for me. I have spent decades of my life rebelling against Sistine Chapel Guy, and I am not about to allow him in now.

But my years of research on *Fiddler on the Roof* have imbued me with a profound "attitude of gratitude." I recently heard someone say: " 'God' is the address where we send our Thank You cards." Right now, that is as close as I can get. Thank You, God. I hope you like this card.

✡ ✡ ✡ ✡ ✡

My years of research on *Fiddler on the Roof* have also suffused my life with profound respect for Judaism. Once I took Sistine Chapel Guy out of the picture, I found a great deal to love about Judaism. "These are the rules that you shall set before them…" I do not believe the point of Judaism is to keep all these rules; I believe the point of Judaism is to keep trying.

This, I learned, is the miracle of the minyan. It takes ten. So what if you want to stay in bed under the covers? You must still make every effort, because you might be number ten. Somehow Jews figured out some simple truths about human nature, and these truths have sustained us as a people through thousands of years of dispersion.

You have to stop once a week to count your blessings. Jews call this day Shabbat (the Sabbath). You have to stop once a year to say you are sorry. Jews call this day Yom Kippur (the Day of Atonement). You have to keep promising to do good all the while knowing that whatever you do, it will never be good enough. Jews call this "tradition" (flavored with Ashkenazi, Sephardic, Mizrachi, Ethiopian, and even secular spices).

I am grateful to all the rabbis and teachers, scholars and writers from whom I have learned so much since I began my research on *Fiddler on the Roof.* Simon Schama's quip "Judaism is a suitcase-ready religion" is profoundly true. "Wherever you go, there you are," so look for more Jews and keep on keepin' on. "Shema Yisrael, Adonai eloheinu, Adonai echad." (Hear, O Israel, Adonai, our God, is one.)

Counting just from May 20, 2000, I have seen more than two dozen live performances of *Fiddler on the Roof.* Many were in Metro Chicago, of course, but I also went to regional theaters from West Palm Beach, Florida, to Regina, Saskatchewan. And I saw both Broadway revivals—in 2004 and 2015—three times each (first just to "enjoy" and then to take notes).

I have seen some very famous actors play Tevye on stage (including Theo-dore Bikel, Danny Burstein, Harvey Fierstein, Alfred Molina, and Chaim Topol), and I have seen some actors in supporting roles who were not well-known then but are fairly well-known now (such as Erik Liberman, Sally Murphy, and Robert Petkoff). I know for sure that many of these actors were Jewish, but most of them probably were not.

I owe each and every one of these performers (the known and the novices) a huge debt of gratitude. Every single stage performance of *Fiddler on the Roof* has been a source of inspiration to me. No matter how many times I see it, I am never bored. It is always different. Seeing the actors stretch—as they step into the TRADITION of *Fiddler on the Roof*—is always thrilling. I have learned more from watching Anatevkans do their thing on stage than I have learned from all the books, articles, reviews and interviews in my queue.

© Hirschfeld (1989)

And the same goes for all the people working behind the scenes (directors, designers, choreographers, musicians). They each work tirelessly to make their own production of *Fiddler on the Roof* memorable, and they always succeed. Whatever the constraints of budget, cast, etcetera, *Fiddler* always wins!

So I thank the entire team who created the original Broadway production of *Fiddler on the Roof* in 1964, as well as all those who provided the source materials (most especially Sholem Aleichem and his many English translators). And I bow before the awesome genius of Jerome Robbins. Through the force of his will and the intensity of his commitment, Jerome Robbins compressed all of these disparate elements into the brilliant diamond called *Fiddler on the Roof.* No, Jerome Robbins was not God, but he is certainly a god to me.

At this point, I must make a decision. Should I credit everyone connected with this project in Chicago, Brooklyn, cyberspace and beyond, and risk leaving someone out… or just mention the people actually responsible for getting this book—this physical thing—into your hands? I have decided to take the narrow approach.

298

Here are the names of all of the people who have worked in various capacities to help me complete production on *Diamond Fiddler: New Traditions for a New Millennium* (ranked according to years spent on Team *Fiddler*):

Bonnie Kustner (writing coach)
Brigid Presecky (proofreader)
Dana Sinn (transcriptionist)
Pilar Wyman (index consultant)
Allison Nordin (design consultant)

I also received interim copy editing assistance from Sharon Lynn Bear, Julia Lasker, and Trudy Obi. My debt to each of these individuals is enormous. I am exacting, demanding, and headstrong—and just like Jerome Robbins—I am sure I am often exasperating. So I thank them all for their patience as well as their technical skills. My profound gratitude to cartoonist Sharon Rosenzweig, and to my tireless project manager Katherine Factor.

✡ ✡ ✡ ✡ ✡

My parents (Helene and Edwin Huttner) and my in-laws (Juanita and William Miller) are not gone. They live on—in my heart and in my mind—with every breath. Gloria Golub Schneider (my father's sister) and Edmund Hecht (my mother's brother) will always be constants in my life too.

✡ ✡ ✡ ✡ ✡

And finally, a few words spoken directly to the two people—my husband Richard Bayard Miller and my BFF Dorthea Juul—who keep me grounded on Planet Earth: Without you two to cling to, I would be adrift in the world with no home. My rest comes in your love.

She-hekh-ee-ah-nu

Barukh atah Adonai, Eloheinu Melekh haolam, shehekhehyanu, v'kiy'manu, v'higianu laz'man hazeh.

Our praise to You, Adonai:

For giving us life, sustaining us, and enabling us to reach this season.

Dreamscape

*Top row from left: Maroussia Rabinowitz (Marie Waife-Goldberg),
Soloman Rabinowitz (Sholem Aleichem), Julia Migenes (as Hodel in 1964),
Jerome Robbins, and Bea Arthur (as Yenta in 1964).
Bottom row from left: Sharon Rosenzweig and Jan Lisa Huttner.*

ABOUT JAN LISA HUTTNER

I am a graduate of St. John's College in Annapolis, Maryland ("the Great Books School"), and I hold master's degrees from Harvard University (EdM, Educational Psychology), the State University of New York at Binghamton (MA, History and Philosophy of the Social and Behavioral Sciences), and the University of Chicago (MA, Human Development). I received an Affirmative Action grant while at SUNY-Binghamton, and fellowships from the Thomas J. Watson Foundation and the G.D. Searle Foundation.

I gave three different presentations during my grad school years at annual meetings of the Jean Piaget Society. One of these presentations later appeared in *International Studies in Philosophy* as an article called "Egocentrism: A Defense of Pre-reflexive Experience." But after several years as a member of the Committee on the Conceptual Foundations of Science, I left the University of Chicago without completing my PhD. (Long story. Don't ask.)

From 1984 to 2002, I worked as a healthcare computer consultant for two "Big Eight" accounting firms—Coopers and Lybrand (now PricewaterhouseCoopers) and Peat Marwick Mitchell (now KPMG)—as well as Superior Consultant Company (a boutique healthcare consulting firm). During these years, I carved out a niche for myself as a nationally recognized expert on behavioral health, home care, and long term care, publishing regularly, and making frequent appearances at professional conferences. I left consulting in 2002 to attend to family health issues. (Long story. Don't ask.)

I began writing professionally in 2003, quickly amassing local and national awards for my print pieces and online posts. I received three "Silver Feathers" as writer of the year from the Illinois Woman's Press Association in 2005, 2006, and 2010. Several of my submissions were also sent up from IWPA to the National Federation of Press Women (NFPW), where I won further recognition in 2005 and 2010 in their multi-state contests.

In 2004, when I was Director of College & University Relations for AAUW-Illinois, I started the WITASWAN project (**W**omen **i**n **t**he **A**udience **S**upporting **W**omen **A**rtists **N**ow). In 2007, I began collaborating with Martha Richards of WomenArts (the Fund for Women Artists) to turn

301

WITASWAN into an international holiday called SWAN Day. In 2011, I published *Penny's Picks: 50 Movies by Women Filmmakers*, with introductory chapters on the history of WITASWAN and International SWAN Day, as well as reviews of 50 films by women directors and/or screenwriters. The first International SWAN Day was celebrated in 2008, primarily in the USA. Since that time, International SWAN Day has been celebrated at more than 1,500 separate events all around the world.

I relocated from Chicago to Brooklyn in September 2012 when my husband made a job change. This proved to be a happy occurrence which enabled me to spend unlimited time doing archival research (especially in the extensive collection of Jerome Robbins papers) once I lived a short train ride away from the New York Public Library for the Performing Arts at Lincoln Center.

Early in 2014, I decided to self-publish "something" in honor of the Golden Anniversary of the first Broadway performance of *Fiddler on the Roof.* The result was *Tevye's Daughters: No Laughing Matter*, which I fondly describe—with a wink and a nod—as "my appetizer course."

Diamond Fiddler: New Traditions for a New Millennium is not only the culmination of 18 years of research on *Fiddler on the Roof*, it is also the embodiment of all the hopes and dreams contained within the heart of this "Good Jewish Girl" from New Jersey.

ABOUT SHARON ROSENZWEIG

Sharon Rosenzweig is an investigative cartoonist. Her work examines religion, politics, care giving, and her ongoing adventures with renegade hens. She holds a BFA in Painting from Indiana University and an MFA from the School of the Art Institute of Chicago (where she taught painting and printmaking for a decade). She also studied at the Art Student's League in New York.

Sharon frequently works in collaboration with her husband Aaron Free-man (a much-loved stand-up comedian with deep ties to National Public Radio and Chicago's famous Second City troupe). Together, they co-created two books: *How to Say "I Love You" in Thirty Languages* (published in 2006 by Rat Riding Press) and *The Comic Torah* (published in 2010 by Ben Yehuda Press). They have also published political cartoons together in *Huffington Post*, and created graphic short stories for the *Annals of Internal Medicine*.

ABOUT US

Sharon and I have a wonderful "meet cute" story.

On February 16, 2006, we both happened to hear radio host Terry Gross interview Israeli artist Amitai Sandy on her NPR program *Fresh Air*. Amitai had just launched a worldwide search for anti-semitic cartoons by Jewish artists. As he explained it to Terry, the trigger was an Iranian newspaper's competition for cartoons on the Holocaust in response to the cartoons depicting the Prophet Mohammed which had been published in the Danish newspaper *Jyllands-Posten*.

> No Iranian will beat us on our own home turf… Jews can offer sharper, more offensive satire of themselves than anyone… This is fighting fire with humor.

Back in 2006, I was still writing monthly columns for the *JUF News* under the byline "Second City Tzivi," so I was always on the look-out for interesting content. I signed on and started following Amitai's website. One day, I saw a cartoon that made me laugh so hard that I had to know more. So I sent an e-mail inquiry to Amitai in Tel Aviv asking about the artist, and he sent me Sharon's contact information that same day.

Amitai had no idea that this cartoonist—who could have been from anywhere—was actually my neighbor. And I had no idea that this cartoonist—who could have been married to anyone—was the wife of "Darth Vrdolyak" (the villain in Chicago Public Radio's infamous Council Wars series). I just knew I had to do an interview with this hilariously subversive local cartoonist for the *JUF News*, and so, I did.

I published my piece on Sharon in the April '06 issue of the *JUF News*, and soon after, I asked her if she would do a cartoon of me for the header of my new blog. She may not have won the contest itself, but Sharon had

Second City Tzivi Typing Away

Second Avenue Tzivi Fiddlin' above Broadway

certainly won my heart. Her cartoon for the Jewish Anti-Semitic Cartoon Contest is posted on my blog:

www.ff2media.com/secondcitytzivi/2010/01/22/how-to-say-i-love-you-in-thirty-languages/

The avatar of me for my blog also became my avatar for all Jewish purposes (including the header of my *JUF News* column) for years afterwards. I would go to events at places like Spertus Institute for Jewish Studies on State Street, and people would instantly recognize me. "You're Second City Tzivi," women would crow as I washed my hands in the ladies room.

When I moved to Brooklyn in 2012, Sharon created an update that we call "Second Avenue Tzivi" in honor of Maurice Schwartz.

In 2014, when I decided to self-publish *Tevye's Daughters—No Laughing Matter*, I spent a great deal of time and money securing permissions for wonderful photos and art works, all of which look very nice in the ebook version (where they appear in color), but not so great in the print-on-demand version (where they appear in black and white).

So when the time came to map out my plans for *Diamond Fiddler*, I decided to start fresh with Sharon. After all, I said to myself, commissioning an artist to do original drawings honored the tradition established by Ben Shahn (who did original drawings for *The Collected Stories of Sholom Aleichem*) and Manuel Bennett (who did original drawings for the Pangloss Press edition of *Tevye the Dairyman*.)

What a joy it has been to work on these drawings for *Diamond Fiddler* with Sharon Rosenzweig! Her tremendous talent is matched by her enormous patience. Somehow, she transformed my stick figure sketches into marvelous snapshots of critical players in the story of *Fiddler on the Roof* as they lived and breathed in my imagination.

In most cases, I was able to find actual photos for Sharon to work from (aging the faces up as needed). As far as I know, however, there are no extant photos anywhere of Sholem Aleichem's mother, Chaya Esther Rabinowitz, so Sharon created her facial features as best she could from photos of her son and her husband. Better that, we agreed, than to leave such a critical woman out of her family's tableau.

To Sharon: My gratitude for your contributions to my life is without measure. My gratitude for your contributions to this book knows no bounds.

BRIEF NOTE ON NAMES

Just like in the case of C-H-A-N-U-K-A-H versus H-A-N-U-K-K-A-H, there are choices to be made. Is the English name of this great Yiddish author "Sholem Aleichem" or "Sholom Aleykhem"? Was his real name Solomon Rabinowitz or Sholom Rabinovich? Was his second daughter's name "Lyala" or "Lola" or "Lala"? In all cases, someone has before them a name that was originally written in either Cyrillic characters or in Hebrew characters, but in a world of search engines, where does one look for the "right" English translation? I have looked everywhere!

In general, for the sake of consistency, I have chosen whatever name was used by the creators of *Fiddler on the Roof* because these are the English names which are most familiar to us now. But when I am quoting someone else, I don't change the actual text of the quote. And so, for example, when I quoted from the Regina Mantell essay in the 1948 *Sholem Aleichem Panorama*, I kept the names the way she spelled them: "Madame Sholom Aleichem" and "Hodl."

For the sake of ease in finding various sources, I have cited the translators of Sholem Aleichem (in lieu of the author's penname) parenthetically in the body text. In this, as in all cases, all the final editing decisions were made by
me (most especially with respect to style and punctuation).

BIBLIOGRAPHY

Key Texts

Sholem Aleichem's eight Tevye stories
    1948 English translation by Frances Butwin
    1996 English translation by Hillel Halkin
    2009 English translation by Aliza Shevrin

Fiddler on the Roof, published in arrangment with Crown
    Publishers, Inc. New York: Limelight Editions, 1964.
    Book by Joseph Stein, music by Jerry Bock, and lyrics by
    Sheldon Harnick.

Waife-Goldberg, Marie. *My Father, Sholom Aleichem*. Shelter Island, NY: Sholom Aleichem Family Publications, 1999.

Etz Hayim Torah and Commentary. Philadelphia, PA: Jewish Publication Society, The Rabbinical Assembly, 2001, 2004.

The Holy Scriptures: JPS Tanakh. Philadelphia, PA: Jewish Publication Society, 1917.

Selected Books & Stories by Sholem Aleichem

A Treasury of Sholom Aleichem Children's Stories, trans. by Aliza Shevrin. Lanham, MD: Jason Aronson, 1996.

Favorite Tales of Sholom Aleichem. New York: Crown Publishers, Avenel Books, 1983.

From the Fair: The Autobiography of Sholom Aleichem, trans. by Curt Leviant. New York: Viking Press, 1985.

From the Fair: The Autobiography of Sholom Aleichem, edited by Marvin Zuckerman, trans. by Curt Leviant. Plunkett Lake Press, 2012.

Inside Kasrilevke, Three Stories, trans. by Isadora Goldstick. New York: Schocken Books, 1973.

Nineteen to the Dozen: Monologues and Bits and Bobs of Other Things, trans. by Ted Gorelick. Syracuse: Syracuse University Press, 1998.

Old Country Tales, trans. by Curt Leviant. Shelter Island, NY: Sholom Aleichem Family Publications, 1999.

Selected Works of Sholem-Aleykhem, edited by Marvin Zuckerman and Marion Herbst. Malibu: Pangloss Press, 1994.

Some Laughter, Some Tears: Tales from the Old World and the New, trans. by Curt Leviant. New York: G.P. Putnam's Sons, 1968.

Stempenyu: A Jewish Romance, trans. by Hannah Berman. New York: Melville House, 2008.

Stories and Satires, trans. by Curt Leviant. Shelter Island, NY: Sholom Aleichem Family Publications, 1999.

Tevye Stories and Others, trans. by Julius and Frances Butwin. New York: Pocket Books, 1965.

Tevye the Dairyman and Motl the Cantor's Son, trans. by Aliza Shevrin. New York: Penguin Press, 2009.

Tevye the Dairyman and The Railroad Stories, trans. by Hillel Halkin. New York: Schocken Books, 1996.

Sholem-Aleykhem's *Tevye the Dairyman*, trans. by Miriam Katz. Malibu: Pangloss Press, 1994.

Tevye's Daughters: Collected Stories of Sholom Aleichem, trans. by Frances Butwin. New York: Crown Publishers, 1949.

Tevye's Daughters: Collected Stories of Sholom Aleichem, trans. by Frances Butwin. Shelter Island, NY: Sholom Aleichem Family Publications, 1999.

The Adventures of Menahem-Mendl, trans. by Tamara Kahana. Shelter Island, NY: Sholom Aleichem Family Publications, 1969.

The Best of Sholom Aleichem, edited by Irving Howe and Ruth R. Wisse. New York: New Republic Books, 1979.

The Old Country, trans. by Julius and Frances Butwin. New York: Crown Publishers, 1946.

Additional Primary Sources

Austen, Jane. *Pride and Prejudice*, introduction by Anna Quindlen. New York: Modern Library, 2000.

Burrows, Abe, and Helen Jerome. *First Impressions*. Music and lyrics by Robert Goldman, Glenn Paxton, and George Weiss. New York: Samuel French, 1959.

Chagall, Bella. *Burning Lights*, trans. by Norbert Guterman. New York: Schocken Books, 2013.

Chagall, Marc. *My Life*, trans. by Elisabeth Abbott. Cambridge, MA: Da Capo Press, 1994.

Granger, Farley and Robert Calhoun. *Include Me Out: My Life from Goldwyn to Broadway*. New York: St. Martin's Press, 2007.

Herzog, Elizabeth and Mark Zborowski. *Life Is with People: The Culture of the Shtetl*. Foreword by Margaret Mead, introduction by Barbara Kirshenblatt-Gimblett. New York: Schocken Books, 1995.

Lapid, Shulamit. *Valley of Strength*, trans. by Philip Simpson. New Milford, CT: The Toby Press, 2009.

Perl, Arnold. *Tevya and His Daughters*. New York: Play Service, Inc., 1958.

Roth, Philip. *Goodbye Columbus and Five Short Stories*. New York: Vintage International, 1993.

Singer, Isaac Bashevis. *The Collected Stories of Isaac Bashevis Singer*. New York: Farrar, Straus & Giroux, 1983.

Updike, John. *Too Far to Go: The Maples Stories*. New York: Random House, 2009.

Selected Secondary Sources

Altman, Richard and Mervyn Kaufman. *The Making of a Musical: Fiddler on the Roof.* New York: Crown Publishers, 1971.

Boym, Svetlana. *The Future of Nostalgia*. Paris: Basic Books, 2002.

Butwin, Joseph and Frances Butwin. *Sholom Aleichem*. Woodbridge, CT: Twayne Publishers, 1977.

Cohn, Rella Israely. *Yiddish Given Names*. Lanham, MD: Scarecrow Press, 2008.

Dauber, Jeremy. *The Worlds of Sholem Aleichem: The Remarkable Life and Afterlife of the Man Who Created Tevye*. New York: Schocken Books, 2013.

Englander, Nathan. *The Ministry of Special Cases*. New York: Alfred A Knopf, 2007.

Erikson, Erik. *Childhood and Society*. New York: W. W. Norton & Company, 1993.

Ezrahi, Sidra DeKoven. *By Words Alone: The Holocaust in Literature* (excerpts from "Menachem Mendel's Letter" by Natan Alterman). Chicago: University of Chicago Press, 1982.

Grafstein, M.W. *Sholem Aleichem Panorama*. London: Jewish Observer, 1948.

Harman, Claire. *Jane's Fame: How Jane Austen Conquered the World*. New York: Picador, 2009.

Hobsbawm, Eric and Terence Ranger, editors. *The Invention of Tradition.* Cambridge: Cambridge University Press, 2012.

Isenberg, Barbara. *Tradition: The Highly Improbable Ultimately Triumphant Broadway-to-Hollywood Story of* Fiddler on the Roof, *the World's Most Beloved Musical.* New York: St. Martin's Press, 2014.

Kagan, Andrew. *Marc Chagall.* New York: Abbeville Press, 1989.

Kruckman, Herbert. *Our Sholem Aleichem: The Story of a Great Jewish Writer.* Whitefish, MT: Literary Licensing LLC, 1946.

Kugelmass, Jack. *Key Texts in American Jewish Culture.* New Brunswick: Rutgers University Press, 2003.

Lambert, Philip. *To Broadway, To Life! The Musical Theater of Harnick and Bock.* Forward by Geoffrey Block. Oxford: Oxford University Press, 2011.

Lawrence, Greg. *Dance with Demons: The Life of Jerome Robbins.* New York: G.P. Putnam's Sons, 2002.

Meyer, Franz. *Marc Chagall.* New York: Harry N. Abrams, 1964.

Miron, Dan. *From Continuity to Contiguity: Toward a New Jewish Literary Thinking.* San Jose: Stanford University Press, 2010.

Rich, Frank and Lisa Aronson. *The Theatre Art of Boris Aronson.* New York: Alfred A. Knopf, 1987.

Roskies, David G. *A Bridge of Longing: The Lost Art of Yiddish Storytelling.* Cambridge: Harvard University Press, 1995.

Solomon, Alisa. *Wonder of Wonders: A Cultural History of* Fiddler on the Roof. New York: Metropolitan Books, 2013.

Strom, Yale. *The Book of Klezmer: The History, The Music, The Folklore from the 14th Century to the 21st.* Chicago: Acapella Books, 2002.

Suskin, Steven. *Opening Night on Broadway: A Critical Quotebook of the Golden Era of Musical Theatre.* New York: Schirmer Books, 1990.

YIVO Encyclopedia of Jews in Eastern Europe. New Haven: Yale University Press, 2008.

Troyat, Henri. *Tolstoy,* trans. by Nancy Amphoux. New York: Grove Press, 2001.

Vaill, Amanda. *Somewhere: The Life of Jerome Robbins.* New York: Broadway Books, 2008.

Vincent, Isabel. *Bodies and Souls: The Tragic Plight of Three Jewish Women Forced into Prostitution in the Americas.* New York: Harper Perennial, 2005.

Wolf, Stacy. *Changed for Good: A Feminist History of the Broadway Musical.* Oxford: Oxford University Press, 2011.

Selected Articles Quoted in Text

Fiddler on the Roof (2015) Study Guide. fiddlermusical.com.

Henneberger, Melinda. "50th Anniversary of 'Fiddler on the Roof' Reunites Tevye's Many Daughters." *WashingtonPost.com.* June 12, 2014.

Walgrove, Amanda. "The Aristocrats." *TabletMag.com.* January 13, 2012.

Wecker, Menachem. "Marc Chagall: The French Painter who Inspired the Title 'Fiddler on the Roof.'" *WashingtonPost.com.* October 23, 2014.

ADDITIONAL HUTTNER MATERIALS

"Everybody's *Fiddler*: A Researcher Finds a Link Long Denied Between Chagall and Sholom Aleichem." September 5, 2003. *ff2Media.com* (originally published in the *Forward.com*).

"From Halsted Street to Broadway: Jan Chats with Chicago Actress Sally Murphy." April 1, 2004. *ff2Media.com.*

"In the Eye of the Beholder: New Revivals of *Fiddler on the Roof* Open in Chicago and New York." July 1, 2004. *ff2Media.com* (originally published in *WorldJewishDigest.com*).

"Who was Boris Aronson?" July 12, 2004. *ff2Media.com.*

"Schwartz's *Tevye* Receives the Royal Treatment from NCJF." December 1, 2004. *ff2Media.com.* (*World Jewish Digest* distributed internationally by the Jewish Telegraphic Agency, *JTA.com*).

"Tevye's Family Adjusts to Life in America." August 1, 2006. *ff2Media.com* (orginally posted in *All About Jewish Theatre*).

"Jonathan Wilson's 'Jewish Encounter' with Marc Chagall." March 1, 2007. *ff2Media.com* (originally published in *JUF News*).

"Munster's *Fiddler*." April 1, 2007. *ff2Media.com* (originally published in *JUF News*).

"Sholem Aleichem's *Stempenyu* Newly Reissued and Available in Paperback!" December 20, 2008. *ff2Media.com* (originally published in *JUF News*).

"Jan Chats with Klezmer Musician Steve Greenman about *Stempenyu's Dream*." February 15, 2009. *ff2Media.com* (originally published in *JUF News*).

"Chaim Topol's Farewell Tour." June 10, 2009. *ff2Media.com* (originally published in *JUF News*).

"*Fiddler:* Stage versus Screen." November 11, 2011. *ff2Media.com* (originally published in *JUF News*).

"*Shylock and His Daughter* Opens in Oak Brook Tonight." July 26, 2012. *ff2Media.com* (originally published in *JUF News*).

"Anatevka is Alive and Well on the Fox River." March 20, 2013. *ff2Media.com* (originally published in *JUF News*).

"Jerome Robbins, Jewison and *Fiddler on the Roof*." August 2, 2013. *ff2Media.com* (originally published in *JUF News*).

"Alisa Solomon Brings 'Wonder of Wonders' to Chicago Area Nov. 22." November 20, 2013. *ff2Media.com* (originally published in *JUF News*).

PHOTO CREDITS & PERMISSIONS

18. In William James Hall with Jane Platt (1975). © Huttner/Rosenzweig (2015). All Rights Reserved.

32, 192. Perchik Tears down the Mechitzah. © Huttner/Rosenzweig (2015). All Rights Reserved.

48, 273. *Fiddler* Timeline 1963-1965. © Jan Lisa Huttner. All Rights Reserved.

52. *Fiddler* Timeline 1965-1971. © Jan Lisa Huttner. All Rights Reserved.

54. Stempenyu plays for Sholem Aleichem and Marc Chagall. © Huttner/Rosenzweig (2015). All Rights Reserved.

57. *Green Violinist* painting by Marc Chagall. © Artists Rights Society (ARS), New York/ADAGP, Paris. Permission granted 2018. All Rights Reserved. https://guggenheim.org/artwork/802.

58. *Fiddler on the Roof* original playbill (1964). © PLAYBILL, INC. Permission granted 2017. All Rights Reserved.

67, 204. *Green Violinist* (bottom right corner). From *Chagall Stained Glass Coloring Book, Rendered for Coloring Marty Noble*, page 6. Dover Pictorial Archive Series, 2000. © Dover Publications, Inc. Permission granted 2017. All Rights Reserved.

70, 182. Dueling Yentes: Molly Picon Onscreen vs. Bea Arthur Onstage. © Huttner/Rosenzweig (2016). All Rights Reserved.

87, 231. Yente/Yenta: Name vs. Noun. © Wikipedia, 3/8/11.

94. Siberia? There wih my love I'm home. © Huttner /Rosenzweig (2015). All Rights Reserved.

117. Loyeff Family Tree, based on Marie Waife-Goldberg's *My Father, Sholom Aleichem*. © Jan Lisa Huttner (2016). All Rights Reserved.

118. Perchik teaches lessons from the Bible. © Oceanside High School, New York (circa 2000). Permission granted 2017. All Rights Reserved.

121. Rabinowitz Family Tree, based on Marie Waife-Goldberg *My Father, Sholom Aleichem*. © Jan Lisa Huttner (2016). All Rights Reserved.

124. Sholem Aleichem's "Republic." © Huttner/Rosenzweig (2016). All Rights Reserved. Based on photos in Marie Waife-Goldberg's *My*

Father, Sholem Aleichem. Note that this is an imaginative reconstruction. These specific people were never in the same room at the same time. Furthermore, as far as I know, there are no known photographs of Chaya Esther Rabinowitz (Sholem Aleichem's mother).

132. *First Impressions* (1959). © The Al Hirschfeld Foundation. Al Hirschfeld is also represented by the Margo Feiden Galleries Ltd., New York. Signature: HIRSCHFELD Philadelphia. Permission granted 2017. All Rights Reserved. www.AlHirschfeldFoundation.org.

137. *The Five Daughters of Zelophehad* sculpture. © Judith Klausner (2010). Permission granted 2017. All Rights Reserved.

140. Three Scenes from the Life of Jerome Robbins. © Huttner/Rosenzweig (2015). All Rights Reserved. Based on Amanda Vaill's 2006 biography *Somewhere: The Life of Jerome Robbins*.

172. Two Scenes from the Life of Jan Lisa Huttner. © Huttner/Rosenzweig (2016). All Rights Reserved.

185. Motel's Tailor Shop at Dusk, photograph. Collection of Lisa Jalowetz Aronson. Permission granted 2004. All Rights Reserved.

193. Golde (Paula Scrafano) and Yente (Rebecca Finnegan) conspire against Tevye. © Marriot Lincolnshire Theatre (2010). Permission granted from Actor's Equity Association 2017. All Rights Reserved.

196. Yente Suffers in Silence. © Hutner/Rosenzweig (2015). All Rights Reserved.

217. Frances Butwin's Literary Progeny: Sample of story collections published in English since the premiere of *Fiddler on the Roof* in 1964, photograph. © Jan Lisa Huttner (2018).

229. Yente Abramovitch with her granddaughter (circa 1915), crop. © The Archives of the YIVO Institute for Jewish Research, New York. Permission granted 2018. All Rights Reserved.

230. Abramovitch Family (circa 1915), photograph. © Archives of the YIVO Institute for Jewish Research, New York. Permission granted 2018. All Rights Reserved. Sheynem Dank to Vital Zajka.

236. Yes! The noun "yenta" acutally appears in the Yiddsh text of "The Great Windfall" (the first of the eight Tevye stories). © National Yiddish Book Center (1999). All Rights Reserved.

240. Jan builds her *Fiddler* platform, venn diagram. © Jan Lisa Huttner (2003). All Rights Reserved.

CONTEXTUAL INDEX

Please note that particular attention has been paid to providing specific details about (1) The members of Sholem Aleichem's family aka The Rabinowitz Family, (2) The work of Sholem Aleichem, (3) The various ways the titles of Sholem Aleichem's eight Tevye stories have been translated over the years, (4) Names for the members of the Rabinowitz Family come from Marie Waife-Goldberg's *My Father Sholem Aleichem* and Sholem Aleichem's Ethical Will (see Zuckerman and Herbst).

Bennett, Manuel 305
Bercovitch, Reuben 219
Bercovitch, Sacvan 219
Berdichev/Berditchev (Russia) 232–234, 234
Bergen, Polly 130, 132, 134–135
Berkeley Free Speech Movement 48
Berkowitz Family. *See* **Rabinowitz Family**
  Ernestina (daughter of Sholem Aleichem)
  Isaac David aka I.D. (husband)
  Tamara Kahana (daughter) 234
Berman, Hannah 199
Best of Sholom Aleichem, The collection
  218–221
Bielke (fictional character) 8, 11, 13, 76, 81,
  84, 109, 160, 244
Bikel, Theodore 72, 297
Block, Geoffrey 178
Blue Violinist, The painting (Chagall) 38,
  200, 202, 203
Blum, Etta 219
Bock, Jerry 49, 144, 194, 201, 207
  awards 136
  compositions 90, 157, 178
Bolideus 295
Boston Pops 26
"Bottle Dance, The" dance 289–291
Bowman, Sylvia E. 226
Boym, Svetlana 165-166, 274
Brazile, Donna 292
Broken Barriers film 73
Brooks, David 277–278, 288
"Bubble Bursts, The". *See* Tevye stories.
  (Sholem Aleichem) 210
Buenos Aires (Argentina). *See* "The Man
  from Buenos Aires" 209, 210, 211, 222
Burrows, Abe 129, 134, 135, 139
Burstein, Danny 297

Butwin, Frances 17, 223
family of
  Joseph (son) 226–228, 246
  Julius (husband) 208–209, 216, 236, 271
works by
  Collected Stories of Sholom Aleichem, The
    86, 88, 208–209, 236, 271, 305
  Old Country, The collection 207, 208,
    210–211, 216, 236, 271
  Sholom Aleichem monograph 225–227,
    246
  Tevye's Daughters collection 86, 88, 208,
    209–210, 211, 215, 216, 225, 236, 271

C

Cariani, John 253
Chagall, Marc 63, 67, 146–147, 159, 189–190,
  203
family of
  Bella Rosenberg (wife) 159, 189–190
  Ida Chagall (daughter)
  Franz Meyer (son-in-law) 203
books about
  Marc Chagall book (Franz Meyer) 203
  Marc Chagall monograph (Boris
    Aronson) 204
paintings by
  Blue Violinist, The painting 38, 200, 202,
    203
  Dance mural 37, 60
  Drama mural 37, 60
  Genesis painting 36
  Green Violinist, The painting 4–17, 37, 38,
    56, 60, 61, 67, 198, 199, 201–205
  I and the Village painting 185
  Literature mural 37, 60
  Music mural 5, 24, 37, 60, 204

Jan Just Keeps on Schleppin'

Whatever the obstacle, my father's advice was always the same:
"Jan, just keep on keepin' on."

PLEASE TELL US WHAT YOU THOUGHT OF

DIAMOND FIDDLER:

NEW TRADITIONS FOR A NEW MILLENNIUM
WHY FIDDLER ON THE ROOF *ALWAYS WINS*

Thank you for purchasing this book. It is a labor of love
representing almost two decades of research! I know you could
have picked any number of books to read, but you picked my
"meal" and for that I am extremely grateful. I hope that it adds
value to your love for *Fiddler on the Roof.*

I would be so grateful if you would share a post about it
on Facebook or Twitter. . . or if you would post a review on
Amazon and/or Goodreads.

This is a unique book by an independent author. Therefore
your feedback is critical.

PLEASE FIND AND REVIEW THIS TITLE AT **.AMAZON.COM**

Contemporaries of Tevye's daughters, they all traveled far from the homes they loved and—collectively—they gave us life.

To Life! To Life! L'Chayim!

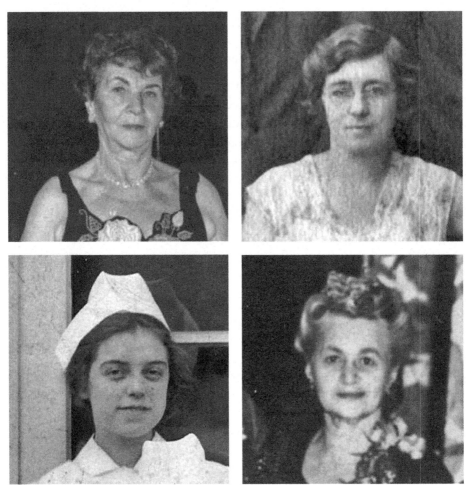

"SAFI"
Clockwise from top left:
Sophie Slotnick Hecht (~1961)
Audrey Berryman Miller (~1932)
Fanny Silverkeit Hatoff (~1949)
Isabel Hayes Richards (~1918)

334

Made in United States
North Haven, CT
02 February 2022

15524138R00192